World Disorders

World Disorders

Troubled Peace in the Post–Cold War Era

Stanley Hoffmann

ROWMAN & LITTLEFIELD PUBLISHERS, INC.
Lanham • Boulder • New York • Oxford

ROWMAN & LITTLEFIELD PUBLISHERS, INC.

Published in the United States of America
by Rowman & Littlefield Publishers, Inc.
4720 Boston Way, Lanham, Maryland 20706

12 Hid's Copse Road
Cumnor Hill, Oxford OX2 9JJ, England

British Library Cataloguing in Publication Information Available

Library of Congress Cataloging-in-Publication Data

Hoffmann, Stanley.
    World disorders : troubled peace in the post-Cold War era /
Stanley Hoffmann.
       p.   cm.
    Includes bibliographical references and index.
    ISBN 0-8476-8574-8 (cloth : alk. paper).
    ISBN 0-8476-8575-6 (pbk. : alk. paper)
    1. Peace.   2. War   3. Security, International.   4. International
cooperation.   5. International organization.   I. Title.
JZ5538.H64   1998
327.1'09'049—dc21   98-29541
                                                          CIP

Printed in the United States of America

Contents

Part Three: Ethnicity, Nationalism, and World Order

Preface

This book is a collection of most of the essays I have written about international affairs in the past decade. My earlier essays dealt largely with the universe of the cold war; many of the recent ones try to make sense of the complicated international system that has replaced it. They pay particular attention to the issues of nationalism and intervention in the domestic affairs of states, two of the most visible features of this system. My interest in the political philosophies (and philosophers) of world affairs has persisted,[1] and my concern for the ethical aspects of international relations[2] is central in this new collection.

I have purposely omitted the essays I have written on Europe[3] and on the Yugoslav tragedy.[4] Inevitably, among essays written over a short number of years, there is some overlap—for instance, between chapter 4, "Beyond Realism and Idealism," and chapter 17, "Principles of a Liberal Ethics for International Relations," as well as between chapter 4 and chapter 5, "The Crisis of Liberal Internationalism." I apologize to the reader; but I remember that when the Nobel Prize economist Wassily Leontief, the late psychologist Henri Tajfel, and I once toured France on an OECD (Organization for Economic Cooperation and Development) mission, and Tajfel teased Leontief about his tendency to make the same points again and again, Leontief replied with a smile, "When you have a good idea, repeat it!" I don't know how good my ideas are, but I have certainly repeated them.

I have not tried to update these essays. This means that I have made no effort to correct mistakes in my analyses. The reader will note that chapters 6, 7, and 8 refer to the Soviet Union. I did not predict the great disintegrations of 1989–1991, and below, I try to understand why. I have left intact my essay written during the crisis over Kuwait. It was a plea against launching a war that I thought much more full of risks and perils

vii

than it turned out to be. Like many other observers, I was surprised by the ease of the coalition's victory. But if I was wrong in expecting far worse, I remain troubled by two points. First, for all the progress in precision bombing, which allowed for far fewer civilian casualties than in earlier wars, the destruction of Iraq's infrastructure resulted in conditions that did lead to misery and death for many civilians. Second, while Kuwait regained its independence and Saddam Hussein's armies and arsenal were badly battered, he is still in power and still trying to regain a dangerous capacity in weapons of mass destruction. Marching on Baghdad and eliminating him in 1991 would have been highly unpopular in the United States and might have led to a breakup of the coalition (as well as of Iraq). But failing to do so has left us with a recurrent headache. The dilemma faced by the United States in the last days of the war was tough: what to do when a just cause cannot be promoted by moderate means and may not have a reasonable chance of success? This same dilemma has reappeared in subsequent crises with Iraq.

These essays try to make sense of an international system in which forces contained or repressed during the cold war are asserting (or, like nationalism, reasserting) themselves. It is also a system in which, long after decolonization, the failure of the colonizers to prepare adequate state institutions for the peoples they had dominated, and the failure of many of the leaders of the newly emancipated peoples to build such structures, have led to violence and disintegration. This system is part of a world society in which economic and technological globalization, economic, social, and cultural modernization, and "americanization"—the spread of American techniques, ideas, mores, and popular culture—are hard to disentangle. No single, simple concept—or theory—can provide a satisfactory answer to the puzzles and riddles of this new world.

—*Stanley Hoffmann*

1

Introduction:
From This Century to the Next

Wе are at the end of an incredibly turbulent and often terrifying century. If we look at the world since 1914—a little longer than what Eric Hobsbawm has called the short twentieth century—where do we come from, where are we, and where are we going?

Of the many lessons taught by the avalanche of events, six are particularly weighty. First, the combination of human passions—ethnic, ideological, and so on—of state struggles for power and of modern technological advances has put into the hands of leaders and followers an extraordinarily large capacity for destruction. Eighteenth- and nineteenth-century dreams about the obsolescence of war, or its gradual ritualization, and about the gradual pacification of humanity have been shattered, Hegel's philosophy of history seems quaint, and Kant's ideal still distant.

Second, the twentieth century brought something entirely new: the modern totalitarian state. It represented the culmination of the messianic aspirations to "forge a new man" that began with the French Revolution. This time, these aspirations were exploited by powerful states with the determination and the ability to reach into every corner of society and were upheld by ideologies that divide the world into the good and the evil, reducing the latter to subhuman status. The concentration camps, the gulag, and the killing fields followed. These efforts ultimately failed because they demanded more than human nature, for all its malleability, can give. But the cost to humanity has been enormous, not only in victims but also through the corruption of the subjects of such power, so well analyzed by Vaclav Havel. Those who aimed at mobilizing their faithful

1

and their followers into armies and communities ended up reducing them to atoms.

Third, this century produced—for a while, at least—a remarkable social democratic synthesis of liberal and social values of individual freedoms and, if not equality, at least welfare. The record of this synthesis is not perfect. It succeeded in improving the living conditions of millions of people and provided them with safety nets against life's major vicissitudes and against the fluctuations of the capitalist market. However, the costs of welfare keep rising, social programs have bred an often stifling bureaucracy, and plans conceived as ways of recreating a sense of community have, paradoxically, fed an insatiable demand for rights, countless battles of entitlements, and escalating litigation.

Fourth, this century has seen a generalization of the great movement for emancipation from traditional customs, hierarchies, and yokes foreseen by Alexis de Tocqueville. Totalitarianisms and mass wars helped this movement more than they thwarted it. The liberation of colonized peoples, the mergence of many individuals situated at the bottom of society from poverty and humiliation, the transformation of the condition of women and of the young, and the struggles against racial and other discriminations have amounted to a gigantic political and social revolution.

Fifth, during half of this period, another innovation reigned: the cold war, a planetary bipolar conflict that did not lead to a war and avoided repeating both the scenario of 1914 and the sad mess of the 1930s, thanks to the nature of the main actors and to that of nuclear weapons, so that "rules of the game" gradually developed. And yet in many respects it was like a war: it dominated the international agenda, it resulted in a multitude of interventions and proxy wars, and it ended with the defeat of one of the contenders, which collapsed in utter political and economic bankruptcy.

Sixth, the successive revolutions in communications have shrunk the world. Since World War II—partly because of its global character and of the global nature of the cold war, partly because of these revolutions and of the phenomena huddled under the term *globalization*—there is a single, worldwide international system. And although interdependence is to a large extent a construct, the product of deliberate policies, agreements, and regimes (to that extent, it is reversible just as the laissez-faire world liberals had striven for in the nineteenth century was partly undone at the end of that century and later destroyed by the Great Depression); it is also a condition, one that leads to almost instantaneous reactions, contagious vulnerabilities, and information overloads.

Where are we now? Much of this book tries to suggest answers to that question. Three remarks suffice here. First, the current international system presents us with a bill for what we bought during the cold-war era. The former tense and costly concentration of the superpowers on their contest has led, in the United States, to various forms of battle fatigue—fatigue with battles, fatigue both with unilateral interventions and with multilateral agencies and operations not controlled by the United States—and to various withdrawal symptoms, insofar as the diplomatic-strategic arena is concerned (the expansion of NATO [North Atlantic Treaty Organization] appears to contradict this statement, but it amounts more to an insurance policy against a decreasing American influence on the European continent that to a hegemonic tool). The Weinberger doctrine became the Powell doctrine and the Cohen doctrine. As for the Soviet Union, it has dissolved; its fragments are experiencing big difficulties in establishing democratic institutions and the rule of law in countries with little experience of the former and mainly an experience of authoritarian and totalitarian arbitrariness disguised as law. Moreover, societies that suddenly face increasingly inequalities, rising corruption, and much-diminished protection provide only fitful support to, and cause great turmoil for, their political systems. Long-repressed ethnic tensions degenerate into conflicts both in the former Union of Soviet Socialist Republics and in Yugoslavia; former Communists, to stay in power, have become converts to nationalism. As for the new states that emerged from the collapse of empires, many of them had been artificially held standing by the superpowers in need of clients; they have often turned out to be artificial and shaky in their institutions and borders; hence the large number of failed, troubled, and murderous states (see chap. 11).

Second, the system of sovereign states is doubly undermined: from below, so to speak, by this crumbling of the Westphalian floor—the collapse of states whose claims to sovereignty are untenable—and from above, by two revolutions. One is the empirical revolution of globalization and interdependence. It deprives states of much of their operational sovereignty, for instance, over their currencies and their budgetary policies; and it transfers power from the state to a private global economy—of investors, business people, traders, communication experts, bankers, and speculators—that is largely uncontrolled, since global capitalism is not matched by international regulations and institutions in the way in which national capitalisms were matched by the power of the national states. In recent years, onslaughts by financial investors on European currencies (1992–1993) and Mexico, Thailand, Malaysia, and Indonesia have exposed the weakness of the state and its financial reserves when faced with such attacks and transfers. The delicate balance between capitalist efficiency and the equity functions of the state has been destroyed because of the weakening of the state and the deficiencies of international governance.

The second revolution against sovereignty is normative. Human rights norms and regimes, moves (still fragmentary) toward environmental regimes and international criminal justice, the march (still incipient) toward norms limiting the ability of states to engage in terror or to develop weapons of mass destruction, and experiments in both dismantling and pooling sovereignty, such as the European Union, can be mentioned in this connection.

Third, we live as a result in a world of great originality, complexity, and uncertainty. It is still a world of states, yet many of its problems cannot be solved unilaterally by them—environmental problems, or the desires of consumers for cheap and varied goods, for instance. Many of the levers states used to hold are now in the hands of the mass of private actors in the global capitalist market who control communications, financial services, and much of technology. It is a world that moves in two opposite directions at the same time. One is the greater *integration* fostered by market mechanisms and the spread of modern technology—that is, by private forces—and also by public international regimes ad institutions, a vast domain in which the main promoters have been the United States and Western Europe. The other direction is *fragmentation*, resulting partly from globalization itself (see chap. 4), partly from ethnic and religious conflicts, or from the increasing attachment to national or local culture (as a way either of resisting globalization or even of benefiting from modernization without, however, abandoning distinctive customs and values—as a way to gain from economic and technological progress without being "Americanized"). Another cause is the spreading desire for greater democracy, a desire that often seems more attainable at the local or regional levels than at a distant center.

It is also a world that lives in different ages. Many of its inhabitants live in the age of global society—a society that is cosmopolitan, English speaking, connected through professional bonds and the internet, addicted to acronyms, and relatively peaceful. Others live in the age of traditional interstate conflicts and rivalries, where national histories, myths, and prejudices still flourish and where force and heroism, rather than rational calculations and efficiency, remain essential. Finally, there is the somber age of state disintegration, chaos, and genocide so widespread in recent years.

This world, united and split, has problems both with its floor and with its ceiling. The problem of the floor is the crisis of the state, no longer a very effective agent, often under attack, even when it is solid, and certainly not solid everywhere. The problem of the ceiling is that of world governance: we have, at present, neither a concert, or society, of great powers nor sufficiently powerful and authoritative international organizations. The only remaining superpower, the United States, may well be indispensable, but it acts fitfully and sees less far than its leaders think.

Where are we going? We face two large question marks. First, is this global anomie temporary—and if so, what is it a transition toward: a renewed bipolarity? a global multipolarity? a fully asserted American hegemony? Also, will a steering capacity at the global level develop? Second, will the "floor" be repaired? This would require not merely the panacea of free-market economies but also workable political, legal, and social institutions in societies that do not or no longer have them and effective regional organizations providing assistance to their development. Otherwise, there will be a grave risk of chaos, and the prospect of a two-tiered international milieu, with one tier made of effective states and one of poor, isolated, or distintegrating ones.

In trying to answer these questions, we are not much helped by our conceptual tool kit. It has several components. One is the stock of political philosophies that have tried to account for international affairs. Marxism has neglected the importance of the nation, overestimated that of class struggle and intercapitalist contests, and underestimated the autonomy of the state. Realism and liberalism have also been flawed: realism (and its impoverished heir, neorealism) has ignored the importance of the multiple restraints that have softened and partly tamed the old "anarchy" of world politics, and liberalism, which foresaw the importance of transnational economic links, did not want to see the darker side of the triumph of an open and largely privatized global economy; it has tended to dismiss cultural and political resistance to the upheavals and to the inequities this economy has fostered—the permanent redistribution of inequality—as mere nuisance and atavism. Its own heir, liberal institutionalism, has focused primarily on interstate relations. Both realism and liberalism have assumed rational states, deriving evident interests from their geopolitical position and their resources in realism's case, agglomerating private interests in liberalism's—a far too simple view of what has happened so often in this century.

Another conceptual component consists of prophetic hypotheses. In chapter 4, I mention two: Francis Fukuyama's end of history, which tends to confuse the success of capitalism and of the market with the triumph of liberal democracy, and Samuel Huntington's clash of civilizations—the West versus the rest—which offers a series of undemonstrated links, rides roughshod over the complexities and divisions of existing civilizations, and overlooks the fact that the West has infiltrated, and sometimes reshaped, all other civilizations.

The last tool is social science. But it suffers from two enormous flaws. On the one hand, it is, in its display of "economics envy," increasingly abstract and remote from the realties and the substance of world politics. Models based on rational-choice assumptions and on game theory rest on hypotheses that are productive only in limited parts of the field. As Raymond Aron argued long ago, the simplifications that economic theory performs do not violate the essence of economic behavior; but those that the "scientific" theorists of world politics commit distort and betray the essential realities of foreign policy behavior. Some frameworks, such as Robert Putnam's two-level game, are useful and stimulate research, but they are not to be mistaken for models or theories. The search for general laws remains a quest for the white whale. It has led to such absurdities as the anathema thrown on case studies. It is really better to compare, let us say, the aftermath of forty peace treaties—analyzed superficially—than to study in depth three or four cases or to study one case in such a way as to derive from it conclusions that can then be tested, modified, and enriched in equally serious examinations of other cases? Also, the fashion of single explanatory theories (and for the discarding of alternative explanations) often leads to absurdities. Many "dependent variables" are the products of different factors—at one moment or at different times. Squeezing a complex and ill-defined phenomenon (say, imperial overstretch) into a straitjacket (such as coalitions of interests) is rotten history and bad social science.

On the other hand, however hard the scientific approach may try, the capacity of social science to predict remains limited. We may be able to predict the effects of what Aron called one "causal series" in isolation, but historical events are the products of the collision and interplay of many such series. We may be able to forecast broad material trends but, as Daniel Bell has argued, there is often a disjunction between the material (economic, demographic, technological) infrastructure and the cultural and political superstructure (Marxists know well how that disjunction demolished Marx's prophecies). The capacity of people to affect the pace and the path of these trends is the result of the freedom human beings enjoy, in contrast with what happens in the world of nature. Indeed, the role of individuals in history, and the role of ideas, introduces major elements of unpredictability and innovation; they shape events in ways that are far easier to reconstruct *ex post* than to foresee *ex ante*.

The most recent example of our trouble in predicting is the collapse of the Soviet empire and Union and the end of the cold war (a more folkloric earlier example was May 1968 in France). That collapse was not explainable in realist or neorealist terms, insofar as these theories concentrate on the distribution of primarily military power, and the Soviet Union fell at a time when many Americans feared that its armed might could overtake that of the United States. To some extent, liberalism provided a clue—the importance of the links between East and West, and of the penetration of Western ideas, that the detente policies of the 1970s had made possible—but few believed that this limited opening would have such colossal effects. What happened was that social scientists did not pay sufficient attention to the following factors.

Many of us were in the grip of two beliefs. One was the received idea that empires do not voluntarily release their captives. After all, the Soviets had crushed revolts in 1953, 1956, and 1968 and had found ways to keep a restive Poland under control. That the Soviet leadership would, at the end, behave in a way more comparable to British than to French or Dutch decolonization was not foreseen. The second belief was in the somber hold of totalitarianism, in the capacity of totalitarian regimes to crush dissidents and to control populations with methods of terror and propaganda merely authoritarian regimes did not possess.

These beliefs would have been shaken if more importance had been given, first, to the degree to which the links and opening mentioned above had broken the shell of totalitarianism, led the citizens of the empire and of the Soviet Union itself to compare their condition to that of people in the West, and made a new generation of the Soviet elite aware of their country's handicaps. Second, the tendency of international relations specialists to focus on those elements of power that are the currency of interstate politics led them to pay insufficient attention to the domestic weaknesses of the Soviet Union, both material—the increasing inefficiency of the nonmilitary economy, its backwardness in the computer age—and mental—the disappearance of ideological faith and fervor, leaving a backward economy in the hands of an ossified party elite and bureaucracy with no other major project than their own survival. That domestic factors shape the distribution of power in the international system's structure was something that Thucydides had known but neorealism had ruled out of its narrow universe.

Even if more recognition had been given to these facts, predicting what and when the collapse happened would have been difficult for a third set of reasons—the Gorbachev factor. Would another Soviet leader have been as easily disposed to let Poland conclude its historical compromise of 1989, to let the Berlin Wall crumble, and to accept German reunification on NATO terms in exchange for financial assistance from the West? The events of the late 1980s are as difficult to imagine without Gorbachev as Nazism without Hitler or post–1940 France without de Gaulle. Leadership matters. But there also was the *engrenage,* the chain of events, the avalanche, that Gorbachev provoked but did not intend. The Soviet economic and political system turned out to be unreformable: it could be preserved, at a frightful cost, or it could unravel. Gorbachev's half-way house between Leninism and social democracy was a mirage. When a crumbling communism that had kept the Union together gave way to separate nationalisms, fueled by political ambitions, when Gorbachev found himself caught between conservatives he had tried to neutralize through coddling and Yeltsin, who had succeeded in making Russia his fief, the Union itself collapsed. There was a Gorbachev revolution, and the paths of revolution are notoriously hard to chart in advance (yes, Edmund Burke predicted the Jacobin terror, but that was only one of the French Revolution's detours).

Instead of predictions, we can offer scenarios. The worst is that of a world of conflict at all levels: among the major powers (for instance, between China and the United States and between the United States and Russia) and among smaller powers endowed with a formidable capacity for mass destruction, through various forms of terror spreading across borders, or through the prevalence of disintegration over "globalization," the triumph of autarchic reactions against economic interdependence (for instance, if a major recession should occur or if the financial markets were shaken by a worldwide contagion of bank collapses and investors' turbulence). All this could be accompanied and aggravated by environmental disasters and by mass migrations provoked both by economic and political turmoil and by the failure of some large states to curb the growth of their population. The best scenario envisages the co-existence and overlap of a number of "security communities" in many parts of the world (already, in Europe, we have the OSCE [Organization for Security and Cooperation in Europe], NATO, the European Union, and the Council of Europe) and extensive cooperation on the global problems of population, the environment, perhaps even migrations and refugees.

We can list the conditions that might bring us closer to one or the other extreme and thus alert ourselves to what needs to be done to avoid the former and to bring us closer to the latter. In this connection, it is useful to draw attention here to a few empirical data and to a few normative notions.

On the empirical side, nothing deserves more reflection than the collapse of the distinction between what is domestic and what is international (this is a major aspect of the crisis of the state). Internal phenomena are the subjects of interstate negotiations, of transnational lobbies and agreements, of collective external interventions; the affairs that dangerous states—Iraq or Serbia—claim to be internal are deemed international by much of world society. Conversely, many international phenomena are shaped by domestic events and processes. The change of regime in Russia, a possible change in China, the collapse of banks in South Korea, the flows of refugees provoked by genocide in Rwanda and by turmoil in former Zaire, these are all domestic factors that affect the character of world politics. It is particularly necessary to pay attention to the domestic disruptions caused by global interdependence, especially by the mobility of financial and industrial capital. Also, the understanding of international relations now requires a sophisticated knowledge of foreign societies and political systems (at a time when much of political science disdains such knowledge as "mere" anthropology and seeks to replace empirical investigations with the manipulation of data culled from countries whose history, institutions, and languages can be happily ignored).

A second empirical datum is the geopolitical centrality of Asia. It is the locus of many traditional interstate conflicts, of several weak states and questionable regimes. It is the scene of great-power rivalries—four of the five major powers are located or involved there. It is an area of spectacular economic development but frequently also of weak political and financial institutions, as the financial crisis of 1997–1998 has shown.

A third empirical fact is the fragile stabilization of Europe. Its stabilization results from, and takes the baroque form of, the European Union, this halfway house that is far less than a federation and far more than a collection of states. Its fragility results both from its dependence on the outside world—on what happens to the global economy, or in Russia, or in North Africa—and from nationalistic and fascistic reactions against "Europeanization," Americanization, and globalization in several countries.

Finally, let us turn to a few normative points. What we get results in part from what we do. If we want a world order that is both peaceful and fair, here is a list of urgent concerns. One, we need to develop more global norms by consensus (with some regions or regional agencies pushing ahead) with respect to the environment, human rights, international criminal justice, criteria for intervention, and obligations of assistance to states and people in need.

Two, we need to find the right balance between the indispensable, and still weak and spotty, institutions of global governance and the desire of people to preserve their distinctive identities and cultures. The unfettered rule of the market within and across borders produces injustices that only strong public institutions ensuring collective goods at the national, regional, and global levels, can attenuate or wipe out. Conversely, local chauvinisms or racisms need to be tamed by an arsenal of norms, for instance, for the protection of foreigners and minorities (see chap. 17).

Three, we need to invent new forms of citizen representation and participation to prevent the extremes of withdrawal, indifference, and cynicism, on the one hand, and sudden surges of disruptive discontent and antidemocratic movements, on the other.

Finally, we must redefine security so as to take into account not only security against physical threats to state but also the various insecurities international relations inflict on states and on people. Also, we should reconsider the concept of interest. Especially in American political science, it tends to be a synonym for material advantages—a far too narrow view. We ought to understand that interests consist both of imperatives and preferences or desires; and we ought to ask not only what are the imperatives and the preferences of states but also what are those of the people in (or outside) the states. We should also ask ourselves how the satisfaction of those imperatives and desires can be obtained in other than purely selfish ways, that is, not at the expense of equally valid claims.

A vast program, indeed! What is crucial for the future of the discipline is not that it tries, once more, to imitate more "scientific" ones but that it concentrates on substance. We should be methodologically ecumenical: for some issues, one method may be the best, for other issues, it may be another method. We should look at theories as disposable stimulants, not as straitjackets or as the sole or even the main purpose of political science. It is a world of human beings that we are trying to understand. Which questions we need to ask should be driven not by methods and theories but by our substantive concerns. Causal explanation is but one aspect of our work. Understanding, evaluation, eventually policy recommendations are equally important. The patterns, the mysteries, the shocks that surround us are sufficiently fascinating to keep us at work.

Part One

Theorists, Theories

2

Hedley Bull and His Contribution to International Relations

It was an honor and a privilege to be asked to review Hedley Bull's contribution to the study of international politics. Over the years we had discovered many affinities. We had a common way of looking at the theory and practice of international politics, even if we did not always give the same answers to the questions we both asked. I was always impressed by the extraordinary clarity and lucidity of his arguments, and by their fairness—by his way of taking into account all the points in his adversary's case and all the objections to his own arguments and assumptions. Both of us looked at a discipline that had developed in the United States after World War II as outsiders who did not support all the premises of its main practitioners and theoreticians.

I was always an admirer of the extraordinary sweep of Hedley Bull's mind, and yet when I reviewed his work I was left with an inevitable sense of incompleteness. He accomplished so much, but there were also so many more directions in which he might have gone and in which he was beginning to go.

The most striking aspect of his work is its extraordinary unity and the coherence of his approach: the unity of method and of substance and the consistency and continuity of his concern about international society and those contemporary issues which are decisive for the survival of an international society. However, there were also significant tensions in his work: they gave it its density and make it particularly instructive and thought provoking.

13

Hedley Bull's Worldview

At first sight it appears to be obvious where Hedley Bull fits in to the discipline of international relations. He seems to take up a position close to realism, the school of thought that looks at international relations as the politics of states in their external aspects, to quote from his own account of Martin Wight's approach.[1] Realism starts by rejecting all forms of utopianism, as Bull himself did. His most magisterial criticism of utopianism is to be found in *The Anarchical Society,* where he disposed decisively of such concepts as world government, a new medievalism, a regional reconstruction of the world, and revolutionary schemes for change.[2] Even in his first book, *The Control of the Arms Race,* he had been incisively critical of proposals for world disarmament.[3]

And yet things are not so simple. Unlike many destroyers of utopias and many realists—I have in mind George Kennan and Henry Kissinger—Bull never showed great enthusiasm for giving policy advice to usually indifferent princes. Many contemporary realists have been attracted to policy guidance like moths to a flame. Bull had no particular objection to scholars giving policy advice as long as it went to a morally acceptable government;[4] he himself served as an adviser to the British government on arms control matters for several years. Yet, on the whole, he showed more tolerance than enthusiasm for this task. His attitude was similar to that of Raymond Aron: in the field of international relations, as indeed in political science in general, what Aron called "wise counsel" was quite naturally derived from scholarly research, but the main purpose of scholarship was to advance knowledge.

To be sure, not all realists have felt a need to outdo the bureaucrats on their own ground (certainly Hans Morgenthau never did). But there were two other very important differences between Bull's approach and that of the realists. The first came from his distrust of the realist model of state behavior, which lies behind the realists' prescriptions. Morgenthau was the one who put it most forcefully in the first few pages of *Politics among Nations:* one can derive from the study of history, from the logic of interstate relations in the international milieu, and from the geopolitical position of a state something like a rational set of rules for the conduct of its foreign policy.[5] Instances of departure from such rational behavior are treated, in the realists' works, as aberrations. Hedley Bull was no believer in the ordinary rationality of states, nor in the usefulness of developing prescriptions for rational action, because he was even more pessimistic than the realists. To them, departures from the norm are exceptions; to Hedley Bull, stupidity, folly, miscalculations, and mischief were always possible.

The second major point of difference between Bull and the realists lay in his point of departure. He did not begin his study, as the realists do, by looking at the state and its power, a concept about which he has rather little to say. (And what he does say about power is actually quite close to the realist emphasis on military power as the heart of the matter.) Bull's whole body of work takes as its point of departure the group, or milieu, or "ensemble" which states form by interacting. It is the international system, and, above all, international society. When, in his famous article attacking the so-called scientific approach, he drew up a list of important questions to be asked in the study of international politics, Bull's first question was, "Does the collectivity of sovereign states constitute a political society or system, or does it not?"[6] Similarly, in his critique of E. H. Carr's *Twenty Years Crisis,*[7] written thirty years after its publication, he concluded that "in the course of demonstrating how appeals to an overriding international society subserve the special interests of the ruling group of powers, Carr jettisons the idea of international society itself. This is the idea with which a new analysis of the problem of international reactions should now begin."[8] Bull's interest in this idea was constant. Between the late 1950s and the 1980s, American scholarship moved away from general theories toward greater specialization, and it has tended to split into two groups—the strategists and the political economists. Bull never separated his interest in strategic questions from his investigation of the nature, history, and evolution of international society.

Method and Substance

Thus we come to what I called the unity of method and substance in Bull's work. The most fruitful way of grasping this is to start with his critique of the scientific approach to international relations theory: his rejection of "propositions based on logical or mathematical proof, or upon strict empirical procedures of verification."[9] He attacked the practitioners of the scientific approach for a number of reasons. In the first place, this method kept its practitioners from asking what were, according to him, the essential questions about international relations. The practitioners of the scientific approach seemed to Bull like characters who, having lost a watch in the dark, look for it under a light even though they did not lose it there, but because the light happens to be there. As Bull put it himself, their method "keeps them as remote from the substance of international politics as the inmates of a Victorian nunnery were from the study of sex."[10] Second, he disliked the scientific method because he thought its practitioners were obsessed by the quest for a far greater degree of precision than the field of international relations allows. Hence his harsh critique of Karl Deutsch's "measurements," which, according to Bull, ignored the connections between the units being measured and the significance of what was being counted. Hence also his sarcasm about the abstract model-building technique displayed by Morton Kaplan, whose models, according to Bull, were scientifically disguised versions of reality which either lacked rigor and consistency precisely because rigor and consistency are not to be found in international reality or achieved those qualities at the cost of a complete divorce from reality. They were not like economic models, which often manage to remain not only faithful to, but capable of explaining, the way in which economic variables interact. Third, Bull thought that the practitioners of the scientific method were obsessed by an urge to predict and to resolve the issues which they tackled, and he accused them of brashness. These criticisms were addressed primarily to the behaviorist school of the mid-1960s. In "International Theory" (see note 6) he kindly exempted from blanket condemnation such kindred souls as Raymond Aron, Kenneth Waltz, and myself. However, in his major work, *The Theory of International Relations* (Reading, Mass.: Addison-Wesley, 1979), Kenneth Waltz himself subsequently became a prime example of the very approach which Hedley Bull had condemned many years before. Mercifully, Hedley spared Waltz's book, which, as far as I know, he never reviewed.[11]

What was his own preference? He talked about "a scientifically imperfect procedure of perception and intuition," which sounds remarkably like Max Weber's concept of understanding.[12] In Bull's view, in other words, beyond the causal explanation of events or of sequences of events, the social scientist still has to travel one more step and try to grasp the meaning of the whole; and this requires, above all, judgment in the construction and testing of hypotheses. Interpretation, the attempt to seize the meaning of what has been explained, is an artistic enterprise rather than a scientific one. Unlike many of his colleagues in the field, therefore, and unlike Kenneth Waltz in his last book, Bull did not begin his study of international relations with the requirements of method. (Waltz, for instance, begins by laying down a very interesting and rigorous notion of theory, and then, by applying it to international relations, manages to leave most of the substance of the field outside the straitjacket.) Bull started with the questions which were essential to him: questions about society and culture, about the place of war and the conceptions of it, about the relations between the influence of the system and the nature of the state in the determination of events, about the right of states to intervene in each other's affairs—and so on.

To begin with such questions is to realize, first, that they can only be understood by reference to the works of the political philsophers who have discussed and sharpened them. Secondly, they can only be answered comparatively across time and place; for instance, to be able to talk intelligently about what looks like the extraordinary amount of intervention that occurs in the present-day international system, or about the seemingly original network of contemporary transnational relations, it is useful to be able to compare the present system with past ones—something which led Hedley Bull to conclude that the amount of intervention today was not all that unusual, and that the network of transnational relations was far less original than many have claimed. Thirdly, to begin with these questions is to understand that they can only be evaluated by reference not merely to the state's power but also to the rules which states observe, and particularly to that quite special category of rules which constitutes international law.

Bull called this approach a traditional one, and it was indeed traditional if one considers that the study of the history of ideas and of diplomatic history is the very thing from which the modern scientific approach had tried to emancipate the discipline of international reactions; but it was a traditional approach at the service of as rigorous an understanding of international relations as the field allows. In this way, Bull's work is very different from that of traditional international lawyers or diplomatic historians. His very concern for a systematic understanding of international relations leads him, as it had led Raymond Aron, to insist on conceptual distinctions in order to make a clear analysis possible. In *The Anarchical Society* one finds whole forests of distinctions: between the different meanings and kinds of order in international affairs, between the different meanings of justice, between the different functions of war, between intervention and inequality, different types of balance of power, and so on.

Hedley Bull's Humanism

Ultimately, Hedley Bull's work is a blend of intelligent social science and humanism. I insist on his humanism because it takes so many forms.

Predominantly, it takes a Weberian form. Weber wanted the social scientist to respect and empathize with the meanings which political actors gave to their actions, just as he wanted him to be aware of and to highlight the frequent divorce between actors' intentions and the results obtained. It is because of this divorce that it is possible to talk about a system—which might be described as a net of interacting variables which often foul up the intentions of the actor—but it is because human beings are the actors and have the intentions that there is no need to look at the system in the way in which, for instance, Morton Kaplan seems to have done: as a divinity which determines the acts of the various players as if they were puppets on a string. To illustrate this point one can say, as Bull often did, that a balance of power in the international society, or the current balance of terror, can develop even though their creation or preservation was not the deliberate policy or intention of all the participants in international society. On the other hand, how this balance will turn out, how stable it will be, will depend to a very large extent on the participants' intentions and policies.

Humanism is also manifest in the extraordinary density of the historical knowledge in Bull's works, particularly the most recent ones—something which is not to be found in the works of many of his American colleagues. Lastly, humanism is manifest in the importance of moral concerns in Bull's works.

Ethics and International Relations

Hedley Bull's writings on ethics and international relations are more suggestive than systematic. The interest shown in ethics by specialists in international relations has increased enormously in the last ten years, as Bull himself noted. His own concern with this issue started much earlier, but even in his work an increasing emphasis on ethics can be traced in the last years of his life. His thoughts on the subject can be summarized as follows.

First, as far as the study of international relations is concerned, international society has a moral basis; indeed, Bull's concern for international society and his interest in moral conceptions are inextricably linked. The belief of the members of the international society cannot be reduced to their interests and strategies of power—a reduction for which Bull criticizes E. H. Carr sharply, particularly in pointing out that the famous principle *pacta sunt servanda* cannot be described merely as a cynical expression of the interests of the strong. According to Bull, the beliefs of the members of the international society influence the historical evolution of that society. Consequently, the study of international relations must address the question of moral beliefs, in particular in order to establish which beliefs represent a consensus of members, what the substance of that consensus is, and where its limits and weak points can be found. This was a task which Bull performed rigorously in the last years of his life, both as regarded conceptions of justice in the present sytem[13] and in his essay on South Africa. There, taking up the argument of South Africa's defenders, who complained that the white South African government was the victim of a double standard, he argued:

> There is not a world consensus against communist oppression, or oppression by military governments, or of one Asian or African ethnic group by another, comparable to that which exists against this surviving symbol of a white supremacism that all other societies in the world, to different degrees and in different ways, have repudiated over the last three decades. . . . While this should not lead us to fail to protest against . . . other [violations of human rights], we should also recognize that it is not now possible to unite the international community on any other basis than that of a clear repudiation of white supremacism.[14]

Secondly, Bull believed that the social scientist must recognize that there can be no value-free inquiry; and, he added, if it were possible it would be of little interest—another reason for Bull's distrust of the purely scientific approach.[15] Nevertheless, while the presence of values is one thing, to smuggle them in or to peddle them explicitly is quite another. There are many warnings in Bull's work against this—against models of the future into which the writers inject their value preferences by indulging in excessive "salvationism," and against moral preaching in writings on arms control and international justice which oversimplify highly complex moral issues and disregard some of the costs of the solutions they recommend. Indeed, Bull is critical of moral generalizations. To him they are impossible, because of the complexity of concrete situations and because of the very difficulty of the choices faced by statesmen. For instance, the avoidance of war is not always the highest imperative (Bull was writing about Munich); justice and order cannot always be reconciled; the universal promotion of human rights can be "subversive of coexistence" because of the absence of any substantive consensus in this field.[16] Bull was painfully aware not only of the gap between moral imperatives and political reality but also of the multiplicity of moral perspectives in the contemporary world. As he pointed out in his critiques of works by E. B. F. Midgley[17] and Michael Walzer,[18] neither natural law nor Walzer's brand of liberal individualism is acceptable as the truth: for instance, they have been rejected by revolutionaries and by absolute pacifists.

On the other hand, as early as page 25 of *The Control of the Arms Race* we find the following statement: "Moral judgements . . . should never be overridden or sacrificed." The social scientists need to ask broad moral questions. These questions—about the role of the great powers, or the claims of the Third World, or the virtues of the states system—Bull always asked. He did so because he believed that moral issues were susceptible to rational investigation and could even be settled if the parties shared the same moral premises or if the premises involved were universally held—the respect for human life, for property and the sanctity of agreements.[19] Both the multiplicity of moral alternatives and the possibility of moral argument led Hedley Bull to demand that social scientists and philosophers dealing with moral issues in foreign affairs should try to transcend subjectivity and lay out the foundations of their positions. (This was the rationale behind his critique of Michael Walzer, whom he commended for his determination to revive just-war theory but blamed for refusing to explain his own moral theory from the ground up.) However, it must be said that Bull himself never did lay out fully the foundations of his own moral position; he also recognized that, ultimately, there is often no rational way of choosing between moral ends.[20]

The third point to be made about Hedley Bull's thoughts on ethics and international relations is that this omission did not prevent him from making explicit prescriptions (in just the same way that he would have liked a "self-proclaimed realist" like E. H. Carr to have made out a moral case against Munich). It is not surprising to find two sources behind Bull's own explicit prescriptions: the natural law tradition and the values of the West. Natural law, "a doctrine which proclaims that rules are valid among all mankind quite irrespective of the social and cultural facts of the time," he found particularly interesting, "now that there exists a global international society that has clearly outgrown its originally European social or cultural base, . . . and doubts may be entertained as to whether any genuinely universal society or culture has yet taken its place.[21] It was the values of the West which he evoked in his argument for "some degree of commitment to the cause of individual rights on a world scale,"[22] as well as in his condemnation of South Africa and of

Western, primarily American, arguments for supporting the white regime there.[23] It is natural law, tempered by his awareness of the limits and fragility of consensus in the realm of justice, which informs his recommendations about the concept of justice we should embrace in the present international system. Taken together, Bull's writings show that he heeded his own advice about the need to go beyond the language of the sociology of moral belief to that of morals—to that of rights and duties.

Hedley Bull's View of International Society

We now come to Bull's view of international society. Here is where his originality lies: it is *society* rather than *system* which he, virtually alone among contemporary theorists of international affairs, stresses and studies. *System* means contact between states and the impact of one state on another; *society* means (in Bull's words) common interests and values, common rules and institutions. His point of departure is what has sometimes been called the Grotian approach. More will be said about this below. Here we find one of the differences between Bull and Aron or Waltz: unlike him, they start with the international system. A second feature of Bull's originality, a consequence of his emphasis on society over system, is his theory of change, which is very different from that of Waltz or Robert Gilpin. Gilpin attributes change in international affairs to the rise and fall of hegemonic powers; Waltz sees change as the result of shifts in the distribution of power between states, leading from a bipolar to a multipolar system, or vice versa. In contrast, Bull is interested in the cultural change which produces a different perception of common interests in a context of coexistence and cooperation. He is, in other words, emphasizing the passage from a mere system to a society, or from a narrower society to one that includes many more members. He is also interested in the effects of major upheavals like the Reformation, the French Revolution, and the Russian Revolution, which introduced drastically new beliefs and rules into the international society.

What was the origin of Bull's concern for the international society? It seems to have started with his dissatisfaction with alternative approaches. Bull rejected a purely Hobbesian view of international affairs as a state of war or a struggle of all against all. He refuted Hobbes by using some of Hobbes's own arguments, so as to explain why the state of war between nations was more bearable than the state of war between individuals and why there was therefore no need for a universal Leviathan (the state's ability to protect the industry of its subjects, the lesser vulnerability of the state compared to the naked individual because of its greater power, the unevenness of states compared to the puny equality of individuals in the state of nature).[24] Moreover—unlike the Hobbesians— Bull denied that it was only the existence of central state power which could make possible the emergence of a society or could prevent its collapse or disintegration; anarchy *is* compatible with society, because the state is not the only reason for obeying rules in society. In one of his first published essays on the British commonwealth of nations, he noted the incompatibility of theories of Realpolitik with the reality of a group of states whose mutual relations were not inherently antagonistic.[25]

On the other hand, Bull also rejects what he considers to be Kant's universalism and cosmopolitanism, and he criticizes Kant for inconsistency[26]—although, in my opinion, he misreads Kant, who was much less cosmopolitan and universalist in his writings on international affairs than Bull suggests. Kant never advocated a world state or government, after all, and Bull failed to distinguish here between two conceptions which Michael Walzer, for instance, separates carefully: cosmopolitanism, which tries to overcome the barriers to the unity of mankind set by the existence of nations and by national borders; and what Walzer calls the "legalist paradigm," which looks at international relations as a society of states with mutual rights and duties, a conception which is not only similar to Bull's but actually quite close to Kant's.

The second source of Bull's view of international society is his intellectual sympathy for historical authors whose work stressed society even at a time when (as he recognized) reality was really more like a jungle than a society—the theologians and international lawyers of the sixteenth and seventeenth centuries, and particularly Grotius. Clearly there is a parallel between these men, writing at a time when, amid considerable strife and chaos, a radically new system was being created out of the disintegration of the medieval one, and today's expansion of the international system into the first truly global one.

Bull's approach to the study of international society is marked by one important tension, which gives rise to a number of unanswered questions. This is the tension between his realism and his emphasis on the rules and institutions which dampen anarchy—international law, the balance of power, even war as a means of preserving a balance, the role of the great powers with their special responsibilities to international society, the rule of nonintervention. He also emphasizes the community of culture that makes international society possible and requires, if not ideological homogeneity, at least the toleration of ideological differences. In other words, he stresses elements which, taken to an extreme, cause him to appear perilously close to the construction of Hans Kelsen, which he himself criticizes. Kelsen analyzed international law, both as the product of a system in which states interact in pursuit of their separate interests and as the product of an organized society which collectively delegates functions to its members for the enforcement of the common good. In one of his very last works, on international justice, Hedley Bull wrote about "the concept of a world common good" and about the need, "in the absence of a supranational world authority, . . . for particular states to seek as wide a consensus as possible, and on this basis to act as local agents of a world common good." In the next sentence, however, we are reminded that "states are notoriously self-serving in their policies, and rightly suspected when they purport to act on behalf of the international community as a whole"; such a pretense can be "in fact a menace to international order."[27] The same oscillation can be found in some of his writings about questions of military security: in *The Control of the Arms Race,* Bull's concern, he tells us, is not national security but international security, the security of the society of states as a whole—a concept which I myself, with a view of international relations a little more Hobbesian and less Grotian than Bull's, have always found difficult to understand, since in the matter of security "international society" consists of members who distrust one another and spend most of their time if not actually attacking each other then at least protecting themselves from attack.

Bull's own kind of realism, however, was never left far behind. He always managed to correct his Grotian inclinations by an infusion of what he called Oppenheim's pluralism. As a reader of Oppenheim, Bull had commented on the inadequacy of a domestic model for the understanding of the nature of international law or international society; and he stressed the role war plays as an ordinary instrument of state policy rather than as a crime condemned by international society or a sanction enforcing that society's principles. Bull had commented that the adherence of states to international law does not mean that they respect it. He had expressed his skepticism about what he called "the neo-idealist fashions" of today—the recent tendency of some American scholars to depreciate the continuing importance of force in international affairs and to celebrate the emergence of a transnational society.[28] Bull was aware of the fact that in the period following World War I the revival of Grotianism had let to a utopian attempt to reform the international milieu into a society in which war would be banned unless it was an exercise of collective security—an effort that may have been detrimental to the placing of limits on the conduct of war (Bull cites such cases as the Italian invasion of Abyssinia, the Nuremberg trials, and the Korean War).[29]

The questions that Hedley Bull left unanswered are two kinds. In the first place they have to do with the delicate balance between Kelsen, or Grotius, and Oppenheim, or Hobbes—the distinction between society and system, which Bull never expounded systematically. He showed that anarchy was compatible with society; but how much society, as it were, is likely to flourish in an anarchical structure? Conversely, could the factors of society ever hope to overcome the antagonisms which are built into and grow out of an anarchical structure?

Bull's own work laid stress on the emergence of a universal international society, a society previously dominated by Western states and gradually extended, first to non-Western states which accepted European values and then to all the new states which emerged from decolonization after World War II. This expansion raised a question which Bull had only begun to address in his most recent work: can one have a universal society without a common cultural framework, with a cosmopolitan ideal that is only an ideal, indeed, one that is not even shared by all the cultural systems? Bull's final answer was yes, so long as there are still common interests.

The second kind of question which Hedley Bull left unexplored, and which is sorely missed, concerns the distinction, not in theory but in international reality, between different types of international society, in the way in which Martin Wight had distinguished different kinds of states systems. From the point of view of the international order (and this was always Hedley Bull's), there must be a difference between an international society endowed with a common culture and one whose only cement is provided by the (perhaps very short-lived) common interests of its members. From that same point of view, much depends on the kind of culture which underlies a given international society, on the nature of its values, and on how broad or deep the culture is. These are questions which Bull had only begun to address in his writings about the present-day international system.

Hedley Bull and the Contemporary World Scene

The three aspects of Hedley Bull's work that will be taken up here are, first, Bull's analysis of the nature of the contemporary world scene; second, Bull and the nuclear conundrum; and third, Bull's writings on the superpowers and the power balance.

Bull's analysis of the nature of the contemporary world scene is extremely rich; but it is marked by considerable ambivalence and unresolved tension. The question he asked was, what is the degree of society present today? His reply is complex and ambiguous.[30] He produces considerable evidence to show that there has been a dangerous weakening of the elements of society in the current system. He lists the following factors. First, obviously, there is the superpower conflict. Surprisingly enough, this is the factor Bull writes least about, perhaps because he believed his American colleagues were writing about almost nothing else; there is particularly little in his work about the ideological aspects of the superpower conflict. In the second place, Bull finds that the balance of power has been preserved, but, in contrast to that of the nineteenth century, it continues without a common culture as its basis. Third, in addition to the balance of power, there is now mutual nuclear deterrence; but Bull finds it extremely fragile, for reasons to be mentioned below.

The fourth factor in the weakening of current society that Bull discusses, particularly in his most recent work, is the "revolt against the West," the positions taken by the developing nations. This revolt he sees as triply dangerous. It is dangerous, first, because it entails a partial repudiation of the preexisting rules and institutions of international society. He mentions practices by Third World states which violate the principle of diplomatic immunity; he refers also to multiple interventions by some of these states in the affairs of others, as if the barriers against intervention existed against intrusions by the West only. In his 1983 lectures on justice at the University of Waterloo, he added that many countries of the Third World repudiate the Western view that the rights which states enjoy in international law must be compatible with their obligations to the international community. The revolt against the West is dangerous, second, because it results from and contributes to the increasing cultural heterogeneity of international society. In a conference on international relations held in April 1968 at Bellagio—the conference attended by Aron and Morgenthau where Hedley Bull complained about the primitive character of Hans Morgenthau's theory—he remarked that we were now living in a worldwide international system that had "outrun its cultural basis." In his lectures on justice he gave as examples of increasing cultural heterogeneity the differences between Western and Third World conceptions of self-determination, human rights, and economic justice. Last, the revolt against the West is dangerous because it increases what might be called structural heterogeneity, on two levels. On the one hand, as he pointed out, many of the new states are states by courtesy only. And at the level of the system, the demands of the Third World aim at attaining not only greater racial, economic, and cultural equality but also a redistribution of power, which, according to Bull, raises insoluble issues, particularly in the military realm, where the need for order (he had in mind the need to preserve the world from further nuclear proliferation) must sometimes supersede demands for justice.[31]

Hedley Bull's Optimism

Ultimately, however, Bull's reply to this question—what is the degree of international society today—is reasonably optimistic. Here again, several factors must be listed. First, the attractiveness of war as an instrument of policy has diminished, at least between the superpowers. Second, the superpowers themselves have set up various arrangements in order to preserve peace, although these arrangements—which include the Non-Proliferation Treaty of 1968—are not always in strict conformity with justice. Third come the many influences which reinforce the norm of non-intervention. Bull deemed these forces more powerful than the opposite forces which weaken it, and he presented them as a mixture of external power factors, domestic ones, and ideological or cultural beliefs. However, many of the factors which deter intervention are themselves ambiguous, because they are also facets of the revolt against the West: many barriers against intervention were set up by anticolonialist actors, by the revolt against racism, by the demands for greater economic justice. This ambiguity complicates the problem.

The fourth factor to mention, according to Bull, is the gradual acceptance by the non-Western states of the basic elements of international society, despite all the breaches of it which I have mentioned above. Bull thought that such essential ingredients of international society as the principle of state sovereignty, international law, and international organization were being accepted, in theory and practice, by the non-Western states. He also gave to their demands for greater power and greater justice a reformist rather than a revolutionary interpretation. Fifth, in his lectures at the University of Waterloo, he talked about an emerging consensus on certain common notions of distributive justice—despite the lack of agreement on who should be the distributor, the principles of distribution, and any theory of the concept of distributive justice in international relations. This emerging consensus may also have been one of the aspects of the contemporary cultural change which Bull saw as a positive factor: it would bring the different cultures which today coexist closer together. Last, he stressed his belief that it is possible for an international society to exist without a common culture, so long as there is a solid network of common interests; he pointed out that one should not identify, and confuse, present-day international society with the quite exceptional one of the nineteenth century. (One cannot fail to be struck once again here by the importance Bull attached to values and beliefs, as opposed to "rules of the game" and what American theorists call "international regimes," in his account of the components of present-day society.)

The Direction of Contemporary Change

This balanced analysis raised the question of the forces and directions of change in the current international system. Bull answered this in two ways. Analytically, his answer is somewhat ambivalent. On the one hand, he sees no evidence of the world moving "beyond the states system." In *The Anarchical Society,* he asserts that the states system is neither in decline, nor obsolete, nor dysfunctional. In his opinion, none of the schemes which have been presented for its reform are likely to be realized. On the other hand, he detects the beginning of a "wider world political system of which the states system is only part";[32] but, having given us this tantalizing glimpse, he proceeds to remove it from our sight by attempting to prove that what many scholars have presented as entirely new and beyond the states system—for instance, nonstate actors and transnational society—either is not new at all or is really only the states system (or, rather, one dominant state, the United States) in disguise.

The second part of Bull's answer to the problem of contemporary change lies in his prescriptions. At the end of *The anarchical Society,* he recognizes that the book constitutes an "implicit defence of the states system," in particular, a defense of the principle of state sovereignty as the best contemporary way of protecting human beings against forcible external interference. Yet Bull was clearly aware of the need for change beyond the status quo, in a number of directions. Most important of these was his plea for a broadening of the consensus on common interests among states in a way that would include the countries of the Third

World. The need to take into account the demands of the "have nots" was the one positive element he had found in the work of E. H. Carr. Bull's recommendations on justice in international relations showed his desire to satisfy the legitimate demands of the developing countries without in any way giving up essential Western values. This is why he insisted that the recognition of the rights of states should be kept subject to and limited by the rights of the international community and why he emphasized the importance of what he called a profound change in the perception of justice in international law: "The rights and benefits to which justice has to be done in the international community are not simply those of states and nations, but those of individual persons throughout the world as a whole."[33] Indeed, the most striking prescriptions in his most recent work concern the need to develop the cosmopolitan elements in the present world culture, not only as they affect the rights of individuals but with reference to the new conception of a common good for the human species. In both these domains he was aware of the broad range of disagreements among states—especially on human rights questions—and of the absence of any consensus on the means and institutions for stemming "the dangers of nuclear war, disequilibrium between population and resources, or environmental deterioration." Nevertheless he tried to suggest ways of moving in this direction, which might be called, if not "beyond and after the states system," at least a "states system plus," a states system within a wider one that borrowed elements from the "domestic model." Society would thus be sought not only within the (anarchical) states system but beyond.

Ultimately, in this part of his work we find one tension that could also be detected in the work of E. H. Carr: a tension between Bull's awareness of the special importance of the great powers because of their evident stake in preserving international society (a stake which he thought greater than that of other powers) and his awareness of their inadequacy in a global international system in which they cannot fulfill their traditional functions alone any more—for two reasons: because of the greater capacity of smaller powers to resist and because of the greater potency of ideologies of resistance and of international equality. Like Carr, Bull resolves this tension by an argument in support of a much broader definition by the great powers of their own interests—and of the common interest.

Hedley Bull and the Nuclear Conundrum

One of the main perils threatening the human species is the nuclear predicament. Hedley Bull's work on arms control is of considerable importance to students of international affairs. First, it was planted firmly in a political context, unlike, for instance, the contribution of Thomas Schelling. Like Schelling, Hedley Bull emphasized the unity of strategic doctrine and of arms control; but unlike him, Bull also believed in the unity of all military policies (whether strategic or arms control) and foreign policy. Second, the political context Bull had in mind was never just the superpower rivalry with which his American colleagues were obsessed. Bull tried to analyze the possible contribution arms control might make to international society as a whole, since contemporary society rests to such a large extent on a recognition of common interests. It is always from this point of view that Bull asserted that superpower arms control alone was inadequate.[34] Third, although he thought it far more realistic than disarmament, Bull remained extremely skeptical about the value of arms control as a panacea. For him, it could become one, perhaps, but only if states had arms control as their central objective (and most of the time they do not) or if states behaved entirely rationally. But, once again, he greeted the concept of "the rational action of a kind of strategic man" with derision, on the grounds that it was good only for "formal theorizing." Strategic man, he wrote, is "a man who on further acquaintance reveals himself as a university professor of unusual intellectual subtlety."[35]

What were his main contributions to the study of arms control? They may not appear deeply original today, but they certainly were in 1961. Along with Aron's, his was the main non-American voice in the early—and still the best—chorus of "nuclear theorists." In the first place, Bull very soon became aware of the conditions for the stability of nuclear deterrence and of the risks of destabilization. As early as 1961, in *The Control of the Arms Race,* he had defined the conditions of stability as the absence of any capacity for a disarming first strike and the absence of any capability to defend one's population and one's industries. Destabilization could therefore result both from weapons of increasing accuracy and payload—Bull was disturbed by the appearance of multiple independently targeted reentry vehicles (MIRV)—and from the development of antiballistic missiles or strategic defenses in general. Many years ago, Bull reviewed the arguments which had been presented, particularly by the late Donald Brennan, in favor of strategic defenses.[36] He analyzed them with great fairness: he sympathized with the doubts Brennan and Dyson had expressed about the "rationality models" that underlie deterrence theory. But ultimately he rejected their case: he thought that defenses would lead to a dangerous escalation of the arms race, largely because of the countermeasures which each side would obviously be eager to take in order to restore the supremacy of the offensive.

Bull's second contribution to the study of arms control was his awareness of the fragility of arms control as a basis for international order. At the end of his life he seemed to be more optimistic about the stability of nuclear deterrence, in spite of the fact that the theoretical vulnerability of land-based missiles was growing—something which was driving so many Americans crazy. He thought that countermeasures could make these missiles less vulnerable and that stability could survive the vulnerability of one element of the triad of sea-based, land-based, and air-based nuclear systems. Bull wrote that stable deterrence did not depend on or require the doctrine of mutual assured destruction. He thus acknowledged the possibility of what McGeorge Bundy would later call existential deterrence: a condition in which the nuclear powers deter each other from the use of nuclear weapons whatever their strategic doctrine may be.[37] Nevertheless, Bull believed that strategic nuclear deterrence could never serve as a satisfactory foundation of international order, for a whole series of reasons. First, deterrence concentrates on a set of means, whereas the important question for Hedley Bull concerned states' ends. Second, it focuses attention on military issues when the important issue in avoiding war is the management and control of political crises. Third, deterrence deals with the prevention of war but leaves out of discussion what states should do if deterrence fails and war breaks out. Fourth, deterrence is based on that assumption of rationality which Bull always distrusted. Fifth, strategic nuclear deterrence is an intensely bipolar phenomenon in a world in which nuclear weapons are spreading. Sixth and last, a point which Bull made in passing with his usual discretion: peace based on nuclear deterrence alone is "morally disreputable".[38] It is the same awareness of fragility which made Bull skeptical about the scenarios—so often favored by American scholars—of limited nuclear war used to compensate for Western conventional inferiority.

Bull's own recommendations in the nuclear realm were conspicuous for their realism. He could be scathingly critical of pleas for unilateral disarmament or for complete and general disarmament. He was skeptical—more, perhaps, than I would be—about the prospects of comprehensive arms control agreements; he showed more sympathy for unilateral and parallel restraints, and he thought partial agreements more probable. He was aware of the impossibility of distinguishing offensive from defensive weapons; and he did not think it was possible to distinguish between weapons on the basis of the different missions assigned to them, since each weapons system is capable of performing a whole variety of missions. He realized that many weapons systems, including antiballistic missiles and multiple independent warheads, could be both stabilizing and destabilizing. All these points contributed to his doubts about the chances of comprehensive negotiated arms control. Such negotiations, Bull noted, had actually generated new increases in armaments.

Nevertheless, Bull did not give up on the subject of arms control. He had his own prescriptions. He did not think states needed to put the threshold for mutual assured destruction as high as they did. In other words, it did not make much sense for the superpowers to have (as they now do) something like ten thousand strategic nuclear warheads each. But he was aware of the fact that if the threshold was set too low, the risks incurred in case of a violation—or, put another way, the incentive to attempt to disarm the adversary by a first strike—would rise correspondingly. He was hesitant about the best formula for arms control. In 1969, before the first large-scale superpower agreements, he suggested the superpowers should try to limit the numbers of deployed launch vehicles; in 1979, after the mixed record of the SALT process, he wrote that the formula of parity in numbers of deployed launch vehicles followed by reductions was unsatisfactory. He wanted nuclear weapons to serve only to deter from the use of other nuclear weapons—a position which anticipated the stand taken by McGeorge Bundy, George Kennan, Robert McNamara, and George Ball, among others, against any first use of nuclear weapons in case of a conventional attack. (Bull himself doubted, however, that the conventional capabilities of NATO would allow it to adopt such a doctrine.) Finally, he advocated much greater urgency in the task of preventing nuclear proliferation, and he blamed the superpowers' "high posture," their constant escalation of their nuclear arms race, for encouraging third parties to become nuclear states.

Hedley Bull and the Present-Day Balance of Power

Two interesting tensions are to be found in Bull's work on the subject of the balance of power in the present-day international system. The first of these is a tension between two modes of international society.[39] In the first mode, society can be, as he put it, "contrived" or deliberately arranged. In this respect Bull pointed to the role of the great powers: they form a club which has special rights and duties and performs important functions even in the conflictual bipolar world of today. Bull stuck to this notion, largely because of his remarkably non-Manichaean view of the contemporary international system. He emphasized the set of "rules of the game" developed by the superpowers in the 1960s and expanded during the period of detente of the 1970s, which he greeted as a period of progress. But in the second mode, society can be more "fortuitous." In this perspective, Bull's emphasis was on a rather more mechanical and contentious balancing of power than the agreements between the superpowers or their observance of mutual respect for each other's spheres of local preponderance. For Bull, the balancing of power was a necessity for the survival of international society; and this conviction led him to repeat frequently an interesting argument, which enraged many Americans. According to Bull, in the world of today, only the Soviet Union is capable of balancing the power of the United States. Bull used this argument to explain, or perhaps explain away, the Soviet military buildup.[40]

There was another tension in Bull's work on the balance of power: a tension between two approaches to universal society. At one point Bull depicted universal society as resting on a single culture. In the 1968 Bellagio conference, he pointed out that the United States was providing the only basis for the new global society, because American culture had spread through most of the world. He wondered whether the removal of this common basis would not be disastrous, since it could lead either to the risk of Soviet hegemony or to the multiplication of troublesome and potentially nuclear powers. But at a later stage he thought that the universal society which had been formed through the extension of membership to the nations emancipated from colonialism and which was characterized by the revolt against the West, could only survive by accommodating all the different cultures which exist in it today—even if this kind of compromise provided a much weaker common basis than that which European culture had constituted for the international society of previous centuries.

It appears to me that Bull made one attempt to reconcile these divergent notions: in his plea for a Western European entity capable of providing its own defense system. It is one of the paradoxes of recent years that non-Europeans have often been more militantly in favor of a European entity than the Europeans themselves. Bull's rather belated but spectacular conversion to "Europeanism" was a way of achieving a synthesis of his different concerns. First, he saw in the European entity an answer to a problem which he saw as increasingly pressing: the need to balance the power of a United States which in recent years had repudiated detente and appeared to be seeking superiority or even hegemony. Second, a European entity was needed to balance the power of the Soviet Union, which had not repudiated detente and whose policy Bull interpreted as probably defensive in its inspiration, but which would remain defensive in action only as long as there was a strong Western guard. Clearly, Bull had become deeply disillusioned with both superpowers. Already in 1980 he had denounced them as ill fitted to the role which great powers had traditionally played—the United States because of its peculiar past and its tendency to proselytize its own vision; the United States and the Soviet Union together because of their instinctive belief that the menace of superior power can be canceled by virtuous intentions. Both superpowers seemed to him to be insufficiently dependent on the world economy, and plagued by what he called the domestic self-absorption of very large societies.[41] If neither one nor both together could claim to be regarded as trustees for mankind, maybe Europe could.

Bull believed that Europe had a special link with the Third World, largely because of the combination of a colonial past and a sense of guilt about the colonialism. He thought that Europe was uniquely qualified to conduct in the Third World the policy of accommodation which, according to him, the Reagan administration had abandoned and repudiated. Bull also believed that the Europeans would not follow Mr. Reagan's America in a policy of "constructive engagement"—for instance, appeasement of South Africa—which he deemed strategically as well as morally wrong and attributed to cold war obsessions and oversimplification in Washington. Finally, he thought that the construction of a European political and military entity was vital for Western European dignity.

In other words, the Western European undertaking seemed to Bull to represent the choice of universalism over "Americanism" in culture and a mixed policy combining balance (between the major powers) and deliberate contrivance (in the relations with the Third World) in international society. Bull's objective was still to strengthen that society: Western Europe, he thought, was the area where the greatest recognition of the need for international society was to be found; and he wished Western Europe to become a great power so as to prevent the rift in the superpower club from becoming irreparable. But, once again, the only thing missing has been the capacity and the will of the Europeans to play such an ambitious role.

In *The Control of the Arms Race,* Bull had written that "the world is very much more complicated than the arguments" he had presented, and that "the destinies of nations are not determined by simple choices of the soul."[42] But Hedley Bull's work has illuminated these complications in a way which is unique and original precisely because of the rich tension and dialogue between the Grotian elements of his work and the more pluralistic, conflictual views; the choices of this particular soul were never simple, but always generous and wise. This is why his disappearance at a tragically early age is such a serious loss for all students of international relations. In such a small number of years he has given us at lest three reasons for admiring his achievements and continuing his effort. He provided us with the first comprehensive defense and illustration of arms control in an age dominated by the nuclear threat. He gave us the most panoramic and incisive analysis of the rules, institutions, and prospects of the "anarchical society" constituted by the modern states system. And he showed that one can recognize "the limits of rigour and precision" and be "on guard against their misuse" without ever "abandoning rigour and precision in favor" of sloppiness or stridency.[43] His was a highly civilized voice, in which skepticism and hope were admirably balanced. There are few such voices left.

3

Ideal Worlds

Moral and political philosophy have had little to say about international affairs. Rousseau and Kant told us that we would never be truly free beings as long as wars pitted societies against one another and made it easier for authoritarian leaders to rule arbitrarily. But political and moral philosophers have remained concerned with the quest for the good life within society and for the just political state. Insofar as international affairs preoccupied them at all, some of them, the realists, told us that the "state of nature," in which states find themselves competing for power, ruled out moral behavior and allowed for no better conditions than those the balancing of power would produce. Others told us that the triumph of representative and constitutional government at home, and of the principle of national self-determination, would produce a harmonious liberal world of cooperating nation-states, which reduced powers for mischief. Still others, the Marxists, informed us that the revolutionary triumph of the proletariat would result in the "withering away" of the state and, therefore, of the division of the world into competing states as well.

The failure of both the liberal and the Marxist prophecies seemed to abandon the field to the cheerless "eternal verities" of realism, warning us that the need for order—always threatened by the states' contest—takes precedence over the quest for justice.[1] Far from stifling the hunger for a philosophy that might offer some picture of a better international society, realism—rejuvenated by E. H. Carr, Hans Morgenthau, George Kennan, and Henry Kissinger—exacerbated it. Realism seemed inadequate in a world of clashing sovereign states that could be destroyed by nuclear weapons: this time, the struggle for power risked destroying the whole field of players, not just some of them—even Morgenthau concluded that a nuclear world of states, without any central power above them, had become intolerable. Indeed, in the early 1960s and again in the 1980s theologians and philosophers fought fiercely over nuclear ethics, arguing about both the probability and the morality of nuclear war and over whether a resort to nuclear weapons could ever be justified.[2] At the same time, formerly colonized states raised the issue of distributive justice—how unfairly resources and wealth are distributed—in a world whose parts were increasingly interdependent yet divided by a widening gap between rich and poor. A third reason was the relatively recent but powerful concern for the environment—the awareness that the onslaught of human activities against the world's resources, climate, and species could not be addressed by the old methods of leisurely diplomacy. Finally, after the horrors of World War II, there was the spread of a new variant of liberalism: the ideology of human rights. It concentrated not on the virtues of liberal nation-states, as before, but on the crimes committed against human beings in a large number of states. The advocates of human rights pointed out that the very notions of state sovereignty and national self-determination that nineteenth-century liberalism had endorsed were being used by governments and militant nationalists as a shield protecting a broad range of violations of individual and group rights from external scrutiny and correction.

In other words, the time had come to apply the traditional concerns and queries of political and moral philosophy to international society as a whole. Debates about the principles to apply to the issues I have mentioned were mainly over what John Rawls in his *Theory of Justice* calls "non-ideal theory." It deals, on the one hand, with overcoming those "natural limitations and historical contingencies"[3] that prevent "the poorer and less technologically advanced societies of the world" from attaining "historical and social conditions that allow them to establish just and workable institutions"[4] and, on the other hand, with "principles for meeting injustice,"[5] that is, how to handle evil and aggressive regimes. What was missing, however, was ideal theory. In Rawls's terms, when (as in *A Theory of Justice*) ideal theory addresses justice in a national society, it provides "the principles that characterize a well-ordered society under favorable circumstances"[6]. When it deals with international society, it sets rules of behavior for "well-ordered" societies, that is, societies whose citizens accept the same principles of justice, whose institutions satisfy those principles, and whose governments comply with the rules of conduct they have endorsed. Such a theory would serve as a yardstick with which the existing international society could be judged and provide us with directions for reform. The distinction between ideal and nonideal theory is an old one. Rousseau's social contract gave us ideal theory, the principles and institutions of a perfect democracy; in his essays on Poland and Corsica he adapted it to nonideal, specific historical cases.

It is not surprising that Rawls should be the one contemporary philosopher who tries systematically—in a short set of lectures delivered at Oxford—to provide us with an ideal theory for international society. He uses his "social contract doctrine" to develop what he calls "the law of peoples." This is not international law but "a political conception of right and justice,"[7] based on liberal ideas of justice "similar to but more general" than his central idea of "justice as fairness" presented in *A Theory of Justice* and applied to international affairs. In his famous earlier book, and in his more recent essays in *Political Liberalism,* Rawls had tried to define a conception and principles of justice that would apply to the "main political, social, and economic institutions" of society, conceived as a "fair system of cooperation over time,"[8] and would also be acceptable to men and women who hold very different conceptions of ethics and metaphysics—what he calls different "comprehensive doctrines." The principles are the object of a social contract among "free and rational persons concerned to further their own interests" and the result of Rawls's famous procedure in which he seeks principles of justice that such persons would "accept in an initial position of equality as defining the fundamental terms of their association."[9] For that purpose, he imagines representatives of the individual members of society, in that "original position," as being behind a "veil of ignorance." They don't know their place, class position, social status, fortune, strength, or "even their conceptions of the good or their special psychological propensities"[10]. They have only "the two powers of moral personality, namely, the capacity for a sense of justice and the capacity for a conception of the good."[11] In this state they are to choose the principles of justice they prefer. This procedure formalizes the situation of citizens—free and equal—in the "public political culture of a constitutional democratic regime"[12]. The principles that emerge from it grant to each person an equal claim to "a fully adequate scheme of equal rights and liberties" and tolerate inequalities only if they are "attached to positions . . . open to all . . ." and—this is the famous "difference principle"—only if "they are to be to the greatest benefit of the least advantaged members of society"[13]. These principles are strictly political in two respects: they deal merely with the "basic structure," and they constitute a conception that is "political, not metaphysical." That makes it possible for believers in a wide variety of "reasonable" moral and religious doctrines to arrive at, accept, and endorse this conception of justice. A "reasonable" person is one who is "ready to propose principles . . . as fair terms of cooperation and to abide by them willingly, given the assurance that others will likewise do so"; he is also "ready to discuss the fair terms that others propose"[14]. Furthermore, a reasonable person or doctrine is willing to recognize what Rawls calls the "burdens of judgment"—the inevitability of "reasonable disagreement," given "the many hazards involved in he correct (and conscientious) exercise of our powers of reason and judgment in the ordinary course of political life" (conflicting evidence, different weighing of values, different individual experiences, difficulty in setting priorities, etc.)[15]. In this way, he hopes to reconcile a pluralism of reasonable conceptions of the good (for instance, different beliefs about the role of religion in society) with a single political conception of justice. It is itself a conception of the good, but one limited to the political realm. By endorsing it, citizens "affirm the same political conception of justice"[16]. This means that they share "one very basic political end": supporting just institutions and giving one another justice accordingly. The "good of justice" and mutual self-respect, secured by a just political society, are fundamental needs of all citizens.

Rawls had already sketched what the extension of this conception to the "law of peoples" would look like in a couple of pages of his *Theory of Justice* and had disappointed several of his disciples.[17] The new, longer version has revived and sharpened those disappointments. It is not obvious that the social contract method is the best approach to ideal theory, that the specific features of Rawls's brand of social contract lead to satisfactory results, and that the distinction between ideal and nonideal theory really suits international relations.

Who Are the People?

Rawls returns to the method of the original position and of the veil of ignorance. But this time, the "parties" who, behind this veil, are to adopt the principles of justice for international society are not persons who stand in for you and me. They are (in a first stage) delegates of democratic "peoples": "representatives of societies well ordered by liberal conceptions of justice." They would not know "the size of the territory, or the population, or the relative strength of the people whose fundamental interest they represent" or "the extent of the natural resources, or level of economic development."[18] (It is worth noting that Rawls does not ask them to ignore their political culture, whereas he had asked the parties representing individuals in a democratic political culture to ignore their conceptions of the good: for Rawls, the diversity of political cultures seems irremediable, whereas that of "comprehensive doctrines" can be overcome in the political realm of a democracy.) What principles would these representatives of "peoples" decide to adopt? Rawls argues they would arrive at fairly classic principles of international law: "peoples" are to be free, independent, equal, entitled to defend themselves but not to wage war, obliged to respect treaties, to honor human rights, and not to intervene in one another's affairs. This is also close to what Michael Walzer, in *Just and Unjust Wars,* calls the "legalist paradigm": a morality of and for states.[19]

But this approach begs a fundamental question for social contract theorists—and for other theorists of international society. International society is a society of both individuals (acting across borders, for instance, as investors or seeking protection from abroad against their government) and states. Are we seeking principles for states or for individuals? Do the delegates behind the veil of ignorance represent states or the world's individuals? Rawls's "peoples" are "corporate bodies organized by their governments"—that is, states.[20] To be sure, the "original position" devised by Rawls is, in the first part of his essay, a position for representatives of liberal democracies whose states are based on the citizens' consent and respect the citizens' rights. But even among liberal societies, the state is not a mere agglomeration of citizens, an association comparable to, although larger than, all the others.[21] The state shapes the individual and group interests it chooses to defend, and the state has the monopoly of coercion. Thus, the law of "peoples" runs immediately into three obstacles.

First, what is a "people"? Rawls says that one of his reasons for not starting with "a global original position" in which individuals would ask "whether and in what form there should be states, or peoples, at all" is that "peoples as corporate bodies organized by their governments now exist in some form all over the world."[22] Indeed; but in the nonideal world to which he thus refers, many of these "corporate bodies," such as Yugoslavia, the former Soviet Union, the Sudan, Algeria, and Rwanda, are disintegrating because they are racked by opposing conceptions of what constitutes a people: not only multinational versus national conceptions but also rival philosophies of nationality and citizenship. Moreover, states are also increasingly porous, penetrated by terrorists, refugees, and immigrants, and, as Rawls acknowledges, the right of "peoples" to regulate or exclude immigration is a source of intense ethical controversies among politicians and philosophers in Europe ad the United States. In other words, before we can have an ideal "law of peoples" we need a theory that would tell us what are the legitimate political units, and, if they are states, we need to know which entities are entitled to become states and who is entitled to become a citizen. Such a theory of state formation and membership would include the issues of self-determination, secession, the treatment of minorities, population movements, and the regulation of entry and exit. Rawls merely states that the rights to independence, self-determination, and secession require certain limits, such as respect for the freedom of another people, and he acknowledges a people's "qualified right to limit immigration"[23]. But without much deeper consideration of such subjects, "ideal theory" risks, in the philosopher Onora O'Neill's words, being not just abstract but "idealized," in the sense of applying "only to idealized agents," agents with at least one feature that cannot be found in reality[24]—in this instance, sovereign states whose sovereignty creates, by definition, no problems. Here we find already one difference between ideal theory for domestic society and ideal theory for "peoples": the former provides guidance for the solution of political problems, the latter tends to leave out some of the more fundamental issues from the beginning, such as the issues of what constitutes a "people" and the relation of "peoples" to "state."

This is confirmed by a second difficulty. The "peoples" organized into democratic states often promote the rights and interests of their members across borders in ways that lead to clashes. Japanese-American trade relations, Franco-American political and security relations, and Canadian and Spanish fishing practices are cases in point. They also pursue what might be called "state interests" of a geopolitical nature that are often quite risky, and different from those of the citizens. America's cold-war interventions in Central America or Vietnam, French interventions in black Africa, and American and French support for a variety of repressive regimes easily come to mind. How should states pursue their objectives? Rawls's "law of peoples" gives us only limited guidance. He tells us that states are not supposed to wage wars other than for self-defense and that they are to comply with obligations they have accepted. So far so good: the representatives of democratic "peoples" may well agree on such obligations. However, Rawls goes on to say that "we must reformulate the powers of sovereignty" so as to get rid not only of the right to war but also of the "right to internal autonomy" (i.e., to freedom from external intervention), which "fails in the case of disordered societies in which wars and serious violations of human rights are endemic;"[25] but the principles he proposes—not surprisingly, given the method by which they are arrived at, by imaginary representatives of organized "peoples" interested in protecting their own people from the intrusion of others—entail no such "reformulation." They offer far too thin and conservative a code of behavior, especially in a world in which interdependence empties sovereignty of much of its substance. A couple of sentences about (unspecified) "principles for forming and regulating" possible associations of democratic societies and "standards of fairness" for trade and other cooperative arrangements[26] are all we find in this connection. A world of "peoples" would have no world state: the peoples' delegates would, in Rawls's view, reject it on the same grounds as Kant: because it would be either tyrannical or excessively fragile. If this is so, then a theory of international justice has to address far more specifically the issue of the instruments, means, and methods states should use in their relations. It is an issue that can perhaps be left out of the ideal theory of a "well-ordered" democratic society where the state is assumed to be acting in our behalf and has a monopoly on coercion, but it is a crucial issue for a world of competing states, even when those states are democratic.

Moreover, a world of "peoples"—even democratic peoples—for which principles of justice are being sought is likely to remain a highly inegalitarian world of rich and poor states, given the uneven distribution of the world's resources and wealth. *A Theory of Justice* offered drastically egalitarian guidelines for distributive justice—the famous "difference principle" that has provoked so much debate, which holds that "the social and economic inequalities attached to offices and positions are to be adjusted so that, whatever the level of those inequalities . . . they are to the greatest benefit of the least advantaged members of society."[27] Rawls's ideal theory here simply assumes that the "peoples" will be well-ordered societies maintaining "decent social institutions"—an optimistic assumption—and will agree on "certain provisions for mutual assistance between peoples in times of famine and drought" and, "were it feasible, as it should be," on provisions for ensuring that in all "reasonably developed liberal societies people's basic needs are met"[28]—a vague and limited provision. Here, we find Rawls's ideal theory to be more timid than even the practices of our definitely nonideal international society.

These are the flaws of a theory for "peoples." However, an ideal theory derived from a "global original position" (for individuals, not peoples), requested by some of Rawls's disciples, such as Thomas Pogge, would run into serious trouble also. An ideal "law of peoples," as we have seen, looks a bit empty; but the kind of ideal theory for international society that begins not with "peoples" but with "abstracted" individuals placed behind the veil of ignorance is a blur. Does it concern itself with principles acceptable by all "reasonable" persons, whatever their political culture? These principles risk being both few and elementary, if they are supposed to accommodate cultures that restrict or deny basic individual rights or liberties. Does it seek principles acceptable to reasonable persons who share the political culture of democracy? This would be a richer set but leave the relations between these persons and all the others problematic. (Indeed, Rawls's second reason for rejecting a global original position is that it would treat "all persons, regardless of their society and culture, as individuals who are free and equal"[29], and thereby make the basis for the law of peoples too narrow, since this is only the liberal conception.)

A "global" ideal theory could, on the one hand, reach principles comparable to, or identical with, those of the *Theory of Justice,* including a global "difference" principle dealing with the huge economic and social inequalities that exist in the world. This would require a drastic redistribution of the world's resources. It would thus be hard to carry out in the absence of some kind of world government or of some highly unlikely consensus of states to enforce such provisions. On the other hand, what such a theory would have to say about the fundamental problem of international politics—the division of the world into a maze of separate communities, both states and nations—remains unclear. In *A Theory of Justice,* the parties behind the veil of ignorance are asked only to define principles of justice for an already constituted society and state. In a global origin position, the parties would have to decide how international society should be constituted: as a single society, or as a society of societies organized as states, or as a society of societies less endowed than the present states with the powers usually associated with state sovereignty (such as the rights to wage war, to be safe from external interference, to close its borders). Would individuals who, behind their veil of ignorance, would have "lost" their nationality along with their other distinctive characteristics and beliefs, choose to reduce boundaries to mere administrative divisions in a global polity? This too would be utopian. Would those denationalized persons, aware of the material, cultural, and psychological advantages that membership in a close-knit society (such as, say, Japan) entails, reaffirm the need for separate states on moral grounds—such as the human need to belong to a political society smaller and less remote than humanity as a whole (and in this case, when could a foreign state intervene legitimately to protect the "equal basic liberties" to which each person has an equal right?). A global original position for individuals raises the issue of the moral significance and importance of state boundaries. It is assumed to be great by communitarians (including Michael Walzer and Charles Taylor) and by all those who begin with peoples and states. By contrast, state boundaries tend to be dismissed as arbitrary and morally uncompelling by "globalists," such as Martha Nussbaum. There are intermediary positions, held by writers such as Charles Beitz and Yael Tamir, who deem borders morally important only if they are open and if what happens behind them is just. But the discussion of that crucial issue has only begun.[30] The attempt to arrive at a social contract for international affairs leads to an impasse.

Democracies and Other Regimes

The tension between individuals and "peoples" that plagues the search for a social contract is also at the root of the quarrel between communitarians, who stress the distinctiveness of the values and culture of each society and treat "the beliefs and practices of all recognized subcommunities as equally valid," and universalists, who emphasize the need to protect human rights everywhere "from utilitarian sacrifices, communitarian impositions, and from injury, degradation, and arbitrariness."[31] This tension is particularly visible in the writings of Michael Walzer. On the one hand, he argues that "thick" morality—the "culturally integrated, fully resonant" code of values and principles "elaborated" by every society—can exist only in a particular society; "societies are necessarily particular because they have members and memories . . . of their common life," whereas "humanity has members but no memory, and so it has no history and no culture . . . no shared understandings of social goods."[32] On the other hand, he recognizes that there exists a "thin" universal morality of which he gives a double account. It seems to be what the many "thick," communitarian moralities all have in common; but he also believes that there are some elementary moral demands and protests—for truth, against oppression, for justice, against genocide—that we all formulate and which can unite us at exceptional moments, usually against a common enemy, the "product of a historical conjuncture"[33]. At such moments, he tells us, a "politics of rescue" ought to override the principles of sovereignty and nonintervention, as should have been the case in Bosnia. But Walzer, on balance, is a "minimalist" universalist: the "thick" morality of each society is not based on or derived from the "thin" morality of universal principles; the latter is "only a piece" of the former.[34] As a result, social critics should mostly work from within their community's beliefs, and the world will remain a world of "tribes"—distinctive, often antagonistic ethnic groups (his concrete references cover mainly Eastern Europe, Caucasia, and the Near East). "Tribalism names the commitment of individuals and groups to their own history, culture, and identity, and this commitment (though not any particular version of it) is a permanent feature of human social life"[35]. Parochialism can't be overcome, it must be accommodated. Walzer writes sensible things about the need to make the tribes less destructive of one another and of minorities in their midst—by helping people have and accept multiple, overlapping identities and "divided selves"—but he provides no road map toward this goal, and his final comment is that "the crucial commonality of the human race is particularism"[36] and that the nation-state is "most obviously appropriate in those cases where a particular identity is . . . under siege"[37]. In these essays of "moral argument at home and abroad," there is little about the content of even a "thin" transcommunal morality—indeed, there is nothing at all about international distributive justice.

Rawls's approach is almost the opposite. He presents his doctrine as "universal in its reach," even though his methods are never general principles for all aspects of social life but, rather, principles "for each kind of subject as it arises," beginning with "principles of political justice for the basic structure of a closed and self-contained democratic society" and continuing with, say, principles for the law of peoples and principles for "special social questions." The final result is what he calls "a constructivist liberal doctrine," the sum of all these principles "endorsed on due reflection by the reasonable agents to whom the corresponding principles apply," with its authority resting "on the principles and conception of practical reason."[38] But if it is universal in the sense of being applicable to a variety of social and political issues, it is not universal in the sense of being acceptable to all societies. His principles for the law of peoples are derived from the "common understanding of liberal societies"[39], just as the principles of justice as fairness were embedded in the political culture of Western democracies. A key element of Rawls's law of peoples is his emphasis on human rights. How widely endorsable are these? In accordance with his own attempt, in his earlier work, to distinguish a "political conception" of justice from a "comprehensive" philosophical doctrine, Rawls avoids raising the controversial problem of the foundation of human rights: are they derived from God's will expressed in natural law? from human nature? from human sociability? from the dictates of reason? Each comprehensive doctrine has its own answer. Moreover, many of the world's societies would reject all these ideas as "in some way distinctive of the Western political tradition and prejudicial to other cultures"[40]. And just as he had, in his previous work, derived the principles of justice not from any "comprehensive" doctrine but from the idea of society "as a fair system of cooperation" among philosophically diverse individuals,[41] Rawls wants human rights not to depend "on any particular comprehensive moral doctrine or philosophical conception of human nature."[42] Instead, he states that human rights "express a minimum standard of well-ordered political institutions for all peoples who belong . . . to a just political society of peoples"[43]—that is, human rights are a requirement for a just international society. But two things happen here, which show once again the differences between ideal theory for a domestic society and for international society.

The "domestic" Rawls wants to show that the principles of political justice derived from the original position could be endorsed by individuals who believe in a variety of "reasonable" comprehensive doctrines—for instance, a Catholic doctrine that accepts the principle of toleration and a constitutional regime, a "comprehensive liberal moral doctrine" such as Kant's, and an "unsystematic," pluralist view.[44] This endorsement is what Rawls calls an "overlapping consensus"—without which political liberalism would be merely a doctrine, not a conception providing for political legitimacy and stability. Rawls has a special definition of consensus: he has firmly insisted on the difference between a rallying around principles arrived at first, independently of any comprehensive doctrine—which is what he seeks—and a modus vivendi, that is, a mere compromise among such doctrines or among group interests, which he deems unstable, since each party will keep trying to push forward its own views or interest (the example he gives is that of Catholics and Protestants in the sixteenth century[45]). The object of the "overlapping consensus" is a moral conception "affirmed on moral grounds" and limited to the political domain—the basic liberties and the "basic structure," that is, the main political, social, and economic institutions[46]. (Of course, critics have pointed out that the distinction between the political and the nonpolitical spheres is elusive, that few moral and religious "comprehensive doctrines" are likely to endorse a liberal conception of the political life, and that many such doctrines have their own conception not only of how we should live but also of how we should govern ourselves).[47]

In his Oxford lectures, Rawls wanted again to show that the liberal principles of international behavior, the "law of peoples" devised by representatives of democratic "peoples," could be freely endorsed also by other states, so that this liberal conception could not be denounced by representatives of other traditions as paternalistic or imperialistic. But this time, in order to build his "overlapping consensus," he departed from his previous approach in two ways. First, the principles of the law of peoples themselves were defined in such a way as to be acceptable to more than liberal democracies. Although he presents the principles as an extension of the liberal conception of justice to international relations,[48] it is an impoverished conception that he extends. This is obvious in two respects. He begins by removing from his earlier conception of political justice "the three egalitarian features of the fair value of the political liberties, of fair equality of opportunity, and of the difference principle" in order to reach "greater generality"[49]. Thus the scope of acceptability now shapes the substance. He is particularly explicit about this when he explains his rejection of the difference principle: appropriate for a democratic society, it is not valid for international society (even though we're dealing with ideal theory), because this principle wasn't "framed for our present case" (a rather insufficient explanation) and many societies—even liberal ones—would find it unacceptable. Moreover, the list of basic human rights is, insofar as liberty is concerned, restricted to "the right to life and security," the right to emigration, and "freedom from slavery, serfdom, and forced occupations." Only "a certain liberty of conscience and freedom of association" are mentioned. Freedom of expression and freedom of the press do not appear. These rights are said to be "distinct from the rights of democratic citizenship" (i.e., there is no right to vote) and "politically neutral," not "peculiarly liberal or special to our Western tradition"[50]—a weird statement, for there is nothing "neutral" about human rights, and while, indeed, non-Western states have signed treaties that commit them to respect these rights, they are clearly liberal in origin and substance.

Why is Rawls's list skimpier than the list of rights covered in many of these treaties? The purpose of these restrictions and qualifications is to make such rights acceptable to a second category of "peoples": nonliberal societies whom Rawls calls "hierarchical." Like "well-ordered liberal societies," they are an ideal type. Unlike the former, however, they have no, or barely any, empirical, nonideal counterpart in the real world;

one can, perhaps, think of Jordan, or Singapore, or Tunisia, but Rawls's category is an idealization (in the sense of beautification) of a tiny group of real states. Once again, we find that what is mere "abstraction" in the philosophy of domestic government becomes utopia in the philosophy of international relations. These hierarchical societies, to be well ordered, must be peaceful, "guided by a common good conception of justice" (i.e., a conception "founded on certain religious or philosophical doctrines"),[51] have a legal system that "takes into account people's essential interests and imposes moral duties and obligations on all members of society," and respect basic human rights.[52] Even though they may have an established religion, they don't persecute other religions; even though there are no elected legislatures, there is "a reasonable consultation hierarchy," and all persons are treated as "responsible members of society." The representatives of such societies, placed behind a veil of ignorance, would accept the same "law of peoples" as democratic societies. As one critic of Rawls has pointed out, this is far from obvious: would they really accept to be bound by international law to respect human rights?[53] Are ideological or religiously driven societies likely to respect basic human rights at all? How would we know that their "system of law meet[s] the essentials of legitimacy in the eyes of (their) own people,"[54] since there are no free elections? Whatever the answers, what is clear is that the law of peoples has been shaped so as to appeal to a purely hypothetical group of "peoples."

The fallacy here is in the parallel Rawls seems to draw between an "overlapping consensus" of comprehensive doctrines that endorse a single conception of justice within the framework of a democratic political culture (and do so after the domestic principles of justice have been set) and an "overlapping consensus" of societies based on very different political conceptions of justice, which endorse a "law of peoples" whose thinness can only be explained as the result of an implicit modus vivendi among egalitarian liberal societies based on Rawls's original "justice as fairness," "liberal societies whose institutions are considerably less egalitarian," and "hierarchical" societies. As Thomas Pogge and Bertrand Guillarme, a young French political philosopher, have pointed out, Rawls applied the liberal imperative of toleration in domestic affairs only to nonpolitical matters, where different conceptions of the good were free to compete.[55] Within the political sphere, only his liberal principles of justice ruled, and "unreasonable" doctrines that rejected them—which Rawls expects to be few in a democratic political culture—were not to be accommodated. In Rawls's "law of peoples," we are asked not only to tolerate certain nonliberal regimes (Rawls refers here to "liberalism's own principle of toleration for other reasonable ways of ordering society")[56] but to set up principles of world order that accommodate them. It is as if Rawls had taken too seriously the argument, made by so many repressive regimes, that the liberal conception of justice is "ethnocentric"—as if one could not find believers in liberal values everywhere, and many antiliberals in the West.[57] Rawls is sufficiently aware of the difference between domestic and international affairs to suggest that in international affairs the concept of "reasonableness" has to be relaxed; when he develops his "ideal conception of a society of well-ordered peoples," his principles are meant to include in that ideal society regimes that are "not unreasonable"—neither expansionist nor terrorist.[58] An international law of peoples that goes out of its way to suit at least some of the nonliberal regimes may be a political necessity; it may be a stage in nonideal theory toward the realization of an ideal world; but can it be, as he presents it, a moral conception for an ideal world?[59]

The Quest for an Ethic of World Affairs

What lessons can we derive from the flaws of Rawls's approach? First, the social contract method is difficult to apply to international society because it is both a society of separate states (or peoples) and a society of individuals, who play an increasingly important role in world affairs, as their capacity to disrupt borders and destroy states shows and as the formidable and uncontrolled growth of a transnational economy of private investors and financial markets able to overwhelm central banks, sink currencies, and ruin economies is proving every day. It makes a huge difference whether one places behind the veil of ignorance individual actors or state representatives. To develop an adequate ideal theory for international relations, following Rawls's prescription that "each kind of subject . . . must be governed by its own characteristic principles . . . worked out by a suitable procedure beginning from a correct starting point,"[60] one might need at least three contracts: first, a global one defining the rights and obligations of individuals, whatever "people" they belong to, and defining the structures they would want to live in—a global state, a multitude of states, or entirely new institutions; should the parties reassert the need for states, this global contract would put limits on state sovereignty and autonomy, especially concerning human rights; second, a contract among representatives of states, or of whatever other structures the global contract might have set up, defining the principles of their own intercourse; third, a contract to which the parties would be representatives both of individuals and of states (or of alternative structures) setting up authoritative international institutions and procedures to deal with issues that cannot be left merely to arrangements among separate units or to an unregulated market, such as much of the world economy. There must be easier ways to ideal theory!

This difficulty is magnified by a second problem. Theories of social contract, whether Locke's, Rousseau's, or Rawls's, yield "ideal theory." But in thinking about intentional affairs the best we can come up with, in "ideal theory," is pretty thin. It may produce the idea of a world government, established either by individuals in the "original position," or by states acting as their agents (as world federalists would want), or by states behaving like Hobbes's subjects in the state of nature, impelled by insecurity and the fear of violent death to transfer their powers to a Leviathan. Or else ideal theory can take the form of Rawls's meager law of peoples, which does not add much to old liberal notions of world harmony, and particularly to Kant's provisions for perpetual peace, calling for an end to war and standing armies, and for the establishment of a league of constitutional regimes. Ideal theory based on the social contract method thus leads either to utopia or to a minimal set of principles acceptable by an "overlapping consensus" of "not unreasonable" regimes.

Most of the philosophical and ethical problems of world affairs are the concern of nonideal theory: how to produce both order and justice in a world of different "corporate bodies" and regimes, which reflect different conceptions not only of the social good but of political justice and are based at least as often on coercion and repression as on consent. Rawls, having spent most of his essay on ideal theory, spends only seven pages on what to do "about the highly non-ideal conditions of our world with its great injustices and widespread social evils"[61]. He examines both what he calls noncompliance—how to deal with regimes that "refuse to acknowledge a reasonable law of peoples," which he calls outlaw regimes—and how to deal with societies that lack the traditions, human capital, know-how, and resources needed to be "well ordered." What he tells there is limited, if unassailable. First, well-ordered societies must eventually bring all societies to honor the law of peoples and to secure human rights; but these are matters of foreign policy and political wisdom to which political philosophy has not "much to add"[62], except for suggesting a "federative center" of well-ordered peoples (such as the United Nations) to expose the cruelties of outlaw regimes and granting a right to war against these if they attack "the society of well-ordered peoples" and, "in grave cases," if they violate the human rights of their innocent subjects. Second, well-ordered societies must see to it that basic human needs are met everywhere (even though, in his view, economic injustice results more from domestic factors—"the public political culture and its roots in the background social structure," oppressive governments, corrupt elites, religions that repress women[63]—than from the international maldistribution of resources). Thus, hugely important issues are left in the dark: what is "a grave case" that justifies a war defend human beings whose rights are trampled by an outlaw regime? Is forcible intervention also justified when such rights are crushed in a civil war? How can the authors of international crimes be brought to judgment? If "the duty of assistance is not based on some liberal principle of distributive justice" but is based, rather, on "the ideal conception of the society of peoples itself as consisting of well-ordered societies"[64], what kind of assistance should be granted by the rich, and how can it be made to reach the poor in poor countries? How much of a priority should be given by a state to helping its own poor? How should noncitizens and minorities be treated?

There is another problem. In *A Theory of Justice,* Rawls's domestic ideal theory assumed "strict compliance" with the principles of justice—a not unreasonable assumption, for in a liberal democracy, once citizens agree on what policy should be followed, there is a judicial system and a state with the means of coercion that will ensure compliance. In *The Law of Peoples,* Rawls again relegates noncompliance to the short section devoted to nonideal theory, where he tells us how well-ordered societies should deal with outlaw regimes. But in a world of formally sovereign states and of individuals who trade and speculate freely across borders, with no central executive, legislature, or police and a rarely used World Court, the issue of compliance is fundamental—even among democratic regimes. An ideal theory for "peoples" should no more leave it out than Rawls's ideal theory of domestic justice left out the issue of inequality. The failure to comply is built into the very structure of a society of states; when a state violates the obligations that result from agreements or from a World Court decision, trade conflicts, resorts to force to change borders or to help insurgents abroad, and massive violations of human rights can occur. An ideal theory that does not deal with this issue is left up in the air.

How, then, is moral and political philosophy to proceed? One approach, often followed by Sissela Bok,[65] tries to find a common ground among existing ethical traditions, secular and religious. The problem here is that the common notions are often extremely fuzzy and provide little guidance for action; also, there is more common ground to be found in matters such as individual and family values and behavior than on subjects such as the basic structures of society and its political organization (although the battles over abortion and population control remind us of how hard it is to disconnect those levels and how much disagreement exists over the most basic issues).

Another approach consists in applying to international society what Rawls calls a comprehensive doctrine, in order to promote what it sees as universally and absolutely valid principles capable of establishing both order and justice. Thus, one could imagine a modern version of a natural law ethic, a utilitarian ethic, or a Kantian ethic that tries to formulate universalizable maxims based on the categorical imperative—which Kant saw as a "command of reason" that orders us to act "only on a maxim through which we can at the same time will that it should become a universal law" and to treat human beings "never simply as means but always at the same times as ends"—for the behavior of states and individuals across borders and to see how far, in the real world, one can go in applying any one of them.[66]

The results of the Kantian attempt might not be very different from those of a third approach, which does not require acceptance of Kant's "transcendental idealism" and faith in "the coherence and unity of reason, both theoretical and practical, with itself."[67] This would be an extension to international society of Judith Shklar's "liberalism of fear."[68] Its main purpose is the protection of the individual from cruelty, oppression, and fear. Like Rawls, she wanted liberalism to be a political doctrine, independent of the various philosophical formulations (such as Kant's and Mill's) that had been offered—indeed, independent of Rawls's formulation, also. For unlike Rawls, she wanted to ground it not in a procedure undertaken by equal and reasonable persons seeking "fair terms of cooperation"[69] but in what she deemed a fundamental, common, and immediate emotional experience; the fear of cruelty and tyranny. The memories of "peoples" and communities are all too often distorted and antagonistic. The liberalism of fear is based on the one memory that, Walzer notwithstanding, is common to the men and women of this century: "the history of the world since 1914" and of its atrocities. According to Shklar, it is the only kind of liberalism that can still have a broad appeal, now that the liberalism of hope, of faith in reason, progress, and harmony, has been destroyed.

Given her goal, she saw human rights as necessary "licenses and empowerments that citizens must have to preserve their freedom and to protect themselves against abuse," just as the prohibition of cruelty is a universally necessary "condition of the dignity of persons": the emphasis is on their moral needs as individuals, not on the idea of persons as "responsible and cooperating members of society."[70] (One of her permanent concerns was with refugees, exiles, members of minorities, i.e., involuntary misfits fallen between society's cracks.)[71] To be sure, as Stephen Lukes points out in his own witty and spirited Oxford lectures defending human rights against a variety of "comprehensive doctrines" that ignore or restrict them, what needs to be protected is not only the integrity of the individuals but also "the activities and relations that make their lives more valuable" and that "cannot be conceived reductively as merely individual goods." Individuals do want and need to belong to associations and communities. But human beings also want and need not to be crushed, confined, or defined by them. Associations or communities can, in other words, be dangerous—and the most dangerous of them is the state. From the liberalism of fear and the imperatives of protection from cruelty and tyranny, important principles can be derived. Shklar mentioned both negative liberties, protecting the weak from harm, excesses of power and the kind of inequality that amounts to oppression, and positive measures about the kinds of institutions "without which freedom is unimaginable"; she recommended the division and dispersion of power, effective voluntary associations, procedural fairness, and well-informed and vigilant citizenry.[72]

The great merit of Shklar's approach is that it is less hypnotized than other liberalisms by the problem of philosophical and religious pluralism, by the multiplicity of conceptions of the good. There are many views of the supreme good, she thought, but only one ultimate evil, "cruelty and the fear it inspires, and the very fear of fear itself." She used for her purposes the title of Thomas Nagel's book: her point of view, she wrote, was "the view from nowhere": the view not from any given society or culture or doctrine but rather from everywhere, for there are victims everywhere; and as such her liberalism "makes a universal and especially a cosmopolitan claim." Has there ever been a more withering attack on cultural relativism and on the evils of nationalism?

"Only the claims of universal humanity and rational argument cast in general terms can be put to the test of general scrutiny and public criticism. . . . Unless there is an open and public review of all the practical alternatives . . . there can be no responsible choices and no way of controlling the authorities that claim to be the voice of the people and its spirit."[73] Shklar did not have the time to develop those ideas and to apply them to world affairs. But the liberalism of fear, conceived for a nonideal world, can provide us with the guidelines and principles needed to curb the pretensions and excesses of states and would-be "peoples," with criteria for such issues as the protection of human rights, the treatment of minorities and immigrants, and the problems of famine and poverty. Those ideas would appeal to a "consensus" of the likeliest victims, the least powerful persons, to be found in all societies and cultures. The liberalism of fear modestly aims at damage control—but today that in itself is a revolutionary aspiration. Over time, many people, and their political representatives, may come to share it and to support the measures and institutions needed to turn it into a plan of action.[74]

4

Beyond Realism and Idealism in International Politics

F ar more than political scientists who deal with domestic politics, students of international relations have found it difficult to keep separate two different quests. One is the quest for understanding the rules of the game of international politics; as we all know, international politics is played in an anarchic milieu, in the original sense of anarchy (there is no central power over all the players), and it is a milieu in which there are very complicated relations of competition and dependence. Two dimensions are the competition among major powers—the horizontal dimension, if you like—and the relations of domination and dependence, which constitute the vertical dimension. Thus, there is a first quest, which is analytic, and a second, which is looking for ways of changing this system and of improving it. This second is the normative quest, and the two are almost inevitably mixed.

The Old Debate

The older version of the double quest is the debate about or between realism and idealism, a debate that raged in the field in the 1940s and continued throughout the 1950s. It was a peculiarly American debate. The idealists were essentially Wilsonian liberals who, like all liberals since the end of the eighteenth century, were in revolt against what is in a sense the key feature of international politics: the so-called state of war—in other words, not only the wars that take place but the fact that so much of international politics is the preparation for war or the consequences of war or the balance of power, which tends perhaps to moderate conflicts but which also always entails wars. Liberals and idealists were also in revolt against the domestic causes and implications of the state of war. From Kant on, liberals have always been convinced that wars are essentially the products of authoritarian leaders or regimes and that they inevitably reinforce authoritarianism because they allow leaders to mobilize the public and to get full powers from their people.

The solution that idealists and liberals advocated was, in part, democratization, because of the hope that it would diminish the risk of war, would bring to power people who would conduct rational discussions, and would rest on public opinion, that is, on citizens reluctant to consent to and to throw themselves into war. Another part of the solution was the principle of national self-determination; a third part was to be found in international organizations, in various formulas of cooperation among states and among citizens of different countries. In other words, what idealists promised, if those kinds of links were established across borders and if democratization and national self-determination were pursued, was harmony. Of course, the realists rejected this with great indignation. Realism had a genuine revival, starting in the 1930s with the Englishman E. H. Carr, and it continued in the 1940s with Hans Morgenthau, who exerted a sort of intellectual hegemony for a long time. Realists wanted to warn us all against the various dangers of idealism. There was first of all (and this is Carr's central point in his *Twenty Years Crisis*) idealist hypocrisy; to Carr, idealism was often a mask the powerful put on their interests to befuddle and deceive the weak. For example, the principles of liberalism were used by England in the nineteenth and early twentieth centuries to disguise the expansion of British power, industrial and military. The second danger of idealism was that it could be disruptive of international order. Morgenthau and others pointed out that democratization and above all national self-determination mean turbulence; they mean the dismantling of existing states or revolutions in existing states. The third danger of idealism (on which Morgenthau particularly focused) was imprudence, because reliance on international organization is misplaced trust, given the weakness, for instance, of the League of Nations in the 1930s.

These long debates raging in political science had a rather strange outcome. In academia there is no doubt that realism prevailed. Morgenthau, as I said, was the dominant influence, and the message that prevailed was the "lessons of Munich" message: that one had to put power behind one's interests, one had to be strong, one had to be willing to prepare for war and to threaten war, one should not rely on deceptive and weak international organizations, and so on. Morgenthau's central point was his notion of interest defined as power—which puts together two words each one of which is so full of complexities that I would like to remove them from the vocabulary of political science, but that is rather difficult—they are the central words of the field. If we turn from academia to policy, particularly American policy in those years, we see that what actually prevailed was a rather peculiar blend of realism and idealism. There was on one hand the realism distilled by people like McGeorge Bundy, Zbigniew Brzezinski, and Henry Kissinger. This was the realism of people who had made a heady discovery of American power during and after the war and who, in a sense, reveled in it. It was the discovery that the United States was the only superpower in the West, that it had an abundance of every component of power, and that it could now shape the world. But that realism was combined with a peculiar kind of idealism, which was not the liberal idealism of John Stuart Mill or Woodrow Wilson. It was not the idealism that promises harmony in a pacified world, which aims at solving disputes in a peaceful way; it was the idealism of a crusade against (or, if not a crusade, at least the containment of) the evil empire of the Soviets. Of course, that fighting brand of idealism got the United States into quite a number of sticky situations, I am thinking, for instance, of Vietnam, or Central America, where North American behavior to some extent vindicated Carr's critique of the frequent hypocrisy of idealism. That was the debate of the 1940s and 1950s.

New Forms of the Debate

From realism we have moved to neorealism, and from idealism we have moved to something called neoliberal institutionalism. Realism, the realism of people like Morgenthau or Carr, or before them Max Weber, and before that Machiavelli, and before that Thucydides, was always focused on the state and its foreign policy. In a sense, it was an analysis of foreign policy and a set of guidelines for what a wise foreign policy should be. Neorealism is largely the product of Kenneth Waltz at Berkeley (and Waltz has been as hegemonic for twenty years as Morgenthau had been earlier). It focuses not on the state and its foreign policy but on the international system as a whole and on its structure; what Waltz means by *structure* is the distribution of power in the system, and what he means by *power* is essentially military power: he does not much look at anything else. The old realists, particularly Thucydides (the first and in some ways the wisest of them all) were always aware of the degree to which a state's foreign policy was influenced, if not dictated, by its domestic politics and regime. This is a central point in Thucydides' analysis of the behavior of Athens in the Peloponnesian war. In his search for a sort of self-contained theory of the international system, Waltz denounced as "reductionists" all those who bring into the analysis of international relations the study of what happens within states.

In my opinion the real reductionists are Waltz and his neorealism, because it leaves out of the study, or at least of the theory, of international politics all domestic determinants of foreign policy, all the transnational forces and institutions that exist across state borders; it discounts completely the significance of international and regional norms and organizations; it ignores or plays down the specificities of international economic relations (if one compares them with the diplomatic-strategic domain); and above all it reduces the realm of international politics to a limited and monotonous repertoire of balances of power. Occasionally it isn't balancing that occurs but what he calls bandwagoning, when various states join the dominant or rising one. Limited as realism may have been, there was something rather humanistic about it; neorealism, on the other hand, has resulted in an acute case of scholasticism and anemia.

As for the move from idealism to neorealist institutionalism, what did it accomplish? The intention was to get rid of the overtly ideological elements of the old idealism, in other words, to devise a theory that would not be tied to such notions as democracy or national self-determination. Its champions borrow from the old realism the notion that the actors, whatever their regime and whether or not they constitute a nation-state, are all moved primarily by self-interest, and yet, starting from this transplant from realism, they focus on the possibilities of cooperation, just as the old idealists did. Like them, the new liberal institutionalists stress the possibility for states, even when they pursue their interests, to cooperate by establishing what they call international regimes (which is what people twenty years or fifteen years older used to call international organizations); and they explain how the establishment of these regimes helps change the way in which states define their self-interest, by making it more enlightened and less purely selfish. This constitutes progress compared with the old idealism of the 1940s and the 1950s; however, there is also a certain degree of anemia here, because of a tendency to analyze international relations in terms of a rather simple dichotomy between cooperation and defection. What is interesting in international affairs is not finding evidence of cooperation: we all know that there is cooperation, otherwise we would live in underground shelters all of our lives. The interesting questions are cooperation for what, between whom and whom, and sometimes cooperation against whom, or against what, or in exchange for what? Another thing is bothersome about neoliberal institutionalism. The old idealism was an overt form of liberalism, it embodied the values of liberalism; in that sense it was overtly ideological. But the attempt that the neoliberal institutionalists make to present their findings as a science conceals values, though they are implicit. These are the old liberal values of harmony and cooperation and the preference for cooperation over conflict. There is at the core of the neoliberal platform an act of faith in the good work that these regimes and organizations can perform, while at the same time they present themselves as value free and purely scientific.

Not surprisingly, this double anemia of the new realism and the new idealism has led the field into a whole series of false debates. Two of these deserve particular mention. The debate about whether states seek absolute gains or relative gains has sometimes taken mathematical form, but at the end of lots of equations and charts the conclusion has tended to be that there is no mathematical solution to the problem. I think one could have predicted this because the answer is very simple; first of all, states usually seek both, and second, whether they seek primarily absolute or primarily relative gains depends very much on the issue; if it is an economic issue, certainly there often is an interest in absolute gains (for instance, it is clear at the present time that France has an interest not only in its own prosperity but also in that of Germany, given the intensity of exchanges between the two), whereas in strategic areas we are much more frequently, although not always, in a zero-sum game. There is no simple answer to that question, other than "it all depends," but basically states would like both. The other debate, which is still raging in the journals, is a debate as to whether international organizations and international regimes are important or insignificant, to which again the answer is, it all depends. In some areas they are very important, for example, the international regime of refugees, the world trade regime, the European monetary system, and indeed many of the regimes set up for the environment. Others have been big failures, particularly in security matters or the global (as distinct from regional) human rights regime. Again there is no simple answer, and yet an enormous quantity of intellectual energy has been wasted. A question in political science almost never receives a black-and-white answer; it is always "under what conditions, when, where," and it is the differences, not the generalities, that are most interesting.

Old Approaches vs. the New World Order

If, indeed, a "new world order" exists, then a new theory of international relations, explaining the new "rules of the game," is required, as traditional approaches have proved insufficient. Realism, for all its wisdom, has always been plagued by a number of problems. The first problem is its essential elasticity and indeterminateness. For instance, realists have never agreed among themselves as to whether a good outcome—in other words, a relatively moderate and stable world—occurred even when the major actors, the great powers, were doing a prudent balancing of power for basically selfish reasons, or whether, on the contrary, this good outcome was possible only if the major powers had a consciousness of the interest of the whole system and were concerned not only with their purely national interest but also with the interest of the system as a whole, a point made by the British political scientist Hedley Bull in his work on international society and also by the contemporary American diplomatic historian Paul Schroeder.

What has also always been striking about realism is the multiplicity of policies that could be defended as realistic. I alluded earlier to the Vietnam War: I was always struck by the way in which people who were self-proclaimed realists were all over the place when it came to Vietnam; realists like Morgenthau and Kennan were hostile to the war because they thought it was folly in realistic terms, but others, like Brzezinski and Robert Scalapino, were great defenders of the war in classical realist terms. That realism could be invoked to justify diametrically opposed policies is a little disturbing. There is, of course, an explanation for this; it is what the philosopher John Rawls, in his *Theory of Justice,* calls "the burdens of judgment," the fact that different people interpret the same facts differently and also that people have different values. It is obvious when one discusses the current Yugoslav crisis that people who have the same reasonable state of mind end up with completely different positions, because of differences both in interpreting the facts and in values.

Another problem has been that realism, though it wants to give advice to the statesman about how to conduct foreign policy, has always displayed a certain inability to provide the actors with ends that go beyond their security and survival. That is a bit narrow and tends to equate international politics with fairly inexpiable conflict. These traditional flaws of realism are aggravated today by two factors. The first is changes in the nature of the threats to the states, in the present international system. For realists, the main threat to a state is usually the attempt by another state to establish hegemony or to create an empire; hence, the advice is to balance power, resist potential hegemons, and stop potential trouble-makers. Today, the threat to many states is something much more abstract; it is, for instance, the threat of nuclear annihilation or the threat of terrorism or the threat of environmental disaster. In other words, in the realm of weapons of mass destruction generally we have to go way beyond balancing to measures of arms control, which are not at all of the same nature as balancing and, in fact, entail the cooperation of power for restricting arms. Similarly, states must sometimes go directly to bargaining and cooperation, as in the environmental realm, because no state can resolve these problems by itself.

There is a second contemporary reason for this insufficiency of realism. Not only is the nature of threats to the states different, but also there is a profound change in the nature of the system itself. This has become a cliché: we are no longer in the world of the Westphalian treaties; we are in a post-Westphalian world in which we find not only states but three different levels of interaction among them. One is indeed the traditional level of interstate relations and interstate conflicts, where realism, of course, is of some relevance; but above the states and constraining them, indeed pushing and dragging them sometimes, there is a global world economy that is a mixture of public and private transactions. The power of states that is engaged in this economy is very different from traditional military power—more elusive, more fluid, more shared, less sovereign. The third level is hard to characterize, but I call it the level of people: people have become actors in international relations. The world economy has become an actor by itself with its own dynamism, and people have become both deeply engaged in that world economy and active in calling for protection against the vicissitudes of that economy. Also, they often call for outside protection of their rights against their own state; they can overthrow their states' government when the government is tyrannical, or they can go so far as to destroy states when these states are ramshackle multiethnic constructions. What is so striking in the present international system is the unpredictable and often destructive power that people have over and across states. These are all problems for which the old realist analysis, which deals almost exclusively with relations among states, is really quite irrelevant. Henry Kissinger's last, enormous book, *Diplo-*

macy, is in many ways a remarkable achievement, insofar as he applies his razor-sharp mind to past conflicts among states. But he has almost nothing to say about the present world; on this matter, in the last chapter, his only advice, is to keep balancing power. Is this an answer to the problems of the world economy or to the problem of the disruptiveness of ethnic groups or religious factions, and so on?

Liberal idealism is quite insufficient, also. The assumption it makes, that if countries were democratic they would live in peace, may be right in an ideal world, but we do not live in an ideal world. We do know from experience that democratic countries have waged many wars against nondemocratic countries (and there are many nondemocratic countries left); countries in the process of democratization are often turbulent and tempted by war as a diversion or as an effect of external involvement in their internal turmoil. This notion of democratic peace, which has also produced enormous controversies, is still only a hypothesis. The liberal assumption of harmony resulting from both democracy and self-determination is a dubious one; what we know now is that national self-determination is a powerful dissolvent of existing order. It has also often been incapable—think of many of the countries that were granted self-determination when European empires disintegrated in the fifties and sixties—of creating effective nation states, particularly in Africa and parts of Asia. Moreover, liberals have always been plagued by their own division over the issue of intervention: is it the duty of a liberal to intervene for the spread of democratic and liberal values when they are threatened in the world, or should one stay out of it and respect the sovereignty of existing units? The debate has been going on since the days of Kant, who was against intervention, and this division was particularly serious when interventions took the form of the use of force. Another weakness of liberalism is that it has endorsed four mutually incompatible sets of norms in international affairs: sovereignty, national self-determination, democracy, and human rights. It is extremely difficult to have all four: self-determination often undermines sovereignty, democracy often takes forms like the Jacobin brand that violates human rights, and so on. An implicit assumption of liberalism is that all good things come together, and unfortunately, that is not true.

Finally, the great transnational hope of liberalism, that conflict among states would be dampened by transnational forces, has been frustrated: there was a hope in the formation of a world public opinion that has not entirely materialized because there are still too many regimes that do not allow any public opinion to form or where those who would like to form

it are thrown in jail. The other great hope of liberalism was in the establishment of a powerful transnational economy of private traders and private investors. That certainly has happened, but like so many successes it
has brought with it enormous headaches. It is true that this global capitalist economy greatly hampers the power of states and eats away the
sovereignty of existing states, but at the same time it represents a new
uncontrolled and unaccountable power that is dangerous in itself. When
daily transactions by tens of thousands of private individuals can sink
the currency of a state, shake all the other currencies, and do the kind of
damage to a national economy that was done to Mexico some time ago,
we have to realize that this transnational economy, fueled by the liberated energy of a large number of people operating across borders, creates
enormous problems of its own, if only because of the backlash this sort
of power then creates. Moreover, when it comes to how to handle this
transnational public economy, just as on the issue of intervention, liberals
are divided, as they have been for a century and a half, between advocates
of free trade and laissez-faire on one side and, on the other side, social
democrats of all types or interventionists who would like to limit the
damage this economy can do.

Toward a Synthesis

A new synthesis would begin with two premises. The first one I would
characterize as the primacy of values and choice. When we are dealing
with domestic political science—the analysis of, for instance, the American political system—what makes it possible to conceive a value-free
analysis, a purely objective analysis (even though I think it is always
partly an illusion), is the idea that when we are looking at what Rawls
calls a well-ordered society, we are dealing with a country in which,
thanks to the state's monopoly of coercion, violence has been tamed,
there isn't a civil war in the streets every day, and injustice has been
minimized because the state has taken measures to grant the right to vote
to the population, because the state has taken social measures to include
as many people as possible into citizenship, because welfare systems have
been established, and so on. That explains why domestic political science
often can make the purely analytic dimension prevail over the normative
and meliorative dimension. But in international politics this is simply not
possible. Whatever issue we examine in international affairs, we always
find both violence and injustice, and that is why, however much we

would like to develop a science of international relations modeled after the so-called science of economics, or even after physics, we still need to begin with a map of values and with a clear sense of normative direction.

Now you may say yes, but what is the point? We may talk about justice and about moderating violence, but states can't afford to be moral, there is no room for ethical action in international relations. Indeed, realists and neorealists have made us very familiar with the idea that international relations is the realm of pure necessity, but the argument is unconvincing. World politics is certainly a domain of sharp constraints; clearly the choices that states make are often agonizing and restricted. But constraints are not unknown in domestic politics either, and while it is true that there may be some life-and-death situations in which states find themselves and in which either they shoot first or they get shot, this is not true of all of international politics. Even when they are in a life-and-death situation, states will have choices: French elites had a choice in June 1940: one was Philippe Pétain, the other was Charles de Gaulle. During the week of the Cuban missile crisis, when America's leaders were convinced that we were perhaps on the eve of nuclear war, there was an important choice to be made between bombing the Russians immediately (which would have certainly led to nuclear war, especially since we didn't know then how many nuclear weapons they already had in Cuba) and the measure that was finally taken—the blockade—and turned out to be far more prudent. Even in life-and-death conflicts such as the Arab-Israeli conflicts in the Middle East, the two sides have managed to observe remarkable restraints. There is always some choice.

The second premise I would suggest is in a sense the opposite or the counterpart of the first. I have been talking about the primacy of values and of choice, but I would add immediately that there is also a need for an analysis that would be as realistic as possible (in a nontheoretical sense, in the common sense meaning of realism) of the constraints, opportunities, and problems the international system presents. Willing the good after we have defined our idea of the good is simply not enough; if we think that the game needs to be improved or needs to be transformed, we can do this only by working through the actors themselves; exhortations are not sufficient. We have a duty to show how the idea is compatible or can be made compatible with the actors' self-interest. Normative theory itself has to deal primarily with what Rawls calls nonideal conditions; we have to deal with the world as it is and not assume that perfection has already been achieved.

A new synthesis requires a realistic analysis of the international system as it currently exists. I have already mentioned the three different levels: the global economy, the states, and peoples, or individuals. In addition, three features are essential. The first is a sort of dialectic of integration and distintegration, a mutually reinforcing dynamic, so to speak. We all know what the integrating forces are: what is sometimes called globalization, especially in world finance, in world industry, and in communications. It results largely from the activities of individuals, but it is also created through interstate trade agreements and through international monetary, banking, and trade organizations. Globalization also entails ever more nongovernmental organizations (NGOs) in multiple fields: human rights, population, environment, and so on. NGOs have been visible in many recent UN conferences and will probably continue to grow and certainly play an integrating role.

As for disintegration, the same globalization that creates a world economy also fosters increasing differences between those countries this global economy helps to develop, industrialize, and get rich and those parts of the world some increasingly dismiss as hopeless and which unfortunately include much of Africa. In the parts that develop and modernize, the interplay between global forces and often shaky, imprudent, or corrupt public and private national institutions can cause sudden crises, as happened in much of Asia in 1997. This global economy also increases the disparities within national economies between rich and poor, between the sectors it favors and the backward ones. This, in turn, often produces a backlash that contributes to a second factor of disintegration, what I would call the politics of identity, or the desire that we find now in so many states to protect the autonomy of the nation or of the state against the homogenizing and alienating currents produced by the world economy. Much of Muslim fundamentalism is a revolt against this cultural homogenization; so is the desire to protect national identity against external influences, whether they are the influences of immigrants or the influences of minority cultures. A third disintegrating force, very much linked with the politics of identity, is the problem of the disintegrating states; some have never successfully established an identity of their own, and they are racked by ethnic and religious conflicts. They are also often states in which the state's structures were never really built, as in so many African countries. It is interesting to note that these disintegrating states are largely to be found in areas that used to be parts of colonial empires. It is difficult to say anything good about empires, but we can note at least that the transition from empire to stable nation-states has often been difficult. The advocates of empires have one argument, which is that although empires may be unfair indeed, they maintain (if brutally) a certain form of order and may thus yield a little more oppression, but also considerably less chaos and disorder.

Next to this dialectic of integration and disintegration, a great deal of international relations today is concerned with domestic politics (this is another reason to reject neorealism). Recent commercial negotiations, for instance, have increasingly become conflicts of domestic models. Americans tell the Japanese how to run their economy, and they tell us how we should run our finances; the United States tells the French that they should stop protecting their movies, which nobody except the French has any interest in seeing, and the French tell us that Hollywood is an awful mess and that the French film industry should be protected against the monopoly of the likes of *Jurassic Park*. Many of the issues in trade negotiations these days are about labor standards, environmental policies, and human rights (for instance, products fabricated by child labor): these are all deeply domestic matters in international affairs. The International Monetary Fund's recipes for countries in financial crisis tend to reshape their priorities and their structures. Another such issue is nuclear proliferation. To tell a country not to buy or make or test nuclear weapons, or not to buy or produce weapons of mass destruction, is really interfering with what has traditionally been seen as the heart of domestic sovereignty, the right of a state to arm itself for its defense. A multitude of international conflicts these days deal with domestic affairs: Yugoslavia, Rwanda, Somalia, Angola. We are dealing with an extraordinarily complex system in which we still find all the traditional goals that states used to pursue: prestige, influence, might; even territory is still often important insofar as it is (for instance, in the Arab-Israeli conflict) a component of national identity. And yet next to traditional goals we also have new ones, particularly in the world economy, where one of the main stakes is really the control of market shares. Finally, we confront the problem of the failed state, formidable both because of its human consequences— chaos, civil wars, refugees—and because of the risk of external meddling.

The third and last feature that I want to mention is deficiency of governance. This is an ungoverned world. The UN has no autonomous power; it is what is members want it to be, and usually its members don't want it to be anything much, as we see when we look at the financing difficulties or at the refusal of states to put any permanent armed forces at the UN's disposal. No country at present plays the role that people who study the nineteenth century (and sometimes idealize it) tell us the United Kingdom played at that time. It may be a dubious parallel, because Britain was a major empire and occupied much of the world, but it is true that at present nobody, not even the United States, sole superpower as it may be, plays this sort of a role. In matters of international conflict, the United States is a highly selective and reluctant policeman. Despite America's dominance of the world economy and drive for ever more liberalization, there is a vacuum of authority in the world economy, where a large number of functions are simply unregulated because many states—and private actors in these states—are hostile to global regulations, and many states also fear that if they impose too many national restrictions and regulations the profits will go somewhere else. Whereas at least in domestic affairs the state has often tried to compensate for some of the inequalities the free market always produces, there is nothing comparable in international affairs. There is no steering group at present; except in the world economy, the United States is turning inward, and the other major powers are either not really major or concentrate entirely, like Europe, on constructing their own unity; or else, like Japan, they are still largely one-dimensional or, like China, primarily engaged in their own economic and political transition. There is also a formidable problem of enforcement. Who should enforce whatever resolutions the UN comes up with? If one relies on a great power like the United States, there is always the risk that it will be done only in the interest of that power (which is in a sense what occurred during the Gulf war). Or else the great power will be imprudent, which has also happened, sometimes, when the world relied too much on the United States. When it is said that it is better if things are done multilaterally, too often this simply means accepting the lowest common denominator, as we have seen in Yugoslavia.

The Place of Ethics

Given these problems and this system, where should we go? What we find today, in addition to the false debates that I have mentioned, is two prophecies not about where to go but about what will happen. One that was popular a few years ago, but which few people still take seriously, was Francis Fukuyama's idea that we had arrived at the end of history. Well, history has not ended. What he meant was that we had achieved a worldwide triumph of liberalism, which would make the world rather monochromatic and boring. I am afraid that the world is not going to be very boring, and it certainly is not of a single color. All we have to do is look at religious fundamentalisms, which do not seem to know about the worldwide triumph of liberalism or, insofar as they know about it, don't accept it. Also, when we look around the world, we see that there are quite a number of regimes that are not yet liberal. They may not all be moved by a great totalitarian ideology like communism, but one can have varieties of minitotalitarianism and authoritarianism without any grand ideology, and that does not make the life of the people who live there any better, or their neighbors any safer.

The other great prophecy is my colleague Samuel Huntington's assurance that we are going to see a clash of civilizations, a prophecy much less serene than the end of history. I do not think it makes a great deal of sense. Huntington has a tendency to confuse or conflate religion and culture, or religion and civilization, and to overlook the fact that some of the worst conflicts are within the same civilization. He has not fully clarified the fuzzy concept of civilization nor fully explained how one moves from a civilization to a state: states, not civilizations, are the actors on the world stage. Nor has he made enough of an effort to show how culture or civilization or religion, which are certainly important factors, get translated into or affect specific foreign policies. Without such understandings, his hypothesis is no more than an arresting idea. The trouble is that it is not only an interesting but also a pernicious idea—first, because it tends to distort the analysis of existing conflicts in order to make them fit the model (see Huntington on Yugoslavia), and second, because it suggests that there is something inexpiable, and inevitable, about conflicts among countries that belong to different civilizations.

If we reject those prophecies, what kind of normative thread can we look for? We should start with a definition of our values, and my approach is a combination of two different kinds of liberalism. One is Kantian. Kant's emphasis on universal rules, his categorical imperative, provides an inspiration and a moral doctrine, but there is something highly abstract about Kantianism, and Kant only wrote short pieces about international affairs. The second kind of liberalism—which I think is quite compatible with the Kantian one but is less philosophical, less purely rational, more easily compatible with the calculation of consequences, and based much more on emotions and common experiences—is what my late colleague Judith Shklar called, in one of her essays, the "liberalism of fear." Her argument is that although at the end of the twentieth century the old liberal faith in reason and progress is no longer credible, there is one experience that everybody who has lived through this century shares, the experience of cruelty and fear. Liberalism, therefore, ought to be based on this common existential experience and should be essentially an attempt at protecting, as much as possible, human beings, and in particular minorities, refugees, and exiles, against cruelty, oppression, and fear. It seems to me that this approach, which she did not live long enough to develop fully, provides a good thread through international relations.

The combination of Kantian ethics and Shklar's liberalism of fear results in an emphasis on both human rights and obligations. I am always a bit uneasy with an emphasis on rights only, but we have at least to begin with human rights. An approach that puts human rights first is one that is centered on individuals and on the groups that individuals form, including states, all of which are aimed, or should be aimed, at protecting individuals from the multiple forms of betrayal, violence, exploitation, misery, and cruelty. Today in particular, individuals in world affairs face various categories of threats that also happen to be central issues of foreign policy: for instance, the kind of individual insecurity that results from globalization, from the fact that economic development is not by itself automatically productive of human rights and democracy. The market can be highly unequal, exclusive, and undemocratic, and it needs to be controlled for the protection of human rights. Human rights are defenses necessary to make sure that the development this world economy makes possible is a fair and balanced one. They can provide a sort of common floor to the unevenness of globalization and serve as an antidote to the backlash that resistance to the effects of globalization often produces, a backlash that often takes the form of xenophobia or hostility to immigrants and refugees.

A second threat to individuals is the violence that results from present forms of interstate conflict; it threatens a human right to peace. That is exactly what Kant proclaimed, and this is why, from the point of view of human rights, policies of nonproliferation, not only of nuclear weapons but of weapons in general, are essential. Finally, there is the violence that results from the disintegration of states; here, the notion of human rights can provide a guideline for when to intervene and a rationale for intervening. In the Yugoslav conflict, the West has been delinquent about the duty, in the new republics that emerged from the disintegration of Yugoslavia, to try to protect both minorities against discrimination—for instance, in Croatia—and individuals who happened to be Muslims against genocide and ethnic cleansing in Bosnia. I repeat that I begin with human rights, not democracy: because it is difficult to install and force democracy from the outside, it is much better to focus on human rights, which need to be respected by and demanded from regimes that are not yet democracies. This is one side of the normative dimension.

The other side is obligations, and here again I take my inspiration from Judith Shklar, this time from her book *The Faces of Injustice,* where she points out that injustice does not consist simply of acts that deny justice to people: much injustice results from indifference and neglect. In international affairs, obligations weigh on all the actors, on states as well as on individuals. What are these obligations? Some are what Kant called negative or narrow duties, such as doing no harm; this already provides some guidelines in areas like violent conflict or the environment. Then we have what Kant called positive and wide duties, what he called the duty of beneficence, which we would call today assistance; this provides us with some guidelines about distributive justice, migrations, refugees, and population or about how to help victims of aggression. Another positive duty, again something that Kant wrote about, is the duty to help individuals and states get out of their rather bloody state of nature by providing some forms of common governance; here we have to think about how to strengthen the legitimacy of and give genuine means to international institutions, public as well as nongovernmental organizations, so as to develop their capacity to intervene and to regulate what is an increasingly messy world, a world dangerous precisely because of its interdependence.

If we do not think particularly about these problems of steering and governance, we are going to face an exceedingly unattractive future. We have concentrated for fifty years on one particular kind of nightmare, the nightmare of a bipolar nuclear conflict between two superpowers—the traditional duel of Athens and Sparta, if you like—and it concentrated the mind because the risks were so obvious. I fear that the mind is much more difficult to concentrate on the kind of chaos we face now, which is not that of two giants armed with nuclear weapons, of "two scorpions in a bottle." It is much more like a scene from Buñuel's movie *L'âge d'or:* at one point there is a picture of a street in which one house blows up, a little like the Federal Building in Oklahoma City, and then a second one blows up, and then a third and then a fourth, and then there is no street left—but it all happened piecemeal. The world we are moving into is of that kind, and if we do not think fairly clearly about what we would like to do, leaving things simply to chance, we may awaken someday to find that there is no world left.

5

The Crisis of Liberal Internationalism

ommunism is dead, but is the other great postwar ideology, liberal internationalism, also dying? A recent book by political scientist Tony Smith as well as several speeches by National Security Adviser Anthony Lake have reminded Americans that "liberal democratic internationalism, or Wilsonianism, has been the most important and distinctive contribution of the United States to the international history of the twentieth century," as Smith states it.[1] Lake, presenting the Clinton administration's foreign policy as a pragmatic Wilsonianism, has explained that it aims at expanding democracy and free trade, defending democracy from its foes, quarantining repressive and pariah states, and protecting and promoting human rights.

After two years, however, pragmatism is more visible than Wilsonianism. In a speech at Harvard, Lake stated that the promotion of democracy and the defense of human rights would entail the use of force only if, among other qualifications, there were clearly defined American interests. He also suggested that the spread of liberalism was not ipso facto an American interest—an inadvertent but remarkable concession to traditional realism. As in the Carter years, the different elements of the liberal agenda are again in competition with one another—human rights versus the expansion of free trade, as one example. Whether the liberal agenda should be carried out by multilateral means or, in case of need, by the United States alone has again become a source of confusion and grief, as in Bosnia. Meanwhile, the nation's enthusiasm for bearing the human and financial costs of carrying out a policy of liberal internationalism has waned. Whereas containment had provided a reasonably clear rationale for policy and a lever for mobilizing public support, neo-Wilsonianism seems a guideline made of rubber and has left the American public deeply ambivalent.

This is not new. As Tony Smith establishes in *America's Mission,* the golden ages of liberal democratic internationalism were the periods that followed the two world wars, and, to some extent, the 1980s, when the cold war was being "won" by the West and the "third wave" of democratization occurred. This is not a coincidence; it suggests that in order to understand the current difficulties of liberalism on the world stage there is a need to go far beyond the all too familiar and depressing litany of what is wrong with Bill Clinton's foreign policy. An examination of the plight of liberal internationalism must shift to the flaws and limitations of liberalism itself.

Liberalism, in its various philosophical guises, was and is a ram against authoritarian regimes. It tries to free individuals from tyranny by providing them with the right to consent to their political institutions and to the policies pursued in the framework of these institutions, as well as with a set of freedoms protected from governmental intrusions and curtailments. Whether it was Immanuel Kant's liberalism based on the concept of moral autonomy, Jeremy Bentham's utilitarian liberalism based on pleasure-pain analysis, or the late-twentieth-century variety—"the liberalism of fear"—suggested by Judith Shklar at a time when nineteenth-century ideas of progress seemed hollow and incredible in light of the totalitarian horrors, the essence of liberalism remains the protection of individual freedom, the reduction of state power, and the conviction that power is legitimate only if it is based on consent and respects basic freedoms.

The international dimension of liberalism was never an afterthought: Kant, Bentham, and John Stuart Mill, not to mention Woodrow Wilson, were cosmopolitans in contrast to Jean-Jacques Rousseau, whose ideal was of small, self-sufficient, and inward-looking democratic communities. But the international dimension of liberalism was little more than the projection of domestic liberalism on a world scale. Liberalism was and is, in large part, an expression of revulsion against illegitimate violence: that of tyrants at home and of aggressors abroad. It held and still holds the belief that the elimination of wars of aggression will result from the spread of liberal democratic regimes and, as in Kant's scheme for perpetual peace, from the agreements such regimes sign to ban war and reduce armaments. The vision of a legitimate world order is thus the order that liberal states living in harmony would finally establish. What would make the inevitable competition of states harmless would be the external effect of two fundamental liberal "revolutions." The first is the triumph of constitutional, representative governments based on consent and rational discussion—governments that would be far less prone to resort to war than authoritarian regimes. The second is the emancipation of individuals at home and the resulting formation of a world public opinion and a transnational economic society of free commerce and industry linking people across borders (and creating strong state interests in cooperation and peace). Thus, the constraints put on government at home would expand into constraints on state power abroad.

Contrary to realist charges, liberalism was thus anything but naive about state power, whose reduction and domestication were deemed essential for the preservation of both peace abroad and liberty at home. Nevertheless, the international side of the liberal coin was far less polished than the domestic one. In particular, two questions remained unanswered. One was, How would the vision of harmony among liberal states with reduced power be realized? That is, should one put one's faith in the irresistible propagation of liberal polities (and if so, would international relations in a world divided into liberal and illiberal states not continue to be the kind of "state of war" Thucydides, Niccolò Machiavelli, Thomas Hobbes, and Rousseau had described)? Or should liberal states intervene actively for the propagation of liberalism or for its defense abroad whenever it risked being crushed? The domestic program of liberalism counted on either reform or revolution: the former, whenever possible, through the combined effects of enlightenment and the new capitalism; the latter when reform was blocked (though the French Revolution taught a grim lesson about the deviations—*dérapage*—in which a revolutionary course might get caught). The international side of liberalism offered a vision but not really a program, and the issue of intervention for liberalism turned out to be deeply divisive. Kant's scheme was resolutely noninterventionist—among liberal states. Mill saw a fundamental difference between interventions for self-government (which he rejected) and interventions for self-determination (which he endorsed). The gamut ranged from what we today would call isolationism on the one side to moral crusades on the other.

The other great unanswered question for traditional liberalism was suggested by Mill's distinction. Liberalism, a seventeenth- and eighteenth-century philosophy, discussed the relations of state and society in terms of mutual obligations between the individuals and the rulers—a rational relationship (often symbolized by the idea of the social contract).

But as the people, or a sizable portion of the people, began to play a role in the management of their affairs, a new issue arose: that of loyalty, of the emotional bonds of allegiance that tie the society to the state. This was the issue of nationalism: a new collective consciousness that could evolve from mere feeling to a passion and an ideology capable of being grafted onto every other conceivable political creed. The French Revolution and its wars, the Napoleonic hurricane, and the revolts of 1848 obliged all ideologies to cope with the nationalist phenomenon. Liberalism embraced the principle of national self-determination because it saw in it the external dimension of the principle of consent. A regime was legitimate if it was based on consent. A state was legitimate (and viable) if it reflected the desire of the individuals to form a nation, free of any oppression or intrusion by other nations. Jules Michelet, Giuseppe Mazzini, and Mill became the intellectual champions of liberal nationalism, with Mill being the most explicit and convincing in explaining why multinational states would have great trouble being liberal, given the demand of each national component for self-rule. Thus, self-determination was seen as the necessary corollary of liberal self-government, and it was this conviction that reshaped the vision of final international harmony into a vision of nation-states with liberal regimes: Wilson's dream.

But liberalism's embrace of national self-determination raised more questions than it answered. There was, once more, the dilemma of intervention for the emancipation of oppressed nationalities. In addition, there were formidable new question marks. Nationalities do not come in neat packages. One could conceive abstractly of a world of distinct liberal states, but a world of separate nation-states would leave vast areas of confusion: minorities in existing nation-states, plus the vexing problem of what is the "self" that is entitled to self-determination (what, in other words, distinguishes a group that deserves to become a nation-state from one that does not). There were also questions of whether self-determination was necessarily synonymous with sovereignty and whether a world of independent sovereign nation-states would find harmony as easily as the world of states envisaged by seventeenth- and eighteenth-century liberals—precisely because of the conflicts that were likely to result from the problems of minorities and of who can claim to form a nation.

Second, the national cause might be separate from the liberal one: there could be authoritarian versions of nationalism, definitions of the nation in terms of "blood and earth," not consent—conceptions that make of the individual a pure product of his national community and not the master of his civic fate. Nonliberal nationalisms thus could give new strength and relevance to authoritarian doctrines and might derail the philosophy of historical progress that predicted the gradual triumph of liberal government over tyranny. The replacement, on the illiberal Right, of divine right (or the power of tradition) with the needs and demands of the nation was to give a formidable new lease on life to ideas previously associated with obsolescent aristocracies, a reactionary church, or frivolous courts.

Third, liberalism's embrace of nationalism introduced into liberalism a philosophical incongruity. The appeal of liberalism had been an appeal to reason—the reason embodied in John Locke's natural law, Kant's idea of a good will rooted in human reason, and the rationalism of utilitarian calculations of pleasure and pain. Nationalism has much more to do with will than with reason; its connections are with Rousseau's concept of the general will, which is exclusively that of the separate community, and with Jacobinism. If the legitimacy of power is derived not merely from rational consent to a system of checks and balances and to a careful separation between a public sphere and a domain of individual liberty but also from the existence of a common national will, are there not serious risks that such a will, however democratic, could overrun the restraints on power and remove the barrier that protects individuals? Nationalism, in other words, reopened the inherent tension between liberalism and democracy that had broken out in the French Revolution, and it thus threatened both the liberal program at home and the cosmopolitan vision abroad—by creating new sources of intense conflict between states with different conceptions of the nation and overlapping nationalities and by weakening the two transnational pillars of the liberal international order: a transnational economy and world public opinion.

Liberal Internationalism and Realpolitik

With such blind spots and contradictions, how could liberal internationalism nevertheless have been as successful as it has been at times, particularly in the period that followed World War II? A part of the answer is undoubtedly provided by American hegemony in the vast areas in which the United States was able and willing to exert its influence after the calamitous insulation of the interwar period. It is already paradoxical enough that the progress of liberal vision, in the creation of a transnational economy as well as in the development of cooperation among liberal states, should depend so much on the preponderance of power in one state and on its willingness to provide others with a variety of public goods. After all, the kind of liberal internationalism achieved through hegemony raises questions both about what happens "after hegemony" and about the fairness of the order thus established. But one has to go deeper and examine both why the "hegemon" acted as decisively as it did and why others were willing to accept some of the costs.

The reason is another paradox. Liberal internationalism, a vision of harmony that remained rather vague about how to reach nirvana, has been best at performing what might be called negative tasks. In the economic realm, this was, of course, exactly what the doctrines of laissez-faire demanded. Liberalism has—under the impulse of a hegemon for which self-interest and liberal conviction converged—succeeded in removing a vast number of barriers to trade and communication and thus in establishing that transnational economic society that liberalism itself called for. The same result was achieved within the European Community, where many of the powers given up by the states have gone not to the new central institutions but to the market. And there, progress resulted not from the hegemony of one power but from a consensus among liberal regimes. In the political realm, however, liberalism, in order to reach its conception of peace, had to give priority to battle. Liberal internationalism has both fueled and supported the revolt against colonialism and imperialism, thus carrying forward Wilson's call that "no nation should seek to extend its polity over any other nation or people."[2] Liberal internationalism has spoken up against violations of human rights, especially in the last twenty years. Above all, it waged a protracted cold war against Soviet totalitarianism in order to "contain" it, in the expectation, formulated in 1946–1947 by George Kennan, that the Soviet system would eventually succumb to its internal flaws.

Thus the prelude to liberal harmony had to be a skillful exercise in limited war—limited both because of the liberal aversion to war and because of nuclear weapons. But it was the force of the totalitarian challenge that resolved the ambivalence of liberalism toward international activism and neutralized, for a long while, its noninterventionist potential. Even many of the "positive" missions accomplished by liberal internationalism after 1945—the democratization of Germany and Japan, the establishment of the European Community, the integration of the world capitalist economy—were undertaken or advanced as essential parts of the battle against the Soviet totalitarian threat. It was a remarkable fusion of Realpolitik and liberal internationalism. But that fusion was not without strains. Some were over priorities: Was the containment of Soviet influence or of communism's expansion so overriding a goal that it left little space for the nurturing of liberal democracy in, say, Greece in 1967–1974, in the Shah's Iran, or in Central American and Caribbean countries? Was the Soviet version of communism so dangerous that it became necessary to court and accommodate Moscow's communist rivals—especially in China—and to close one's eyes to the crimes committed by them against human rights? What was one to do when anti-imperialism struck at interests America's main allies deemed essential (Suez) or when there was a dramatic confluence of communism and anti-imperialism (Vietnam)?

There was also a problem of means: did not the battle against communism entail a risk of using distinctly "illiberal" methods, particularly in the realm of subversion or in so-called revolutionary wars like Vietnam? And there was one issue whose importance was barely realized in the momentous sweep of decolonization: the support the United States and liberals in Europe provided to the revolts against colonialism put the demand for self-determination (that is, against alien rule) ahead of any concern for self-government (that is, liberal democracy). These revolts resulted in the establishment of states within the borders arbitrarily dawn by the imperial powers and amounted to a grant of self-determination not to nations but often to heterogeneous collections of peoples living within these borders.

A last question mark hung over the institutions of cooperation a liberal world requires. The United Nations became a double victim of the cold war. Its Security Council was often paralyzed by the Soviet veto and by the division of the world into rival camps; moreover, the huge financial needs that the advanced liberal powers had to meet in the realm of security—the demands of the "military-industrial complex"—left only relatively meager resources for the development of the poorer states. The concern for equity in this respect was, indeed, more characteristic of social democrats than of liberals, who were ambivalent about providing aid to governments that might either waste it or use it to increase their power, or both. The UN was also handicapped by its composition: a congeries not of liberal democracies but of regimes of every type—a fact that severely limited its ability to protect human rights. Liberal internationalism thus had to rely on partial, rather than global, institutions of cooperation, on military alliances such as NATO, or on the hegemon.

In the late 1980s, Mikhail Gorbachev began to try to reform the Soviet Union and moved its foreign policy in the direction of liberal internationalism: arms control, peaceful settlement of conflicts, retreat from the empire acquired abroad, hymns to interdependence, and so forth. It looked as if the golden age had arrived and a new world order based on the principles of liberal internationalism was going to emerge from the sound and fury of the cold war. Ridiculed for saying it, George Bush had in mind something that was not new: his "new world order" was the order underlying the UN Charter of 1945—an order resting on the principle of collective security against aggression and on the cooperation of the major powers, which, with the exception of China, were now all liberal or on the road to liberal democracy. The Persian Gulf war was the one and only triumph of that dream. Once again, "realist" concerns (oil and the security of the Gulf states) and the liberal vision converged, with the United States as the linchpin of the construction and the UN as the provider of legitimacy. But ever since, the liberal vision has been in serious trouble.

Liberalism's Modern Predicament

Basically, the plight of the liberal vision results from the fallacy of believing that all good things can come together. They rarely do, and many that were expected to be good have turned out rotten. More specifically, the liberal vision was focused on one particular enemy: the Moloch of power, wherever found, either arbitrary and excessive at home or imperial and militaristic abroad. Insofar as abuse of power is a hardy perennial, liberalism remains an indispensable source of inspiration and value. But there is another enemy in today's world: not the violence that results from the clash of mighty powers or from the imposition of the power of the strong on the weak but the violence that results from chaos from below. The world today is threatened by the disintegration of power—by anomie, which denotes the absence of norms but can also refer to the collision of norms.

The Wilsonian edifice, its Rooseveltian version of 1945, the Bush coat of fresh paint of 1990, all were undertaken to deal with a world of interstate conflicts. All three assumed that the nature of the regime is a key determinant of state behavior: that liberal nation-states do not fight each other. It is difficult to provide decisive evidence for such a hypothesis, however, and neorealists believe that the anarchic "structure" of international relations imposes the same kind of behavior on all states. But even if that hypothesis is true, wars among states are only one of the perils of the post-cold-war international system. What is now at stake is the very nature of the state. The "Westphalian" system that has inspired all theories of international relations presupposed well-determined states, clashing or cooperating. Both realism and liberalism shared that assumption; Marxism rejected it, but only because of its belief that the "logic" of state behavior was merely an expression of the logic, and contradictions, of capitalism—that states were, so to speak, puppets manipulated by the global economic system. Liberalism—or the UN Charter—finds it difficult to cope with a variety of phenomena: the disintegration of the Soviet Union and Yugoslavia; ethnic conflicts in the successor states; civil wars among rival ethnic, religious, or political factions in countries long ravaged by the cold war (such as Cambodia or Afghanistan) or in much of Africa; the failure of many postcolonial states, especially in Africa but also in parts of Asia, to become nation-states; and the attempts by Islamic or Hindu fundamentalists to replace a secular with a religious and thus highly exclusionary definition of the state. To arrive at a world of liberal polities, there must be a clear idea of the state. If the world consists of disintegrating states, then the cooperative processes and institutions that are supposed to fuel harmony under the banner of liberal internationalism are easily overwhelmed by millions of refugees who flee massacres and disasters and seek asylum in liberal states or call for protection whenever they cannot escape.

Liberal internationalism thus faces a predicament. First, it needs a set of clear principles to set goals. Yet, in two crucial respects all it finds is a cacophony of principles governing two issues that are anything but new: what to do about violations of human rights by tyrannical regimes—in places such as Haiti, Burma, or China—and how to react to the imposition of alien rule on reluctant peoples—such as the Kurds of Iraq (or Turkey), the Tibetans of China, the East Timorese of Indonesia. On both issues the old split about whether or not to intervene is as deep as ever. On balance, however, the noninterventionist impulse is strengthened by the disappearance of the Soviet threat and rationalized with the argument that the propagation of political liberalism will ultimately result from the spread of global economic liberalism. Thus, paradoxically, the principle of state sovereignty (which is not particularly liberal, since many states are not based on consent) is often given precedence over the liberal norms of self-government and of national self-determination. The old argument for nonintervention was that intervention even for liberal causes would multiply violent conflicts, whereas liberalism's aim was to dampen them.

A new argument is that in a world where chaos is now a major peril, intervention even for good liberal causes may only create more chaos.

It is precisely in the realm of chaos described above—the realm of disintegrating states—that the clash of norms is the most evident and paralyzing: sovereignty (as a principle of order and, still, a barrier against aggressive or imperial designs), self-government or democracy, national self-determination (with all its ambiguities and flaws), and human rights (which are not devoid of ambiguities of their own, as debates over the priority of political over economic and social rights and over the rights of individuals versus the rights of peoples and groups indicate) are four norms in conflict and a source of complete liberal disarray. Human rights—the major strand of nonutilitarian liberalism—often cannot be protected without infringing upon another state's sovereignty or circumscribing the potential for a "tyranny of the majority" entailed by national self-determination and by Jacobin versions of democracy. The troublemaking potential of self-determination, both for interstate order and for human rights, is now so obvious that many liberals want to curb it or even get rid of it, yet the demand for it simply cannot be ignored, and denying its legitimacy would rarely be a recipe for order or democracy. Inconsistency is the result of this confusion: the international "community" has recognized Croatia, Bosnia, and Eritrea but not Biafra, Chechnya, or the right of the Kurds and Tibetans to states of their own.

In a search for a threat that would allow them to set priorities and a strategy, liberal statesmen receive little help from liberal philosophers. In his recent lectures, titled "The Law of Peoples," John Rawls fails to discuss the meaning of "peoples." Cosmopolitan liberals, such as Martha Nussbaum, who stress the moral arbitrariness of borders (between states or between nations) step outside the limits of traditional liberalism (which saw the universal values of its creed realized in and through a world of states, not a world state). They also go far beyond what the moral traffic will bear. Communitarian liberals such as Michael Walzer are torn between the cosmopolitan and interventionist implications of their liberalism—when "domestic brutality, civil war, political tyranny, ethnic and religious persecution"[3] become intolerable—and the noninterventionist and relativist implications of their communitarianism. What is needed, and still missing, is a complex and sophisticated rethinking of liberal internationalism; its Ariadne's thread would be human rights (including the right to participate in one's government and the right to be part of, but not a slave to, a national community). It would curtail sovereignty—so that the powers entailed by it could be shared at home and pooled abroad—and it would limit self-determination so that minorities everywhere could have a genuine choice between assimilation and protection of their distinctiveness and so that the desire for self-rule need not take the form of full state sovereignty in every instance.

Intervention and the Use of Force

Liberal internationalism is also in disarray over methods for defending or promoting its vision. Among liberals today, two sets of alternatives intersect. On the one hand, there is an argument over intervention. Some remain sufficiently suspicious of outside interventions (whether unilateral or collective) to prefer not stepping beyond humanitarian operations whose aim is to protect the victims of natural or manmade disasters. Others fear that the politics of band-aids will only allow the do-gooders to feel good and leave unaltered the deeper causes of the disasters: murderous gangs and armies, as in Liberia, Somalia, and Rwanda; ethnic absolutists, like Serbs or Bosnian Serbs; tyrants such as Saddam Hussein, and so on. The logic of that viewpoint leads, of course, to far deeper foreign involvements, indeed to protectorates or trusteeships (Cambodia being one current example).

The other great division is over the use of force. Traditionally, liberalism has tried to limit legitimate force to self-defense and collective defense against aggression. But the scope of state chaos, as well as the murderousness of some contemporary tyrannies, has led many liberals to endorse in principle the idea of an outside resort to force whenever domestic chaos threatens the peace and security of other states (for instance through the mass flight of refugees) or whenever domestic chaos or tyrannical government results in massive violations of human rights, such as ethnic cleansing and genocide. Other liberals are doubly dubious about the resort to force because of a traditional tendency to look at it as an instrument of last resort only and because of a conviction that many of these uses of force could only lead to quagmires and entrapments. Both sides often agree on the dispatching of UN peacekeepers, but when it comes to having these troops actually use force (except in self-defense) or to having "peace builders" with missions far more extensive than peacekeepers, disagreement reappears. The Bosnia fiasco has been the result of all these cleavages. Bosnia has been the victim of the imbalanced compromise between those who gave priority to the restoration of peace, however unfair the solution may be, and those who gave priority to the suppression of what they saw as a double assault on liberal values: Serb aggression and ethnic cleansing.

A final predicament concerns not norms or methods but agents. Who should be the secular arm of liberal action? Great powers (global or regional) claiming to act as enforcers of community norms inspire suspicion, even if, as in the case of India's intervention in Bangladesh, the ratio of self-interest to common good was clearly tilted toward the latter. There is a second problem with hegemonic enforcers: what happens when they choose not to act, failing to realize that the spread of chaos or the triumph of tyranny are antithetical to their interests as great powers? What has happened in the Clinton years, and may happen even more in the second, "Republican" half of the Clinton era, is ominous. Deprived of the relatively clear and widely shared goals that had pushed America to the fore of what was propagandistically called the free world, Washington has been left with Anthony Lake's laundry list of worthy goals but appears incapable of turning them into a coherent strategy. The administration, sensing the reluctance of its public and Congress to have America play the role of world policeman and marked by memories of Vietnam, suggested that if vital interests were not at stake, force would be used only multilaterally. But the story has been one of a double retreat: from military intervention (except in Haiti, where force was coupled with a very limited or ambivalent mandate) and from multilateralism—except when the latter made inaction or minimal action "legitimate," as in Bosnia. Unilateralism has become a way to appease anti-internationalists (a loose collection of realists and American nationalists) and to justify doing very little.

The alternative to great powers as enforcers would be international organizations, but the lesson of recent years is that the United Nations tends to act effectively only when great powers provide the necessary leadership. When the powers are divided or predominantly reluctant, operations become fiascoes, as has been the case in Somalia and Bosnia, or too little and too late, as in Rwanda (largely because of American pressure to keep the intervention small in size and scope). The United Nations—like traditional liberalism—was designed for a world of interstate conflicts: many of the tasks it has had thrust on its since 1991 therefore exceed its capacities. As an institution it suffers from the contradiction between a liberal vision that makes harmony depend on the right kind of state (liberal-national), on the one hand, and an international system that requires a heavy dose of international regimes and organizations aimed at overcoming the drawbacks of state sovereignty, on the other. The fact that the UN has been provided neither with the enforcement institutions Chapter VII of the UN Charter had foreseen for collective security nor with a permanent force capable of preventive action or of peace building in domestic crises has resulted both in calamitous conflicts of loyalty for the contingents that states placed at the UN disposal and in massive inefficiencies. It would be unfair to accuse liberals of having neglected international agencies, but the literature on regimes has focused much more on norms and institutions at the crossroads of interstate economic cooperation and the transnational world economy than on norms and institutions that deal with what I have called the domain of chaos. Liberals have also paid a lot of attention to agencies for the international protection of human rights. But the gap between liberal theory and practice on human rights is wide indeed. It is explained by the existence of so many states with skeletons in their closets and no desire to do more than pass resolutions on subjects as thorny as minority rights, political freedoms, the rights of migrants and refugees, and international criminal justice.

The Rise of Transnational Society

So far, we have analyzed the plight of liberalism in the world of states. What about the other side of its vision for the planet: transnational society, constraining the capacity of states for evil? Insofar as world public opinion is concerned, Wilson's hopes have not been realized for many reasons. First, when one looks only at the public opinion of open and liberal societies, as expressed in their media, one finds a reflection of the diversity of ideological and religious positions, as over population issues. One also finds the diversity of national perspectives, such as the frequent American reluctance to look at economic and social rights as genuine claims. Second, this is still a world half free and half not. A large number of authoritarian regimes still control the formation and expression of public opinion. They succeed, especially in discussions of human rights issues, in hiding their abuses behind arguments for relativism and the defense of local customs and norms. A variety of economic issues have also put up roadblocks on the way to Wilson's vision. In dealing with the problems of distributive justice associated with the allocation of wealth and resources among and within states and with the intragenerational and intergenerational choices in environmental policies, liberalism has traditionally been rather silent. When it has raised its voice, it has been torn between its pure laissez-faire types who favor efficiency over equity, defend the status quo, and maintain their faith in the "trickle-down" effects of growth, on the one hand, and, on the other, more socially troubled or New Deal types who are eager to find safety nets for the poor, to orient free enterprise toward "sustainable human development," and to entrust international agencies with some redistributive functions and resources. As a result, on issues of singular importance for the vast majority of humankind, "world public opinion" has not been a cohesive force orienting governments. It has been divided—often along the lines of the rich versus the poor, with significant elements in each camp crossing over and adopting the arguments of the other. And it has fluctuated over time. This is not to deny the importance of nongovernmental organizations in many areas and their capacity to graduate from "world public opinion" to "transnational actors." But one must face the limits as well.

The formation of a global transnational economy constitutes a triumph of the liberal vision that first appeared in the eighteenth century (when philosophers saw private interests cutting across borders as potential tamers of clashing state passions), but it also provides evidence of the fact that fulfillment of the vision has mounting costs and unexpected consequences. Liberalism has always been a somewhat delicate coalition of two different perspectives on human nature. One of them emphasizes selfishness, defines interests in material terms, and celebrates the (general) benefits from individual greed. The other touts the moral aptitudes of human beings, focuses on rights and duties, and emphasizes both moral self-fulfillment and civic virtues. Many liberal philosophers—particularly the utilitarians—have tried to make the two strands converge. Much of the admiration Alexis de Tocqueville had for America came from his belief that here they had indeed been merged. Many of his doubts about liberal democracy's future came from his fears about the possible victory of greed and individual self-interest. It should not be surprising that in the drive to create a global economy through the dismantling of state barriers, concerns for human rights, democracy, or self-determination have often been submerged or twisted according to the highly debatable assumption that free economies must "ultimately" lead to free polities as well. The assumption may turn out to be correct, but it is fair to say that the jury is still out.

The new transnational economy has not merely, and beneficially, constrained the power of states. It has not only deprived them of much of their capacity to build command economies that ignore the signals given by markets and produce colossal inefficiencies. It has, alas, also deprived them of some of their ability to perform necessary tasks, to carry out basic functions liberalism never intended to remove from them. The free flow of drugs and the free circulation of crime have accompanied the formation of a global world economy. Governments find it difficult to restore against such "bad goods" the controls they have removed to facilitate the flow of the good ones. Moreover, the ability of governments to define their own monetary policies and to orient investments, employment, and growth has been seriously curtailed by the very size and weight of the transnational economy. The case of the European Monetary System and of its two huge crises in the summers of 1992 and 1993, when private capital movements played havoc with the exchange rates set up by the European Community and overwhelmed the efforts of central banks, is an extreme but important example of what is happening. The liberals of past centuries had thought primarily in terms of trade. We are now moving toward an integrated world market of trade, production, and distribution. The new world economy is made of national and multinational corporations operating across borders and of millions of individual bond holders, shareholders, and holders of savings accounts in search of maximal and quick profits across borders. That has two effects, also unforeseen by liberal internationalism, and both contribute to the prevalence of chaos. One is the creation of a huge zone of irresponsibility: the global economy is literally out of control, not subject to the rules of accountability and principles of legitimacy that apply to relations between individuals and the state. States hesitate to impose their own rules unilaterally, out of fear of inefficiency and self-damage. Thus liberalism, successful in reducing the state's power, has created a formidable anonymous new power. It affects both states and individuals but is treated as if it were merely an extension of the individual's sphere of protected freedoms. What is desperately needed is a theory that acknowledges the public aspects and effects of such private activities across borders and establishes a kind of common government for those activities—just as within civil societies liberalism aimed at setting up legitimate central institutions in order to rule out the flaws of a "state of nature."

The other effect has been frequent domestic backlash against he constraints imposed by interdependence in general, a reaction to the sense that the fate of individuals even in liberal polities is no longer under their control or that of their representatives. It is hard to target the force that is most responsible for this loss—the transnational economy—and too late to do more than delay or restrain a bit the removal of barriers to the free circulation of capital, goods, and services that allows this economy to grow in all directions. Thus, the reaction often strikes instead at efforts at interstate cooperation (such as the European Union) and takes various forms of xenophobia, as in attacks on migrant workers and restrictions on asylum. Those are defeats for liberal values. The phenomena one can observe in Europe are now becoming visible in the United States as well.

Because of the difficulties experienced by liberal internationalism in the new post-cold-war world and the inconsistencies in UN and U.S. actions, one can now legitimately fear a discrediting of international organizations comparable to the one that submerged the League of Nations in the 1930s, even though the causes, this time, are the problems of chaos rather than the challenges mounted by a few major powers. As for the United States, one can also fear a new edition of its behavior in the 1920s, when it remained a mighty actor in the transitional world economy of that period but returned to a severely restricted role in the realm of interstate politics. The main triumphs of the Clinton administration have been in the vigorous offensive to pry open foreign markets, through the North American Free Trade Agreement, the General Agreement on Tariffs and Trade, and the Asia-Pacific Economic Cooperation forum. This is an area where liberal internationalists and American realists can find common ground, since for the United States today, as for Great Britain in the nineteenth century, the case for free trade and the expansion of national economic power and interests appear to coincide. However, the main Clinton objective has not been free trade per se but a return to growth, hence to fuller employment at home. The president is more interested in the liberal vision at home than in the liberal vision abroad. Or rather, the latter serves the former. Meanwhile, the realists, repeating the mantra of "interests defined as power," fail to account for the fact that with the same amount of power on the whole as a few years ago, and at a time when it is the only superpower, the United States is in the midst of a crisis over defining its interests abroad. It tends, in a world without signposts, to give a far more limited interpretation of them—one that reveals a wide gap between unchanged liberal aspirations and actual policies.

Liberal internationalism has never been very good at specifying what liberal state interests were, beyond physical security and survival, and whether setting up an international system of liberal states was a vital interest, and not merely a legitimate aspiration, of liberal states. It has not been good at confronting the illiberal aspects of nationalism and the destructive potential of national self-determination. It has not paid enough attention to the contradiction between a cosmopolitan but uncontrolled world economy and a world of sovereign albeit cooperating states. Nor has it heeded the need for strong common institutions capable both of coping with whatever states cannot accomplish by themselves and of regulating what may soon be seen as a transnational Frankenstein monster.

Marxism is discredited. Realism promises only the perpetuation of the same old game and is no better equipped to face the politics of chaos than is liberalism. Liberalism remains the only comprehensive and hopeful vision of world affairs, but it needs to be thoroughly reconstructed—and that task has no proceeded very far, in either its domestic or its international dimensions.

Part Two

From the End of the Cold War to the Search for a New World Order

6

What Should We Do in the World?

There are periods of history then profound changes occur all of a sudden and the acceleration of events is such that much of what experts write is obsolete before it gets into print. We are now in one of those periods, which obliges the United States to rethink its role in the world, just as it was forced to do by the cataclysmic changes that followed the end of World War II.

For more than forty years American foreign policy has been dominated by the contest with the Soviet Union. The strategy of containment, defined by George F. Kennan in 1946–1947 and applied by all American administrations since, often in a manner that displeased Kennan, may not have been an adequate compass at all times. The Soviet Union found ways of leaping across the barriers that the United States tried to erect, with military alliances and bases, all around the Soviet empire. Moreover, the imperative of containment failed to provide clear guidance for dealing with a host of regional and internal conflicts, especially in developing areas. Nevertheless, containment proved to be an extraordinarily sturdy concept. It was flexible enough to serve such diverse policies as the original strategy of alliance building and confrontation, the détente of the early 1970s (aimed at providing Moscow with incentives for self-containment), and occasional attempts at "rollback," including the Reagan doctrine. And while there were constant clashes over the Third World between "globalists," keen on interpreting the politics and conflicts of, say, the Middle East, Central America, and southern Africa strictly in terms of the Soviet-American contest, and "regionalists," who believed that we had to deal with the local sources of trouble, the two groups agreed that the main goal of American diplomacy was to prevent the expansion of

Soviet influence. In the view of the globalists, this goal required reliance on friendly clients and stern opposition to the Soviet Union and its allies; in that of the regionalists, it required the avoidance of moves that could push local nationalists into the arms of Moscow. Similarly, in the 1970s there were those (led by Zbigniew Brzezinski) who wanted a Washington-Beijing anti-Soviet entente and those (led by Henry Kissinger) who wanted a triangular game that would allow the United States to be closer to both Moscow and Beijing than the two were to each other. Still, containment of Moscow was the aim of both groups.

The momentous changes of the past three years have done more than any other trends or events since 1947 to deprive U.S. foreign policy of this overriding rationale. The détente of the early 1970s was a limited rapprochement between superpowers that were continuing to arm even while seeking to control jointly some parts of the arms race. It was a shaky convergence of contradictory calculations, in which the United States was trying to impose its version of stability and its own predominance on the Soviets, while the Soviets were hoping for condominium. Despite the defection of China, Moscow was still the center of a powerful empire. Today this empire is in serious trouble, China appears the more repressive and cruel of the two Communist giants, and Mikhail Gorbachev has gone far toward fulfilling the prophecy of Gyorgy Arbatov, the head of Moscow's Institute of USA and Canadian Affairs, who said that the new Soviet Union would deprive the United States of its main enemy.

As if stupefied by the pace of events, many members of the American foreign-policy establishment behave like the orphans of containment—clinging to the remains of an obsolete strategy and incapable of defining a new one. And yet this is the moment to coolly reevaluate American interests in the world. For many years our perceptions (often mistaken) of the Soviet threat drove our policy and defined, or distorted, our interests. Any great power has fundamental concerns, such as survival, physical security, and access to essential sources of energy, raw materials, and markets. In addition, it works toward what specialists in international relations call milieu goals: promoting its values abroad, or at least preserving chances for the flowering of those values, and shaping international agreements and institutions in such a way that the nation's fundamental objectives and values are served. These very general interests are translated into something that can be called the national interest—a more precise list of concerns that takes into account external factors, such as the distribution of power in specific areas between friends and foes, and internal ones, such as the imperatives and prohibitions set by domestic political and economic forces. In periods of extreme international tension, when there appears to be one global enemy, any move made by the adversary tends to be seen as a threat, creating a national interest in repelling it. A bipolar conflict thus serves as a procrustean bed: each side's definition of its interests is dictated by the image of the enemy. Now that the enemy recedes, a redefinition of those interests becomes possible, and necessary.

In order to understand what the United States ought to do now, we have to begin by taking stock of where we are—of the main features of the international system in which we operate and of the main perils it contains.

The Two World Systems

The traditional theory of international relations that professors have taught their students, and statesmen have practiced, treats international politics as if it were exclusively the strategic and diplomatic game of states as it was played in the days of Thucydides or in the eighteenth century. But the key reality of the post-1945 period is that states play in two arenas. The first is the traditional strategic and diplomatic one, in which there is no broad international consensus and in which power tends to be used in the way it always has been, usually as a contest in which my gain is your loss. The second is the economic arena, in which a variety of games are played—about trade, finance, energy, raw materials, the environment, and so forth—and most countries, but not all of them, are closely linked; they are interdependent in the sense that even the more powerful and less vulnerable are affected by what happens elsewhere. Here, states combine the usual attempts to gain relative advantages with an awareness that this is not a zero-sum game and that every country has an interest in the prosperity of the global economy and of the other players. Here the logic of "anarchy"—the fragmentation of the world into sovereign states—is checked by the logic of, and a broad consensus on, an open global economy. While international organizations are all fragile, and none of them has power over the major states, they are more numerous and effective in the second arena than in the first.

Each arena has its own distribution of power. In the strategic and diplomatic arena, we have been blessed or cursed, depending on one's point of view, by bipolarity—by the dominance of the United States and the Soviet Union. The economic arena, however, has been marked for a very long time by American hegemony. This is still largely the case, although increasingly important roles are, of course, being played by West Germany and Japan. What's more, here there are major players that are not states but, rather, regional organizations and multinational corporations, banks, and speculators whose capital movements, investments, and loans deeply affect the world economy and contradict the efforts of states to preserve, singly or jointly, some control.

Moreover, each arena has its own, unprecedented restraints upon it. In the strategic and diplomatic field restraint has been imposed by nuclear weapons. What is new here, as McGeorge Bundy has shown in his book, *Danger and Survival,* is that above a certain level of force, superiority does not make any difference, because there is nothing one can *do* with those weapons (as Robert McNamara has been telling us ever since he stopped being secretary of defense). Nuclear weapons have restrained the superpowers from all direct military confrontation, which is quite an unprecedented achievement. In addition, these weapons are largely unusable for political blackmail (for it is hard to wrest gains by brandishing weapons that one doesn't want to use), and the result is that on the very field that is dominated by two powers, they are often impotent. What we find, therefore, is a downgrading of the great powers, a relative pacification at the top, and a continuation of the traditional "state of war" among other powers at lower levels, because, despite prophecies about the obsolescence of war, nuclear restraints certainly have not eliminated violence altogether.

In the economic arena the restraints are different but perhaps even more interesting: they are the shackles of economic interdependence. The economies of the main players have become so thoroughly intertwined that any state that tries to exert its power for competitive, immediate, or hostile gains risks creating formidable boomerang effects, as we have seen, for instance, in the case of OPEC (Organization of Petroleum Exporting Countries) and may be seeing in the future with Japan. To be sure, there is a constant tension between the forces of protectionism— interest groups harmed by open borders and external competitors, bureaucracies trying to save their fiscal policy and other instruments of domestic control—and the imperatives of the open capitalist economy. But, paradoxically, the fact that the agenda for this arena is set by the demands of domestic consumers and producers tends to make those imperatives prevail over the occasional domestic backlash against interdependence or the occasional temptation of states to use their economic power belligerently. This is so because very few states, including the biggest ones, are capable of reaching their economic objectives by what has been the basic principle of international affairs: self-help.

Finally, the internationalization of production—the fact that when you buy a product these days it is hard to know what its nationality is—and the global nature of financial markets result in even more restraints on the manipulation of economic power by any given state. Because the use of force is irrelevant in this realm, its politics are, in fact, an unstable hybrid of international politics without war and domestic politics without central power.

The Diffusion of Power

These features have been visible for a while. But some changes have taken place only in recent years. On the strategic and diplomatic front the most interesting trend has been the beginning of the end of the cold war. Some of the reasons for this trend are external, or international, the main one being the extensive limitations on the effectiveness of force to which I have already alluded. In addition to the nuclear restraint, we must consider the increasing capacity for resistance among the victims of external force, especially if those victims get support from the outside, as usually happens, or if, like the Palestinians in the occupied territories, they fight at a level that makes successful repression difficult. Here recent experiences are telling. We have witnessed remarkable parallel American experiences in Vietnam and Soviet experiences in Afghanistan; the Israelis have been thwarted in Lebanon (which also gives Syria much trouble); the Vietnamese are calling it quits in Cambodia; and so on. Plainly there exists a wide inability to use force abroad for the control of a foreign people. These frustrations lead one to a conclusion once expressed by a former French foreign minister (a very shrewd man who liked to talk in apparent banalities): if you can't win a war, you might as well make peace. Thus the bizarre epidemic of peace in 1988. There is another external reason for the beginning of the end of the cold war. Over time, inevitably, there had to be some loosening of the two blocks that have confronted each other; the compression of all the internal divergences and conflicts within them could not last forever. It was largely artificial: they were compressed as long as there was a cold-war condition, a kind of mimicked state of war; once it became clear that war was being postponed indefinitely, there was no reason for the blocs to remain as rigid as they once had been.

Of course the dominant reasons for the ending of the cold war are internal. In the United States, apart from economic factors to which we will come, there is what is quite improperly called the Vietnam syndrome, which is simply the marked reluctance of the American public to become engaged in protracted, uncertain wars for unclear purposes in secondary parts of the world. After all, Ronald Reagan, a rather popular president, did not succeed in getting the U.S. public to support the contra war against Nicaragua, nor did the American public support the presence of the United States Marines in Lebanon, once the awful costs became visible. In the Soviet Union the internal situation is far more serious, and there is a rather desperate need for retrenchment because of the economic predicament.

In the realm of economic interdependence, the evolution of recent years has two main characteristics. One is that despite the considerable difficulties of the past two decades, the economic relations among the advanced countries have developed successfully. To be sure, there has been a creeping erosion of the international principles of free trade established after World War II. Nevertheless, a relatively open and growing international economy has been preserved despite the economic shocks of the 1970s—no mean achievement, especially if one compares this with the situation that prevailed between the wars. The second trend, which is much more disturbing, has occurred in North-South relations; there, we have not been so successful. An increasing differentiation has taken place between the developing countries that have been able to join the industrial world, and whose economic takeoff has been spectacular, and the many other countries that have failed and have fallen more and more deeply into debt. Between the latter countries and the rest of the world the gap has grown ever wider.

Behind this evolution in both fields there is one very important trend, which concerns the distribution of power. The surface manifestation is a diffusion away from the superpowers. But we are not moving back to the traditional world in which several great powers had reasonably equal weight. In the strategic and diplomatic field we now find a coexistence of weakened global superpowers and regional balances of power, which are often unstable and where an important role is played by what are sometimes called regional influentials. In the arena of interdependence an increasing role is being played by a tightening European Community, by Japan, in some areas by Saudi Arabia. The aspect of this diffusion of power that is most significant for us here is the relative decline of the United States, to use the obligatory cliché of the past two years (after all, a cliché is simply a truth that too many people have uttered and that many resist). Many public officials and academics have wrapped themselves in the American flag in the long debate on decline. They keep saying, quite rightly, that—if one compares the United States in the world today with the United States in the world of 1945–1950—a major part of this decline is not only normal but has been planned by the United States. Since 1945, when, after all, the world situation was completely abnormal, the United States has done its best to help the economies of Western Europe, Japan, South Korea, and Taiwan; as a result the American share of world GNP was bound to decrease.

However, there is more to it than that. The United States has become a debtor nation that depends on the willingness of others to provide the funds necessary to finance its budget deficit; we are going to be burdened for a long time by that debt. The United States has also seen its competitiveness decline for reasons that are largely internal and that cannot simply be dismissed by referring to the inevitable growth of other countries. The phenomena of overconsumption and underinvestment; insufficient industrial productivity; rigidity, waste, and short-sightedness in industry; and the problems in American education, particularly technical education, which have been much discussed though not much as been done about them, are the main culprits here. As a result the United States is simply no longer the leader in a number of key sectors in the world economy. Granted, this is less significant than it would have been in past international systems, where declining in key sectors meant a dangerous advantage for a major new military challenger. In the current system the United States faces no military challenger that is in better shape than it is. Nevertheless, this decline means that the American capacity to mold the international system of the future is not what it used to be, insofar as technological predominance often leads to wide influence abroad and technological decline reduces the dependence of others on American civilian and military goods.

Beyond the Cold War

Given these features and trends of the world of the late 1980s, what ought American foreign policy to be? The point of departure must be the recognition of a paradox. The United States remains the only "complete" great power, the possessor of the largest military arsenal and of the most powerful economy in the world. On the other hand, both the diffusion of power in recent years and the partial impotence of military and economic power because of the restraints on its uses make it much more difficult for the United States to impose its will on others and to shape outcomes according to its preferences. We can still lead, toward goals that have a reasonable chance of being deemed by others compatible with their own interests. But we can no longer rule. Games of skill must replace tests of will. Our waning power to command and control needs to be supplemented by the new kind of power that the international system requires: the power to convince and to deal. In order to be effective, we have to define our national interest in a way that has a chance both of preserving a national capacity for steering toward world order (not because we are wiser than other nations but because there is no other candidate for the job) and of persuading others that their long-term concerns and ours mesh.

We cannot replace a fading vision—that of containment—with more short-term management and avoidance of trouble, because the present offers opportunities for a decisive change in direction and because there are simply too many dangers ahead to allow us to stumble from issue to issue in a "pragmatic" way. Nor can we follow the advice of neo-isolationists who believe that the United States ought not only to reduce its commitments and its military presence abroad, now that the cold war is ending, but also to transfer to other powers the responsibility for dealing with the world's perils. That a great deal of what some call "devolution" needs to take place is not in doubt, but there is a gap between devolution and abdication. The truth is that only our continuing involvement is likely to draw other powers into an effort for world order, precisely because our past predominance had led others to rely on our initiatives and has led us to hug political control even as we rhetorically deplore the costs and burdens that come with it.

We have to define first our goals, then our strategy. Our first goal ought to be the rearrangement of our relationship with the Soviet Union, away from both the old cold war and the rather misleading exchange of misunderstandings that was the détente of the 1970s. This new relationship will inevitably be partly competitive, because our two nations will continue to have conflicting interests in many parts of the world, but it ought to be competitive without excessive militarization, and partly cooperative on issues in which there will be or already are converging interests.

A second goal ought to be a to facilitate a transition to a world in which major new threats to world order will be neutralized. One is the threat of fragmentary violence resulting from sharp internal conflicts in many of the weak countries of the world—conflicts in which others will be tempted to intervene—and from the regional conflicts that still rage in many parts of the world. Some conflicts are likely to surface or to worsen once the discipline exerted on each camp by the cold war is no longer there, once often centrifugal or nostalgic nationalisms (in Eastern Europe, for instance) replace artificial and defunct ideological solidarities. Another new threat is the threat of chaos in world economic relations, because of mismanagement by states (of the huge problem of Third World debt, for instance), or because of a victory of economic nationalism over the constraints of interdependence, or because of states' lack of control over the economic activities of private parties whose moves could provoke financial panic. Therefore, our third goal ought to be to bring about more order and more justice—to use a recently coined phrase, a kinder and gentler world.

The domestic precondition for these new foreign-policy goals must be, of course, putting our economic house in order. What needs to be done in this sphere is too familiar from books and articles for me to repeat in here. I would only point to the price that our continuing budget crisis exacts from the pursuit of U.S. interests abroad. In Poland, for example, the pace and reach of reform will be less than if we had been able to make more money available to promote political pluralism and a market economy.

Goals are easy to describe. What matters more is a strategy for reaching them.

The Gorbachev Opening

Even though the Bush administration appears to have emerged from its inauspiciously long initial phase of skepticism toward Gorbachev and grudging annoyance at the pace of his moves, much of what calls itself the enlightened public remains extraordinarily hesitant about what to do with the Soviet Union. The doubt takes two forms: fear that Soviet efforts at reform are still very much reversible and questioning whether the United States really has an interested in "helping" Gorbachev. My answer is that of course much is reversible—in human affairs many things always are, and in politics nothing, not even totalitarianism, is ever definitive—but a great deal of the new thinking about foreign affairs going on in the Soviet Union is not tied exclusively to Gorbachev. It appears to be shared by much of a political generation, because it corresponds to almost desperate domestic necessities that are being proclaimed by a large number of Soviet people who have, by traveling around the world and by reading foreign works, been able to compare the Soviet perform-ance with what goes on abroad. This is one of the interesting, welcome, and unexpected by-products of the détente of the 1970s. Also, the new thinking corresponds to a realistic reading by many Soviet leaders and experts of an international system in which the traditional Soviet mode of behavior—the attempt to impose political control and ideological con-formity on others by force—yields limited results, often at exorbitant cost; in which the arms race and the logic of "absolute security" lead only to a higher, more expensive plateau of stalemate and to new forms of insecurity; and in which, in particular, the contest with the United States for influence in the Third World has turned out to be extraordi-narily unrewarding. Thus, while Gorbachev may ultimately fail and be replaced, while some of his daring foreign-policy moves may be revers-ible, and while we may have only limited leverage over what happens in the Soviet Union, the important question is whether it is at all in our interest to undermine Gorbachev's innovations. The answer is obviously no, because the alternatives that one can think of are worse: a return to the militarized foreign policy that prevailed in the years of Leonid Brezh-nev or a domestic triumph of the sort of Russian fundamentalism—anti-Western, chauvinistic, anti-Semitic, nationalist—that would make any kind of cooperation with the USSR much more difficult.

Thus is would be foolish for the United States to contribute to Gorba-chev's fall, even if the contribution took the form of merely responding too grudgingly to some of his initiatives and especially if it took the form of setting intemperate or untimely preconditions about internal changes or external retrenchment, which could only embarrass and help derail him. Moreover, if Gorbachev should succeed, the result would not be a Soviet Union so much more efficient that it was more dangerous than the one we have known; in fact it would be less dangerous. Glasnost and perestroika are likely to produce a more open society, with a better in-formed and less manipulable public, with a greater role in the arena of interdependence and a smaller role in the military arena—precisely what we have always said we really wanted. Moreover, should Gorbachev fall after the United States had tried to cooperate with him, we would still have the means to return to our second nature—the cold war—especially if we preserve our alliances while pursing a new policy.

Therefore, it is in our interest to respond to Gorbachev's overtures, for all kinds of reasons. First of all, it is probably the best way of preserving the Western alliance; as the instructive few weeks before the NATO summit last spring showed, the more we drag our feet, the more divided we will be from at least some of our major allies—West Germany, in particular.

And, then, we should respond in order to prevent the Soviets from getting too far ahead of us in a competition that Gorbachev seems to understand is more important than the classic military contest or the struggle for physical control of governments, peoples, and resources: the competition for influence. We should, when we celebrate the end of the cold war as a victory for our past strategy and for our values, be careful not to nurture the illusion that Gorbachev wants to preside over the shrinking of Soviet foreign influence and the liquidation of the Soviet empire. In Europe, in the Middle East, in his relations with China, he acts like a man who understands that his country's best chances for affecting the course of world affairs lie in shedding counterproductive or fruitless burdens and attracting broad support, so that even suspicious powers (say, Israel and South Africa) will be willing to acknowledge a Soviet role. United States passivity would only play into his hands. Also, we have a chance, while Gorbachev is in power, of achieving with the Soviet Union not only a nonhostile relationship, which already would not be so bad, but also a number of cooperative arrangements in several areas.

Finally, we and the Soviets have a remarkably convergent interest in reducing the burden of arms that are very difficult to use and whose main purpose is to deter the other side from doing something that it has no particular desire to do. First, in arms control, the time has come to close the famous grand deal on strategic nuclear reductions that we might have obtained toward the end of the Reagan administration and that a large number of players in that administration wanted. It was blocked by the president, because he could not give up his "Star Wars" dream, even in exchange for drastic cuts in Soviet offensive weapons. The Strategic Defense Initiative (SDI) may have been a clever bargaining chip, which contributed to Gorbachev's reversal of previous Soviet positions on verification and on cuts in heavy missiles, but the time has come to agree to limits on SDI in exchange for these reductions. Such limits would amount simply to recognizing the fact that the "Astrodome" concept is unrealizable, that no reliable deployment is conceivable for many years anyhow, and that there are ways of preserving land-based missiles that are cheaper and better than antiballistic defenses. A START (Strategic Arms Reduction Treaty) agreement has also become snagged on the issue of sea-launched cruise missiles. The United States should agree to the Soviet proposal to limit these weapons, which might otherwise multiply threateningly and without any foreseeable possibility of verification. And the two sides should agree to ban antisatellite weapons.

The reduction of NATO and Warsaw Pact conventional forces, which experts have tended to present as a formidably difficult undertaking, appears far less so since the Soviets' agreement to the framework proposed by NATO and President George Bush's decision to accept the inclusion of aircraft, on which the Soviets had insisted. The coming negotiations are still likely to be complicated, if only because of the number of parties engaged in them and the disagreements on the types of aircraft to be included and on the number of states that will have to reduce their armed forces. But the two sides have agreed to concentrate on those forces that are capable of surprise attack and on those weapons—such as tanks and armored personnel carriers—that are primarily offensive, and they have agreed to try to stabilize the restructured alliance forces at levels much lower than the present ones.

As for regional conflicts, whether in Afghanistan, the Middle East, or Central America, the imperative is clear: we must continue to cooperate with the Soviet Union in resolving them without being handicapped by the needless fear that by engaging the Soviets in such negotiations we legitimize their presence in those regions. They are there anyhow, whether we legitimize them or not. The "Finlandization" of Eastern Europe—the granting of internal autonomy in exchange for continuing membership in the Warsaw Pact—is not a fit subject for Soviet-American negotiations: the Soviets appear already to have granted Poland and Hungary the right to proceed in this direction, and evolution in East Germany and Czechoslovakia depends on the domestic situations there more than on Soviet, or Soviet-American, decisions. As for another suggestion that is sometimes made, that we negotiate the neutralization of Eastern Europe with the Soviets, it is most unlikely that they would accept this and its necessary consequence, a total withdrawal of Soviet forces, without asking for at least a partial neutralization of Western Europe—including West Germany—and the departure of American troops and weapons. It would be unwise for us to accept this, because American forces would be even more difficult to send back to Europe in case of a crisis than Soviet forces would and because neither great power has much interest in severing the ties that bind "its" Germany to it and to the other countries of its alliance. (Also, could two neutralized Germanys remain separate for long? And would not a reunified Germany, even if formally neutralized, be a far more powerful and unpredictable independent actor than, say, a neutral Austria or Switzerland is?)

In the economic realm, the real question is not whether we should provide our chief military rival with high-tech goods and military technology; obviously, the answer is no. But what the Soviet Union mainly needs is consumer goods and the kinds of industries that can produce consumer goods. These are not strategically dangerous goods and industries and are something we ought to be able to provide, in exchange for evidence of progress toward a more decentralized economy. If we don't act in this realm, our allies will anyhow. Finally, we should take advantage of the Soviets' cooperative strategy in order to involve them more, as they say they are willing to be involved, in international and regional organizations—including those that promote human rights.

Against Violence

In the long run, strategy on the global front outside the cold war is likely to be most important and needs to become our main foreign-affairs priority. Much of what we will need to do between now and the end of the century can be grouped under three headings. The first of these is "Against Violence" in international affairs. Here the most urgent task ought to be the liquidation of the acute, dangerous, and lasting regional conflicts that are still with us.

In Central America we are a major part of the problem; we should leave the initiative as much as possible to the regional powers themselves. With respect to Nicaragua they seem to be doing a little bit better than we have done: our goal has been to overthrow the Sandinista regime, and it appears that we have finally given up on it, whereas President Oscar Arias Sanchez, of Costa Rica, and his colleagues can be counted on to keep applying pressure for democratization. In El Salvador it is up to us to make further military aid to the government contingent on the elimination of human-rights violations and the opening of serious negotiations with the opposition; the alternative is endless war and horror.

In the Middle East we are perhaps not a major part of the problem, but we are certainly a major part of the potential solution. There will be no solution if we continue to exert only mild pressure on Israel. The Israeli government's proposal for elections in the occupied territories is one more detour to avoid negotiating with the Palestine Liberation Organization (PLO) and reaching a comprehensive settlement by means of an international conference. But if we want such elections, they will have, in order to be acceptable to the PLO, to include East Jerusalem and to occur in the absence of Israeli military control and without crippling restrictions being placed on the role of the elected representatives. If we succeed in obtaining free and open-ended elections, we will still ultimately need an international conference, because it is only with such a conference that some of the decisive parties—the PLO and Syria—could be involved and that each superpower would have an opportunity to exert some moderating influence on its allies or clients. If there should finally be a settlement of the Palestinian issue, which inevitably will be a Palestinian state (for the choice is either continuing occupation, repression and violence, and the internal corruption of Israel or a Palestinian state), the other American role will be to provide security guarantees for Israel after the state is established.

Another important priority in the area of violence will be to try to limit the risk of contagion from the fragmentary violence described earlier. This means taking more seriously, and backing with collective sanctions, the reinforcement of the nuclear nonproliferation regime, signing and enforcing a treaty against chemical warfare, and gradually negotiating both with the Soviet Union and with our allies (the latter being likely to prove resistant) limitations on the indiscriminate export of high-tech conventional weapons and missiles. These exports are already making even more dangerous a world in which many states have reached the stage of producing their own weapons—something about which we can do little. Both dynamics of the arena of economic interdependence—the traditional drive of states for comparative economic advantage and the logic of an open market that treats the trade in lethal goods like any other trade—threaten to make the strategic and diplomatic arena more deadly. Contrary to Kant's prediction, commerce detracts in this respect from the pacification of world affairs, which Kant thought would result from economic interdependence and the increasing horror of modern war.

Against Injustice

Under this second heading, "Against Injustice," we have a double mission. Some of what we should do derives from self-interest. In matters of distributive justice among states, economic interdependence means that we have an interest in the progress toward prosperity of many of the poorer societies, for they can provide us either with markets or with refugees. Moreover, if their states should collapse under the weight of debts, our international financial system might collapse also. But some of our duties go beyond self-interest. We have values, and it is perfectly normal to seek to promote them. In an increasingly open world of instant communications, the claim of states to exert unlimited jurisdiction over the lives of their subjects is anachronistic and repugnant, because there is a connection between such a claim and the external behavior of a government and because there is a constant demand by the American public in the realm of human rights abroad—an unease with any amoral foreign policy. This demand sometimes (as currently, with China) conflicts with the cold calculations of Realpolitik or else absolves the United States of its own exactions abroad, yet it cannot be ignored by American statesmen who seek legitimacy at home for their diplomatic course. We do not have to be apologetic about a human-rights policy as long as it is pursued without either hubris or illusions.

The main areas of policy against injustice would be the following: First, we continue to face the problem of the debt of numerous developing countries; here what is needed is, in the short term, extensive relief measures that will allow developing countries to concentrate on exports and to afford imports rather than having to spend their resources on servicing their debt. We also need a reform of the conditions ritually imposed by the International Monetary Fund, because those conditions have so often turned out to be politically disastrous and recessionary. Any American policy on human rights must seek to be an international strategy; the United States cannot by itself redress injustices against human beings all over the world. If we look at South Africa, we quickly realize how limited American leverage is: American sanctions are not insignificant, but by themselves, they are not very effective. The United States can stop providing military and economic support to, or encouraging its companies to invest in, countries where serious human-rights violations take place. Moreover, there are many parts of the world where the United States by itself can have a considerable influence on the fate of human rights: those areas where it continues to be dominant and where it could use the tools of policy at its disposal to prod clients toward democracy and freedom.

For a More Balanced Order

Under this last heading, "For a More Balanced Order," come the steps we must take in the 1990s to resolve numerous problems resulting from changes in the global distribution of power over the past fifteen or twenty years. We ought to adjust our burdens and privileges to our (relatively shrinking) power and encourage others to play the roles and carry the responsibilities their power now requires. We should encourage the Western Europeans to develop and strengthen their identity. Whether or not they succeed in establishing a unified market by 1992 is a detail; it is not the timetable that matters but the process itself. It may take a little longer, because the issues of pooling sovereignty over money, taxation, and fiscal policy, for instance, are very complicated and because Margaret Thatcher exists; but even without Thatcher the issues would be difficult, and what counts is that things are again in motion. Fears that a "Fortress Europe" will exclude American goods are not justified; many powerful forces in Europe, including Great Britain and West Germany, and many multinational businesses operating in Europe will not allow this to happen. It is in the American interest, in the long run, to encourage the European Community to play a larger role in diplomatic and security affairs, an arena where progress among the twelve members has so far been very limited. If we succeed in lowering the level of armaments in Europe, in agreement with the Soviets, the moment will come when we will indeed be able to withdraw a part of our forces. The NATO alliance will then become more of an even partnership between the United States and its European associates. They are more likely to cooperate with one another on defense if the level of defense is lower overall than the present one. The situation that President Dwight D. Eisenhower, many years ago, thought would come very quickly will finally arrive: we will be able to disengage somewhat, and our allies will engage more. Western Europe has an extremely important diplomatic role to play in the eastern half of the continent. There, the American and European objective ought to be to encourage as much Finlandization as possible. Each country in Eastern Europe is different, and it is much easier for the Western Europeans to pursue a discriminating policy—helping with economic ties and cultural agreements those countries that liberalize most convincingly—than it has ever been for the United States.

We should encourage Japan to be more active in international organizations, particularly in world institutions of assistance, development, and finance. Greater Japanese efforts at helping the developing countries would allow a partial reorientation of Japanese trade away from the developed world, where resistance to the volume of Japanese exports has been growing. Japanese consumers are likely to demand that their nation's economy also shift from the conquest of new external markets to the satisfaction of long-repressed domestic needs.

The last part of a policy toward a more balanced order should consist of deliberately strengthening international and regional organizations. Their decision-making machinery—especially that of world economic and financial organizations—needs to be reformed, so that the distribution of power, which now reflects the realities of the 1950s, will express the realities of the 1980s and 1990s. This means more power for Japan and Western Europe in the World Bank, the International Monetary Fund, and the General Agreement on Tariffs and Trade. We will need international and regional organizations as peace-keepers in areas of conflict. We will need them for information and for inspection. And we will need them on all the economic fronts, where self-help no longer gets one anywhere. There, such collective frameworks for bargaining are likely over time to affect the way in which states define their interests—by injecting a concern for the long term and for the survival of international institutions. A collective defense of the environment is inconceivable without them. But we will also need to strengthen and spread such institutions in the field of security, in particular, for the prevention and limitation of regional conflicts and the monitoring of agreements against the proliferation of conventional and nuclear arms.

A Public Ahead of the Establishment

There are formidable domestic obstacles to the policy I have sketchily described here. One—with us for so long that it is pointless to pin the blame on any administration—is the disjointed way in which American foreign policy is made. We can deplore this, but we could also try to do something about it, so that the amount of disorganization and fragmentation that inevitably results from our constitutional system is minimized. This requires a strongly engaged president (not one like Reagan, who concentrated on only a few, largely ideological concerns), a State Department that tries to balance the need to pursue a strategy abroad and the need to cooperate with Congress (instead of sacrificing one to the other), and a National Security Council staff that can effectively coordinate, but avoids making, policy. It also requires a sharp reduction in the covert role of the Central Intelligence Agency, a role that not only creates more bad will than successes abroad but also often threatens to divert American policy into uncontrolled, harebrained schemes.

Another obstacle is the disorientation of the foreign-policy establishment. It has become accustomed to American predominance and to the comforting ideas that only the United States has a sense of "world responsibility" and that it has a single permanent enemy and a number of reliable but dependent allies. A world that is more fluid, in which we remain "No. 1" but without the ability to control, is unsettling. A world in which the main perils are abstract—damage to the environment, the risk of a global recession, the possibility of regional arms races—is less easy to understand than a world dominated by a contest between two countries representing rival value systems. The Bush administration is largely made up of conservative men whose formative experiences occurred from the 1950s to the 1970s, and while their pragmatism has been evident, they seem, as in the case of the NATO summit, to have been pushed and pulled into the new world rather than to have devised a coherent and long-term strategy for dealing with it.

However, there is at least one element favorable to the redirection of American foreign policy, and it has to do with the public. If one looks at opinion polls, one sees that the public, while quite wisely cautious toward the Soviet Union, is less mired in old modes of thinking than it has been in a long time. It is sufficiently worried about domestic economic trends to believe that the first priority is indeed putting our house in order. The shackles that opinion sometimes puts on the perceptions of leaders are not apparent for the time being.

In conclusion, in the world we have entered there will be many things that the United States can do nothing about. We should accept this state of affairs and, incidentally, perhaps even be grateful for it. It is a world in which war is no longer the principal and often inevitable mode of change; change comes more often now from domestic revolutions, about which we can and should do very little, because usually we do not understand the political cultures and trends of other countries and often we make mistakes. Change also, now that the pressures exerted by the cold war are easing, comes from the rebirth of nationalisms. Many of the new forces of nationalism may lead to explosions and revolutions, about which, again, there will be very little that we or anybody else in the West can do. The task, therefore, is not to eliminate trouble everywhere in the world. Instead, we must devise what could be described as a new containment: not of the Soviet Union (although this will be part of it, insofar as conflicts of interest with the Soviets will continue) but of the various forms of violence and chaos that a world no longer dominated by the cold war will entail. It is a complicated agenda, but it is at least different from the agenda we have had for so long.

If, as I have indicated, statesmen and citizens now operate not in a single international system but in two different fields, with different logics, actors, and hierarchies and tools of power, the question remains whether this duality can persist. An imperative for the United States is to prevent it from ending in the wrong way, as in the 1930s, when economic power was widely used for either self-protection or aggression. This is why we need to strive for the devaluation of hostile forms and uses of power in the strategic and diplomatic arena and against a major recession in the field of economic interdependence. Our new strategy must aim at spreading the sense of common interests in the former and at strengthening it in the latter. It will require more "internationalism" than before, and the novel experience of cooperating widely with associates who are no longer satellites or dependents—as well as with the enemy of the past forty years.

7

A New World and Its Troubles

Someone—an American—has been lying for almost fifty years on a procrustean bed, with a big gun under his pillow and eyes trained on the window, through which a Soviet intruder might burst in. Today, as he is getting up from that bed, he discovers a Soviet in the room, but with an olive branch; he also notices that there are many other people all around him, that his gun is of little use in the crowd, and that the furniture has been rearranged. A bit dizzy, he congratulates himself on having apparently deterred any break-in, but he finds it difficult to make sense of the changes and the bustle, and he experiences some painful bedsores.

In a sense, the "long peace" that John L. Gaddis has written about was a substitute for a war.[1] National security concerns dominated the foreign policy of the two antagonists. In the USSR, the contest combined with the dispositions of a centralized command economy in building up an efficient war machine that absorbed a huge share of the country's resources and left the civilian economy both below, in priority, and behind, in quality. In the United States, as William McNeill observes, "the arms race . . . provided the principal stimulus for . . . remarkably effective political management of the economy." Certainly, the events of recent years amount to the recognition, by the leaders of the Soviet Union, of the USSR's defeat in that long confrontation—both on the ground, where, in Robert Tucker's words, "the Soviet Union has signalled, as clearly as it is possible for a great power to do, that it is no longer prepared to play the role to which it has aspired since the 1950s and in pursuit of which the Soviet people have sacrificed so much," and in the mind, insofar as the new thinking entails a repudiation of almost all the assumptions that had fed a diplomacy and a strategy of bipolar rivalry aimed at hastening the victory of one "social system" over the other that Marxist-Leninism ideology, now in full retreat, had predicted.[2] As in a hot war, the leaders of the two rivals either concentrated on their conflict or treated the trends and troubles elsewhere in the world as opportunities or perils in that conflict.

However, in other respects, the contest was not a war. Indeed, the common triumph of the superpowers was their ability to avoid one. This feat had little to do with the "structural" properties of bipolar systems (Athens and Sparta were the two "poles" of a Greek city-state system that destroyed itself in the Peloponnesian war); rather, it resulted from nuclear weapons and from the plans, ideologies, and expectations of these particular rivals. The fact that the conflict was not a war, and therefore did not end with the losing side's formally begging for peace, is both an advantage and a drawback. It is an advantage insofar as it ought to facilitate that "integration of the Soviet Union into the world community" that both Soviet and American leaders have stated as one of their new objectives. But it is a drawback for the following reason: states fighting a war always aim at returning to peace—through victory or compromise—and therefore usually make plans both for the reconversion of their economies and for the shaping of the postwar order. The "long peace," precisely because of its length, distracted statesmen—and, often enough, scholars as well—from thinking enough about either. Our "victory" has left us dazed.

As a result, there exists today a certain nostalgia for the cold war, not unlike the romantic nostalgia for the days of sacrifice, discipline, and community so often displayed by veterans or by the British after the blitz: "things were simpler when." The need for each "camp" or "bloc" to preserve its coherence compressed, suppressed, or repressed differences of interests and aspirations within each. But at the same time, because the cold war was not a violent interruption and disruption of ordinary life but a regular form of politics for almost half a century, it warped our definitions of security and stability in ways that wars do not. To be sure, we have gradually understood that military security is not a zero-sum game; theorists of arms control taught both us and the Soviets that nuclear weapons create mutual interests even among rivals. Nevertheless, our approach to security remains predominantly military—in matters of economic security, have we ever succeeded in getting much beyond the need to protect ourselves against a sudden disruption of the flow of oil?— and predominantly "bipolar"—preparing, as McNeill puts it, for high-tech war rather than low-grade local violence. And we have tended to equate stability—the goal of nonrevolutionary statecraft in peacetime— with the structures put in place in order to fight the cold war, the institutions of containment. Even though their main purposes have now disappeared, we find it difficult to imagine new and different structures aimed at achieving if not stability (a somewhat absurd objective in a fluid world) at least moderation.

When we try to establish a balance sheet of the cold war, it is its duality that stands out. As a quasi war, it did great damage to both superpowers, although not to the same degree. In the Soviet case, the fit between the regime and the contest delayed modernization and wasted resources to a catastrophic degree. In the United States, much of the relative decline of American power can be attributed to the diversion of resources toward the military and away from increasingly serious domestic problems. As a result, neither power is in mint shape as it faces the international problems of the future. Insofar as the cold war was not a war but a way of life, of organizing a dangerous but not warlike international system, its end leaves us without a clear sense of priorities or criteria for allocating resources and without a clear picture of all the things that happened while we were manning increasingly irrelevant barricades.

And so we find ourselves today confronting simultaneously two agendas for which we are unprepared. The first is one we always knew, vaguely, that we might have to face someday—it is, after all, what the architects of containment had been aiming at: the liquidation of the cold war, beyond the (difficult enough) routine of arms limitations agreements. Here, the old superpowers remain the central players—although even here they must make room for the main beneficiary of their armistice: a reunified Germany. The German problem and European security are the key issues; what makes these so tricky is that the main stake is the relative influence of the two rivals in the heartland of their former contest, as well as their future weight in the new European order. It is an extremely important agenda, but essentially transitional: the answers to both these questions are already emerging, through the retreat of the Soviets and the rise of Europe. The second agenda is one for which we are not prepared at all; it is the "postwar" and global agenda.

Main Trends of the Post–Cold War World

In describing the main trends that are at work, a convenient starting place is the phenomenon often referred to a the diffusion of power and the perspective provided by the long-dominant theory of international affairs, realism. That theory looks at the international system as a milieu in which states compete, seek to increase their power, try to prevent the rise of rivals or hegemons through unilateral moves as well as through balances of power, and depend for their survival and success above all on military might and the economic underpinning of it.

From that perspective, power has been largely concentrated since 1945 in two "poles," the United States and the Soviet Union. The "diffusion of power" means that this will no longer be the case. But where has power gone? Here, we must make an important distinction between two arenas that exist, or "games" that go on, simultaneously.[3] One is the traditional strategic diplomatic arena, which corresponds to the realists' analysis, with its emphasis on the actors' quest for relative gains or (in the case of great powers thirsting for total security) absolute gains in a zero-sum contest. The other is the modern arena of economic interdependence, in which state actors are interested in relative gains, to be sure, but within a world economy whose continuing growth is in their common interest and in which my gains may well require that you make some yourself. The stakes are clearly not the same: physical security, the control of territory in one case, market shares, the creation and expansion of wealth in the other. Nor are the necessary ingredients and possible uses of power the same.

In the diplomatic-strategic arena, we have moved from bipolarity to a much more complex and unprecedented situation. Here, the main actors are still the states; it is in this realm that the United Nations and the various regional organizations have been least effective. The most impressive groupings have been the rival alliances (one of which is now almost defunct, and the other, as Tucker and Ronad Steel point out, is likely to lose most of its purposes)—but neither the Warsaw Pact nor NATO could ever have been regarded as an independent actor anyway. The United States will remain the most important player in terms of global military power, and the United States and the Soviet Union will keep the capacity to destroy the planet several times over. But the Soviet Union's economic weakness and political turbulence have reduced its ability and will to be a worldwide challenger; and the number of active players has increased and will increase some more, because of the proliferation of military technologies, both nuclear and conventional. A return to bipolarity would require a new Soviet-American confrontation; but the condition of the Soviet Union makes this highly unlikely in the foreseeable future. Neither a success of perestroika, a period of revolutionary turbulence and disintegration, nor a repressive regime attempting to re-impose order and control is a good candidate for a return to global ambitions. Security concerns and balances are more likely to be regional than global; and while the United States, because of its military preeminence and its capacity to project might abroad, might see itself as the "sun" at the center of the solar system, there is no obvious need for the "planets" to turn around it in such a fragmented system—now that the somewhat artificial and never totally effective unity imposed by the cold war is waning. In this system, nuclear states and states with an abundance of conventional forces will be the powers of importance in each region. Besides states, the only significant actors in this realm will be private individuals in the business of arms sales.

The picture is quite different in the arena of economic interdependence. Here, the term *diffusion* is both misleading and imprecise. It is misleading insofar as it conceals the emergence of the new "international business civilization"—a worldwide phenomenon spreading out from the industrialized nations of North America, Western Europe, and East Asia. Diffusion of power suggests dispersion, whereas this "supranational capitalism" of banks and enterprises is to a large extent both concentrated in its origin (a limited, although slowly growing, number of countries) and a unifying force, at least because it does not respect borders, particularities, and traditions. Indeed, it is this force that periodically rearranges the distribution of economic and political power.

The term *diffusion* is imprecise because it lumps together a variety of phenomena. One is the fact that many key decisions about the world economy are made not in the political realm of states but by private agents—investors, corporations, firms, banks, speculators, merchants, mafias—either without much control by state authorities or with enough influence to manipulate them. Another fact, which results in part from the previous one—but to which state, trade, business, and fiscal policies contribute as well—is the internationalization or multinationalization of production, finance, and communications. A third is the mutual entanglement of state economic capabilities, either in the form of "pooled sovereignties" (as in the European Economic Community, or EEC) or in the form of states whose power is each other's hostage (as in the U.S.-Japan relationship). A fourth is the inability of many states to reach their national economic objectives by national means alone (a fact that may well be less true for the United States than for most other states). Present-day Western Europe shows all four phenomena at work. They amount to a decomposition of sovereignty, the ability of the state to command and control that may still exist in the traditional arena. Thus, diffusion here means not only, as in that arena, that the field of major state actors is becoming more crowded but two other things as well. First, in contrast to the situation in the diplomatic-strategic domain, there are serious rivals for the United States: the losers of World War II, who became the main beneficiaries of American protection during the cold war, Japan and German (or an EEC in which Germany will be the principal actor). Second, all the state actors, in different degrees, are exposed to the vicissitudes of a global market they do not control.

International politics today is not the preserve of states and businesses: we have to move beyond, or rather under, the two arenas or stages where actors play. The diffusion of power has a third and quite different dimension, which, like the emergence and eminence of the sphere of economic interdependence, moves us far away from the realist analysis of international politics. Realism reduces world affairs to a game played, in Raymond Aron's words, by diplomats and soldiers on behalf of statesmen. Today, we note a worldwide trend (uneven, to be sure, like the "international business civilization")—a trend so messy that there is no adequate term for it. *Democratization* is not quite right, because it brings to mind the spread of representative systems based on consent; in fact, despite recent surges, their triumph is far from universal. *Populism* would be better, were it not for the word's baggage of connotations derived from peasant and farmers' movements in nineteenth-century Europe and America. Maybe demands for *people power* or for *citizens' say* is the best approximation: the information revolution does, on balance, make the control of people's minds and moves by governments more difficult, and it is popular demands and pressures that set much of the agenda of the governments' foreign policies. The notion, inseparable from realism, that this agenda is "objectively" set by the map of geography and by the map of alignments dictated by the "security dilemma" is obsolete. The agendas are either dictated by domestic imperatives or delicate attempts at reconciling these with external constraints.

This third form of diffusion of power is important above all for explaining a shift in stakes, or state preferences and goals. It is a shift away from traditional goals of conquest, control, and coercion. The decline in the utility of force would not have occurred if it had not been for the three factors that were central to Kant's philosophy of history and ethics of foreign policy: the increasing destructiveness of war; the attractions of "greed," or commerce, that is, economic issues to which force is not relevant; and the rise of popular participation. The last raises domestic obstacles to the pursuit of imperial policies, and it also fosters mass resistance among the victims of such policies, which force is often unable to crush. It is a shift toward those economic stakes that are likely to bring to the nation or to its citizens the wealth and welfare people aspire to—which means that the control of market shares is more important, in a world where firms are endlessly mobile, than that of territory and that access to resources and markets through trade and investment is seen as far more effective and sensible than access through force.[4]

If the diffusion of power is a first way of apprehending the sea change, a second and perhaps more fruitful one is to look at the world in terms of a contest not between two domineering states but between three levels. There is the global level, where the "world business civilization" operates, with its own logic and instruments. There are the states, which try to exploit this logic and its carriers in order to increase their countries' wealth or to increase their power and influence over others (since wealth is more than ever a source of power); but the states are, with respect to the world capitalist system, in a doubly uncomfortable position. On the one hand, they are still engaged in another "game": the traditional one, of security fears, calculations, and contests, whose logic if that of Thucydides, not Adam Smith. On the other, they are trying to prevent the logic of world capitalism from depriving them of financial, monetary, and fiscal autonomy and from magnifying the differences between rich and poor states, as well as between modern sectors, fully integrated in the global economy, and backward ones. Thus, the world economy is not their single obsession, and they are ambivalent about it. Moreover, they are besieged by more than the uncontrollable forces—private, at home and abroad, as well as public, in the form of foreign trading and investing states, abroad—of a world economy that is only partly denationalized.

They are also under pressure from the third level, that of the people. The people, to be sure, count on their state to play the game of wealth effectively and want the benefits of growth that the economy dangles before their eyes. But the global requirements of efficiency are not those of equity, and wealth for the nation and for some of its members may be very different from welfare for most. Participation, equity, and wealth: people want all three, but often they can have only two of these, and sometimes none at all. To keep the engines of growth working, there is often a need, in the advanced countries, to attract immigrants as manpower. All of this exposes the state to a double danger. When its political and economic system leads to poverty and stagnation, there is a risk of rebellion, or of such pressure from below that the system collapses (consider the end of the Stalinist system in the 1980s); but when the state's participation in the global economy leads to inflation, unemployment, growing inequalities, or an "invasion" of unassimilable aliens, a populist backlash is always to be feared.

The world economy is thus one of the factors that may disrupt the connection between national unity and territorial boundaries: either when national unity and identity are challenged by mass immigration or when—as may be the case in the destitute but populous countries of North Africa or black Africa, or Mexico—masses of the poor leave for richer places. To use Albert Hirschman's classical categories, voice (of the "natives" against the intruders) and exit (of the poor) may undermine loyalty to a state deemed incapable of protecting its own people. But there is also a second factor that can break the connection. The "fit" between people and state is often missing—for example, in the case of an obsolescent empire, like the Soviet Union, in which many national minorities want to have states of their own, or in the case of weak or artificial postcolonial states, as in Africa and Asia, where different ethnic groups ask for independence. Both insofar as the loyalty of citizens is based on the state's economic performance and insofar as it is based on cultural and emotional ties, the rise of people power can be not only a threat to the state but also a cause of international conflict: either when other states are made responsible for economic injustice, when secessions and local nationalisms provoke external interventions, or when a state succeeds in diverting its people from domestic grievances by indoctrinating them against an external devil.

These are, of course, broad trends described with broad brush strokes. In today's Japan, national homogeneity has been carefully preserved, and the people appear still satisfied with the strategy, aimed at national wealth rather than individual welfare, that has been selected, in the world economy, by the governments they have confirmed in power for so many years. In China, the regime still—but for how long?—seems to have the power to keep demands for economic change compatible with the preservation of a bureaucratic and authoritarian system of command. But there is yet a third way of looking at the global dynamics at work: a simultaneous movement of unification and fragmentation. The capitalist economic system tends to unify the world by internationalizing and integrating the markets of goods and capital and by creating a sort of world elite of managers, private and public. Still, there is a fragmentation of the world into states, with the trappings of sovereignty, including currencies, armies, and national rules and welfare systems for labor: formal fragmentation, if you like—the kind for which Marx, who saw states as mere facades concealing class relations, had little understanding. And there is another kind of fragmentation that he grasped extremely well in his analysis of world capitalism: the substantive one. It results both from the dynamics of the global market, which tends often to exacerbate inequality both among and within states and from the dissatisfaction of many people with "their" state, precisely because, for ethnic, religious, or ideological reasons, they do not recognize it as theirs or else because the government has failed to feed, employ, enrich, or protect them and thus has broken the bonds of consent.

No End of Conflicts

One reason for offering this rather abstract picture is to point out that a post–cold war world will be anything but harmonious. We are entering a new phase of history. It is assuredly not the "end of history,"[5] a silly notion based on a series of mistaken assumptions (that the death of communism means the definitive triumph of Western liberalism, the end of ideology, and the coming of a "boring" era of material concerns and unheroic squabbles); it is a period in which the discrepancy between the formal organization of the world into states and the realities of power, which do not resemble those of any past international system, will create formidable contradictions and difficulties.

Miles Kahler has indicated why even the shift from traditional goals and tools to economic ones is not likely to lead to peace and quiet. First, there is a huge array of possible "traditional" quarrels, in a world where there is at least still one ideology of violent conflict—Islamic fundamentalism—and where the disappearance or decay of secular ideologies leaves nationalism, over much of the planet, as the only glue of loyalty. The Arab-Israeli conflict, Kashmir, and Cyprus are daily reminders of gloomy forms of permanence. Evidence of the declining utility of force for the superpowers and for other major actors, such as the nations of Western Europe and Japan, may not deter those for whom passion overruns cost-benefit analysis and those for whom force seems the only alternative to despair, humiliation, or destruction. If one remembers that the increased economic capabilities of smaller states, alluded to by Joseph Nye in his latest book,[6] allow them to buy or build formidable modern arsenals and to make themselves largely independent of arms shipments by fickle superpowers—and if one believes, as I do, that the latter, no longer chasing each other all over the world, may play less of a moderating role in such regional conflicts now that their potential as triggers of a superpower collision has vanished—there is, then, no reason to expect that the traditional arena of world politics will be empty or boring—except, perhaps, strangely and happily enough, in Europe, prophets of recurrent doom notwithstanding.[7]

Second, the realm of interdependence will also breed conflicts that could be serious. As Miles Kahler says, elites depend on popular satisfaction for their survival in power, and the disruptions and distributional conflicts the "world business civilization" may bring with it could "cause some states to define their security requirements more broadly rather than less"[8] or to divert domestic turbulence toward conflict abroad. Among the advanced countries, the different strategies chosen by the main players in the quest for market shares and wealth may become incompatible if they lead to permanent imbalances. This is already the message of the so-called revisionists who point out that the Japanese brand of neomercantilism—which subordinates the interests of consumers to those of producers, entails a deliberate and long-term strategy aimed at gaining the lead in advanced technologies, and results in a "continued displacement of industrial sectors and the shift of technological capability toward Japan"[9]—may not be reconcilable with America's consumer orientation, lack of industrial policy, and lesser "ability to adapt quickly to changing circumstances."[10] Conflicts over trade and industrial policy ultimately involve as stakes both the power of states, since wealth is a component of power (even though the uses of economic power are often constrained or capable of boomeranging), and the fate of labor at home. Without the restraining force exerted by the cold war and by the need of Western Europeans and Japanese for American protection, such conflicts could become acute.

The potential for trouble, not between the "North" and "South" but between the advanced countries and certain groups of less-developed ones, is equally serious. It is often said that the poorer among the latter cannot cause much harm, whatever they do. This maybe true, in cases other than oil, if harm is defined in purely economic terms. But radical anti-Western ideologies could turn fiercely against the institutions and agents of Western capitalism; also, the weakness and heterogeneity of some of these states, and the pressure of increasing populations, may well lead to violent regional conflicts as well as to formidable quarrels over immigration and refuge to and expulsions from the richer countries. Two of the problems that have become urgent, drugs and the environment, could all too easily lead to confrontations between advanced states eager to protect their health and their future and states such as those of South America that need to cultivate drugs or to forgo strict protection of the environment in order to develop.

Third, the conflicts between state and people must be taken seriously, too—not only because terrorist violence, or popular or populist attacks on ill-constituted states and unacceptable governments, or governmental attempts to divert or punish such attacks, could lead to interstate troubles but also because the victory of "people power" is neither a guarantee of moderate behavior abroad nor at all guaranteed. Popular victories can trample over minority rights and create nationalist explosions. Conversely, democratic revolutions may wilt if the winners get bogged down in party squabbles and parochial issues or caught between the "demands" of the world business civilization and domestic discontent and replaced by authoritarian or military rulers. This, in turn, may be bad both for regional peace and for the cause of human rights.

The United States in the New World

It is not possible for American to walk away from these problems simply because none of them concentrates the mind and creates a danger for our physical security comparable to the Soviet threat. The role of the United States will have to be quite different from that of the past forty years, and the reasons Tucker gives for rejecting both a policy defined in traditional balance of power terms and a mission of world policeman are compelling. However, an American total retreat toward domestic reform would be a serious moral and political mistake, comparable to the return to isolationism in 1919–1920. Indeed, the scope of American involvements abroad (however much the end of the cold war may allow us to reduce them)—"ethnic empathy toward various parts of the world, popular sympathies for the underdog,"[11] and the pressure of interests affected by the global economy—make such a full retrenchment unlikely.

On the other hand, changes in power limit the ability of the United States to set the rules and to provide the solutions. As John Zysman notes in a recent article, the shift from military to economic influence hurts the United States, insofar as others depend less on American military technology, and in the economic realm a United States deep in debt is far from the free giant it was after the war;[12] our ability to extract foreign policy gains from economic power has dropped, and we depend increasingly on foreign sources for important products and technologies. While Susan Strange is right to point out the assets the United States still enjoys, the various failures of American policy that she criticizes and blames for the fate of international economic organizations have their roots in the place that is the real locus of America's decline: not imperial overstretch nor any catastrophic fall in aggregate figures of material resources but the domestic components of power—low savings; insufficient productive investments, especially in leading sectors; the obsession of business with short-term profits; a poor system of technical education; and, above all, a failing capacity to mobilize tangible and intangible resources, which results from the bad state of American infrastructure (especially urban), popular resistance to taxation, and a lack of leadership.

The United States, after a decade of celebration of its ability to deal with the world's problems by its own means, finds itself in a bind. The three principles that have guided its foreign policy—American exceptionalism, anticommunism, and world economic liberalism—are of little help, because others are less receptive, or because "victory" has made anticommunism irrelevant, or because the market itself is the problem (as in U.S.-Japanese relations) or provides no answers (as in ecological matters). Persisting with the trade and budget deficits increases American dependence on creditors; eliminating those deficits could require either measures that would disrupt the world economy (protectionism) or decisions that would bring about a complete and painful reorientation of American fiscal and industrial policy. If U.S. statesmen do not address the domestic issues that deeply worry the people but that, in the absence of leadership, leave it adrift, America's ability to affect world affairs positively will decline further, and we will find ourselves on a road comparable to that on which the Soviet Union is now skidding. However, if the United States addresses its internal problems, the resources it will need to raise will not be available for external purposes. America faces a heavy bill, the product of the weaknesses of its own unregulated and often uncalculating economic system, of those of its decentralized and Byzantine political system, and of the cold war.

The tensions, contradictions, and conflicts described here will therefore not be manageable unless we find the methods and found the institutions of planetary governance that are now indispensable. Laissez-faire and the invisible hand are not capable of resolving such issues as population growth and movements, the environment's destruction, famines and epidemics, and the distributional effects (among and within states) of the "business civilization." It is, of course, true that the demands of the people and the short lives of democratic governments make multilateral co-operation difficult, but they also make it necessary. At this stage, the states remain the only legitimate public authorities and mobilizers of public resources, but the problems they face—those I have just mentioned, but also those of "megascience" and large-scale technology—demand cooperative solutions. Moreover, the very dynamism of the world economy and its restless reallocation of wealth and power require the same kind of political control at the global level that the "political realm" of authority, the state, provides at the country level; and that control, too, can come, so far, only from a pooling of state efforts.

It is therefore, to use Richard Gardner's terms, for a "comeback of liberal internationalism" that one must plead.[13] Each person may have his or her own favorite blueprint, but the main directions are clear. Among the advanced countries (including—or rather, and also—the Soviet Union), the main tasks will be, first, the establishment of a new security system in Europe, which will probably be a mix of a much-reformed NATO no longer dominated by the United States, a Western European defense organization, and an organization set by the Conference on Security and Cooperation in Europe (CSCE); second, an agreement among the main suppliers of arms and advanced technologies to restrict such sales drastically, to strengthen the nuclear nonproliferation regime, and to establish regional arms limitation and conflict resolution regimes; third, a deal to redistribute power—now still largely in the hands of the United States—among the main actors in the international financial and economic organizations, the United States, Japan, and the EEC.

The end of the cold war and of the straitjacket of worldwide East-West security concerns should allow the advanced countries to concentrate their efforts on social, economic, and political conditions in an increasingly diversified "South." Both ecological imperatives and the issue of the population pressure of the poor and the refugees require a set of bargains, thanks to which ample resources will, through multilateral assistance and with the participation of the leading private firms, be made available to the developing countries, in exchange for commitments on environmental protection, health care, energy efficiency, agricultural productivity, and human rights. The demands on the resources of the richer states—caught between the needs and expectations of their own people and the fear of external chaos—will be both so large and so conflicting that organizations for regional and global cooperation will have to be strengthened, through guaranteed revenues, the creation of independent secretariats, and frequent high-level meetings.

Will a world without a central threat and a hegemon be able to create order? It is not certain. What is proposed here is very much a halfway house: not a world government for which states and peoples are unprepared (and that the managers of the world business civilization would not like) but a new experiment in polycentric steering, in which the three major economic powers—plus the Soviet Union, if it overcomes its problems, and perhaps China, once it begins to turn its potential into effective power (something that would require drastic political changes)—would form a central steering group and in which regional powers would play comparable roles in their areas. Nothing like this has ever been tried—but then, the hidden theme of this chapter is the advent of discontinuity in international affairs.

Two big question marks remain. First, will a development of multilateral diplomacy and institutions not merely add a layer to the three—the global market, the states, the people—that exist already, and simply add cooperative inefficiency to market inequities, state erosion, and popular discontent? Will it help global unification or make for more fragmentation (including, now, among international and regional agencies)? The risk exists; the example of the EEC shows that where the will can be found, the danger can be overcome. Second, will the United States be willing to commit itself, and sufficient resources, to such a path? The answer could be yes, on two conditions: if adequate leadership can at last be provided—leadership that would understand and explain that, as Kahler puts it, "unilateral American action is likely to be less effective, and the workings of an untrammeled market . . . less desirable than . . . international collaborations"—and if domestic reform to provide for the underpinnings of power is undertaken. Without such reform, popular turbulence and resentments against competitors will mount. To be sure, such reform will require fiscal sacrifices, and while it absorbs attention and funds, America's own contributions to the needs of others might remain limited. But none of America's problems at home or abroad can be solved if "people power" is equated with no new taxes; and in the immediate future, one of the welcome effects of the diffusion of power is the ability of Western Europe and Japan (already the largest donor of foreign aid) to play a larger role.

A Complex Multipolarity

The world after the cold war will not resemble any world of the past. From a "structural" point of view—the distribution of capabilities—it will be multipolar. But the poles will have different currencies of power—military (the Soviets), economic and financial (Japan and Germany), demographic (China and India), military and economic (the United States)—and different productivities of power—demographic power is more a liability than an asset, the utility of military might is reduced, and only economic power is fully useful because it is the capacity to influence others by bringing them the very goods they crave. Moreover, each of these poles will be, at least to some extent, mired in a world economy that limits its freedom of action. What we do not know is what relations are going to develop among these actors, what institutional links they will set up to manage their relations with one another, and their relations with the rest of the world, in a context of vigilant, demanding, and often turbulently mobilized masses. The fate of this new world will depend on the ability of the "poles" to cooperate enough in order to prevent or moderate conflicts—including regional ones—and to correct those imbalances of the world economy that would otherwise induce some states, or their publics, to pull away from or to disrupt the momentum of interdependence. Above all, it will depend on domestic currents that remain highly difficult to predict. Since foreign policy today is so largely shaped by domestic demands and expectations, the most dangerous remaining tension, and the most difficult to overcome, is that between the global dimension of the issues that foreign policy will have to deal with and the fact that political life remains, at best, limited to the horizons of the state and is, often, even challenging the unity, the borders, and the effectiveness of the state.

The world is like a bus whose driver—the global economy—is not in full control of the engine and is himself out of control, in which children—the people—are tempted to step on either the brake or the gas pedal and adults—the states—are worried passengers. A league of passengers may not be enough to keep the bus on the road, but there is no better solution yet.

8

Delusions of World Order

How states create and maintain order in a world of sovereign powers has been the fundamental and so far insoluble problem of international relations. During the cold war, the superpowers, driven by the fear of nuclear war, devised, by trial and error, a network of rules and restraints aimed at avoiding direct military collision. Now the world faces new circumstances whose implications it is just beginning to discover, and the problem of order has become even more complex than before.[1]

One reason for this is the unexpected increase in the number of independent states; even five years ago no one predicted the end of the Soviet empire in Eastern Europe and the breakup of the Soviet Union itself. A second reason is that the states, while still playing the traditional game of diplomatic and strategic competition, are now also engaged in an intense competition for economic and financial power that does not entail the use of force. In the past, when such activities did not dominate the plans of states as much as they do now, order was provided by the rules set by the economically dominant nation: Britain in the nineteenth century, the United States after 1945. What order there was broke down when the dominant nation's hegemony was challenged (as Britain's was after 1870) or when there was none, for example during the period between the two world wars. Today, the predominance of the United States has been put in doubt, both by Japan and by the rise of a united Western Europe increasingly dominated by Germany.

In any case, world politics, and therefore world order, are no longer monopolized by states; on the one hand, they are constrained by the world capitalist economy, which limits their domestic and external freedom of maneuver, particularly when it comes to supplies of raw materials such as petroleum. On the other hand, the various peoples of the world, as opposed to governments, are more turbulent than ever before. From Algiers to Uzbekistan, they demand participation in public affairs, or a state of their own if they feel oppressed or neglected, in a multiethnic state; and they also want both more wealth and a more equitable distribution of it—demands which are usually both unachievable and incompatible.

As a result, while the world no longer lives under the shadow of a superpower nuclear confrontation, the numbers of actual and possible conflicts, both among and within states, seem bound to grow, whether because of aggressive ambitions, as with Saddam Hussein, or border disputes and rival claims over the same territory, as in the case of Palestine, or domestic crises and policies that have effects abroad, causing other states to threaten external intervention, as with Yugoslavia. The breakup of countries such as Yugoslavia and the USSR is already causing refugees to flee toward their neighbors.

Two sources of international insecurity seem to me especially important. The first derives from the hardly understood workings of the global economy and includes poverty, overpopulation, and migrations. The inequality among states is, on the whole, exacerbated by the capitalist world system, and most of the poorer countries, particularly in Africa and central Asia, are getting poorer without any prospect of reversing the trend. The same can be said for the ecological tragedies, such as ozone depletion, that are too slowly becoming known, the struggle for access to resources such as oil, the threat of the drug traffic, and the highly lucrative arms trade, essential for the favorable balance of payments of many states, including such advanced capitalist countries as Sweden and Switzerland.

No less ominous are the dangers created by the one general ideology that has survived the collapse of communism: nationalism, which is often heightened by or concealed behind religious revivalism. It owes its current success not only to the end of the cold war but to its appeal to the basic emotions of tribal solidarity, which were often suppressed under one form of imperial rule or another. Nationalism can both dissolve states and cause trouble among them. Since many states have advanced weapons, and either possess or could soon possess the means of mass destruction, all these conflicts raise a threat of, at least, regional chaos, and worse, if, as in the Middle East, the region is thought to be of strategic and economic importance, for the entire world.

Virtually all discussions of world order are based on four principles, all of them flawed and in conflict with one another. The first is the principle of state sovereignty. As enshrined in the charter of the UN, it commits all members to preserve the territorial integrity or political independence of any state from threats or uses of force. It has one enduring merit: it can serve as a shield against the imperialist or aggressive designs of other states, which explains why small and new countries cling to it so fiercely. But it is inadequate today when the world economy has already deprived states of much of their theoretical financial, industrial, or commercial autonomy. The United States, still the most powerful country in military strength and the size of its economy, depends on Japanese and European loans and investments to finance its budget deficit. Until the still very shaky experiment with a commonwealth made up of the former Soviet republics, the only nations to give up state sovereignty voluntarily in the modern world are those of the European Community; and notwithstanding years of discussion they have done so only to create a single market, while refusing to give up independence in matters of diplomacy, defense, or immigration. State sovereignty, moreover, by granting each government full and exclusive control over its territory, allows for domestic atrocities that not only offend the sense of justice but can also all too easily foster international disorder, for instance, when the victims, or the parties locked in internal conflict, call for outside help.

Liberals concerned with world order have made much of the excesses of sovereignty. They hoped to square the circle by promoting a second principle; self-determination. From Mazzini to Wilson, they believed that a world of sovereign nation-states—each nationality having fulfilled its destiny by obtaining a state of its own—would be able to live in harmony, or in sufficient harmony to deter and to punish violators. They did not see how this principle can be a formidable factor of disintegration and conflict, as we can observe in Yugoslavia and the former USSR, as well as in Russia itself, Cyprus, Sri Lanka, Ethiopia, Kurdistan, and with the Arab-Israeli quarrel.

Who can define with any consistency the national "self" that is entitled to autonomy or sovereignty? Is every sizable group that is ethnically distinct entitled to form a nation? And if the definition of a nation is based more on people's expression of collective preference than on ethnic identity, is any association of people who want to live together entitled to call itself a nation and demand a state of its own? If self-determination is a fundamental principle, why shouldn't the Ibos have had their state of Biafra? But if it is, what happens to current borders and to the sovereignty of existing states? Does one serve justice by granting statehood to nations that are likely to contain, and often to mistreat, their own ethnic or religious minorities?

Wilsonian liberalism proposed a third principle. World order would emerge if the world of nation-sates was also a world of constitutional governments. Harmony thus was ultimately dependent on the triumph of democracy, because it has been assumed, ever since Kant, that democratically elected governments that respected the rights of citizens would not make war against other democracies and that constitutional government would encourage a rational discussion of the sources of conflict and act as a dam against surging passions.[2] But from the viewpoint of international legitimacy, self-government still has a lower status than sovereignty and self-determination. The UN Charter does not require that all members be democracies (unlike, in practice, the European Community). It mentions the "self-determination of peoples" as one of its basic principles, but when it comes to the way sovereign states govern themselves, it only mentions the promotion of human rights and fundamental freedoms through international cooperation.

In other words, world order still remains tied to the distinction between domestic affairs and relations among states. International and domestic legitimacy remain distinct, in conformity with the doctrines of "realism" based on traditional balance of power, which prescribe that states attempt to affect each other's external behavior but not the domestic conduct and institutions of political regimes. Whereas many theorists, including liberals, have supported external intervention to help a people obtain self-determination, few have advocated similar interventions for democracy. John Stuart Mill, in an argument reformulated by Michael Walzer,[3] sharply distinguished these two cases. They argue that freedom from tyranny, unlike liberation from alien rule, cannot be conferred on nations from the outside. To reverse this rule would open the way to constant foreign intervention, manipulation, and domination.

Not all democracies protect what Isaiah Berlin called negative liberty—individual rights to take action without being hindered by others and by the state. Some are Jacobin democracies that allow no such obstacles to stand in the way of majority rule—in which case minorities as well as individuals may have their rights destroyed. Also, whether a democracy emphasizes "negative" or "positive" freedom, the benefits of both may well be reserved to nationals, with inalienable rights (as well as the power to participate in common decisions) denied to foreigners, including immigrant workers. The issue of citizenship is nowhere a simple one. This is why a fourth notion has gained much intellectual support: the universal protection of human rights, which would allow individuals and groups to survive and flourish under any regime and in any conditions. But scholars and politicians disagree about which rights are essential ones, and states both resist external intrusions in so vital a domestic matter and are notoriously fickle and self-serving about taking up the cause of human rights abroad.

What is clear is how difficult it is for most states to pursue simultaneously the four goals of sovereignty, self-determination, self-government, and human rights. Even though President George Bush said that Saddam Hussein's dictatorial rule was the ultimate justification for the Gulf war, both the United States and the coalition of states that supported it settled for the restoration of Kuwait's sovereignty and for thwarting, by partially destroying, Iraqi power while allowing Saddam Hussein to crush both the Kurds and Shiites, whom we had encouraged to rebel against the regime. When the flight of the Kurds provoked an outcry, the United States took some steps to protect them from Saddam Hussein's wrath but never endorsed Kurdish demands for autonomy. Neither in Iraq nor in Kuwait has self-government, or even modest steps toward democracy, or the protection of elementary human rights, become the goal of U.S. diplomacy.

Obstacles and Handicaps

A policy of world order would require that the many sources of global or regional turbulence be dealt with in ways that would minimize violent conflict among states, reduce injustice among and within states, and prevent dangerous violations of rights within them. The obstacles to such a policy are formidable.

First, the model of world order that underlies both the League of Nations and the UN is unworkable. It is based on the notion of collective security, by which all or most states will come to the rescue of a state that is the victim of aggression and punish the wrongdoers through sanctions or even force. The traditional criticism of collective security attacked the assumption that was supposed to lie behind it—the idea that delinquent states could be treated like criminals in domestic law. The critics pointed out that international society has neither the centralized government, judicial system, and police that characterize a well-ordered state nor the consensus on what constitutes a crime that exists in domestic affairs.[4] And even when such a consensus exists (as sometimes in the case of armed aggression), states are not likely to honor their commitment to punish the crime unless it serves their interests to do so. Collective security tends to work, paradoxically, when a major power is willing to take the responsibility for it and the other nations are willing to fall into line. If it means the possibility of war against a major power, it will probably not be carried out, as is suggested by the fate during the cold war of the system of collective security set forth in Chapter VII of the UN Charter.

Coercion seldom works as an instrument of order in world affairs for other reasons as well. Outright aggression is not likely to be the most frequently or obvious source of disorder among states. Many violent conflicts are not caused by the moving of a hostile army across a well-defined border. The conflict may well be over where a controversial border should be, as in the case of Kashmir, or in the Palestinian-Israeli conflict, or perhaps tomorrow between Russia and Ukraine; or it may be about one state's intervention in another's domestic conflict at the request of one of the factions, as in the cases of Cyprus and Angola or, in the early 1960s, in Yemen and Vietnam. In such instances, looking for an aggressor to punish could be futile and divisive—and this is one of the reasons why, in the past, the Security Council has chosen to treat violent conflicts under Chapter VI—concerning pacific settlement of disputes through diplomacy—rather than under Chapter VII, which authorizes coercive action against threats to peace, breaches of the peace, and acts of aggression.

Moreover, coercion, even when it is effective—indeed, especially when it is—often punishes the innocent even more than the guilty. The people who suffer most are the hapless civilians who have had little say about the evil policies of their leaders. Here again, concepts of order that leave out civilian populations are inadequate. Those of us who advocated a longer period of sanctions in preference to early war against Iraq should have no illusions about who would have suffered most from the shortages imposed by a prolonged blockade. Still, the more violent the methods of coercion, the heavier the price paid by the innocent. Modern war virtually ensures that the troublemaker will drag down with him thousands of noncriminals—not only civilians but soldiers often drafted against their will and driven by fear—unless "enforcement" or world law can be carried out by small and brief police operations. In a full-scale war, precision weapons may avoid the direct massacre of the innocent, only to destroy the conditions for a decent life, as the reports from Iraq describing the desperate fate of hospitals, health centers, water purification, power supplies, and so on have pointed out.

Modern war, fought with late-twentieth-century weapons, therefore almost guarantees a disproportion between ends and means, or between the values saved and the values destroyed, as well as unexpected and damaging consequences. It is not only nuclear war but modern large-scale war that, in Michael Walzer's words, "explodes" the old Catholic theory of the just war, in which justice depends on whether the violence used does not cause far more death and destruction than the aggression that has provoked intervention in the first place.[5] World order may require brief police operations; but if it is based on the violence that accompanies either prolonged or intense fighting, it can hardly be called order. A large number of "Gulf wars" would be neither morally acceptable nor politically manageable; how often, even in cases of unmistakable aggression, will we find the remarkable coincidence of economic or strategic interests that made possible the U.S.-led coalition?

This is why I have argued, along with others, that prevention should be favored over coercion.[6] There are two approaches to prevention, and both present difficulties. The first calls for resolving conflicts by negotiation (as in Chapter VI of the Charter). But diplomacy will succeed in settling intractable disputes only if the major powers, in the world or in a region, are willing to put forward incentives and impose penalties in order to get the parties to budge and compromise. How often will they decide their essential interests are sufficiently threatened by the enduring conflict to engage themselves so deeply? When one sees how reluctant the United States has been to do so in the Palestinian-Israeli quarrel because of the real or imagined domestic political costs to the administration, one has good reason to be skeptical. And the dispatch of peacekeeping (as opposed to fighting) forces by the UN or by regional organizations, to prevent an unsettled dispute from becoming a war under present world law, requires the consent of all the main parties. As in the case of Yugoslavia, many destructive months may pass before such consent is reluctantly given.

The other method of prevention tries to limit weapons at the disposal of the parties to a dispute so as to reduce the capacity for violence or to make coercion more effective if aggression occurs anyhow. But such efforts are likely to encounter formidable technical obstacles, as we can see in the Middle East today. In prohibiting arms sales, should such means of mass destruction as nuclear, chemical, and biological weapons be singled out? If this were done, and long-range missiles equipped with conventional warheads were included as well, it would still be entirely possible to fight highly destructive wars with almost equally lethal conventional weapons, including tanks and planes (as Israel currently argues about its adversaries). And if one adds such weapons to the list, doesn't one provide a powerful incentive to efforts by the smaller countries, already well under way, to produce their own arms? The more extensive the list of prohibited weapons, moreover, the more difficult verification becomes—satellites and ordinary intelligence were far from accurate about Iraq's capacities before and during the Gulf war. It is becoming harder and harder to deny potentially aggressive countries access to technologies that can be used for lethal ends (as the U.S.-sponsored COCOM organization used to do against communist states). It may one day be possible to monitor accurately the uses to which these technologies are put, but scientific advances in monitoring may well be matched by advances in the art of concealment.

As current U.S. plans to sell F-15s to Saudi Arabia show only too well, the goal of prevention often comes into conflict as well with the logic of political alliances, which requires that one supply one's friends. Following that logic will encourage regional arms races; but if one limits arms exports, one's friends will protest that they are treated no better than one's enemies. Also, how many countries would one want to catch in the net of arms limitations? Only those that are currently antagonists? All those situated in a given region, such as the Middle East and the Gulf? In many countries, moreover, including the United States, France, and Czechoslovakia, the national arms industry has a strong domestic constituency, not least because of its contribution to the balance of payments and employment.

If coercion is too violent and prevention is too uncertain, what about deterrence? One can conceive of deterring wars through a process that worked fairly successfully in Europe as a result of the Helsinki agreements of 1975 and of subsequent meetings, including the CSCE in Paris in November 1990. The NATO and Warsaw Pact countries agreed on "confidence-building measures" aimed at preventing surprise attacks, for instance, by notifying other states of military maneuvers, and they also agreed that national armed forces would largely rely on defensive, not offensive, equipment and strategies. But it is not easy to visualize Ukrainians, Croats, Serbs, Israelis, Syrians, or Pakistanis agreeing to such limitations.[7] Another method of deterrence—less radical but often the most sensible available—is based on the presence in a region of military forces, sent by the UN or provided by a regional organization and capable of intervening against a troublemaker. But such forces have not always deterred determined states—especially not in the Middle East, where UN peacekeeping forces were removed, in May 1967, at Egypt's request and pushed aside by Israeli in Lebanon in 1982 and again in February 1992.

Domestic disorder or repression can create international conflict, particularly when a government violently attacks a large part of its own population, whether this corresponds to the legal definition of genocide or not. Humanitarian intervention, including by force if necessary, in order to prevent or stop such massacres has often been advocated. But not only do all the difficulties entailed by the use of force arise again in such cases, but the claim of sovereignty will likely be used to block efforts to intervene. Most governments and international lawyers read the Charter as banning the use of force for humanitarian reasons. And if a nation wanted to move beyond the Charter, by having the Security Council treat such cases as threats to world peace, how can it get the other UN members to agree? Many of them (such as China and Syria) have armies of skeletons in their closets; or they fear that old enemies would take advantage of a humanitarian cause in order to gain advantages (as India did when it helped dismantle Pakistan in 1971 or as Vietnam did in Cambodia); or they close their eyes to atrocities if they are committed by friends, or friends of friends, or foes of adversaries (as the Chinese did with the Khmer Rouge).

A different issue is that of grave violations of fundamental human rights by oppressive regimes—China in Tiananmen Square, South African through apartheid, the late Chilean and Argentinean military dictatorships with their *desaparecidos*. So far, such violations have been deemed by the UN an international threat to the peace only in the case of South Africa; and South Africa may be the last state to be officially labeled as a pariah. Outside the UN, human rights have been defended or ignored depending on whether they were trampled by the Soviets and their satellites or by allies of the free world. This is less likely to be the case now that the cold war is over, but the subordination of an active defense of human rights to political calculations is not about to disappear, as the Bush administration's policy toward China shows. There have also been cases of widespread famine tolerated by the starving country's government (Ethiopia) or caused by a civil war (Somalia); the resistance of such a government to outside assistance, or the chaos in the country, has prevented international rescue efforts from succeeding or even (as in Somalia) from taking place.

Another persistent challenge to any predictability of world order is the clandestine buildup of weapons of mass destruction, especially in states with deep unsettled grievances toward neighbors. Destroying an opponent's facilities—as Israel did in Iraq in 1981—would amount to a recipe for chaos if it should become a widespread state practice; and it is likely to foster revenge.

Where, in any case, is the impetus for a new world order to come from? Who really cares about it? A "new world order" requires three kinds of leadership. It requires international and regional organizations capable of putting forces in place for peacekeeping and enforcement. But most of the existing organizations are inadequately equipped for such missions: their resources are too meager, their staffs too politically constricted, their procedures too clumsy, their agendas overburdened, their legitimacy too contested. (Much of this is true even of the most impressive of all regional organizations, the European Community.) In the UN, the General Assembly is unwieldy, and the Security Council is frozen by the obsolete definitions of the great powers deriving from World War II.

International and regional organizations cannot be effective unless a powerful state, or group of states, is willing to take responsibility for exerting pressure or taking action. (In the European Community, it has been the Franco-German axis.) At the global level, we now face a paradoxical situation. Those who talk of a unipolar world confuse America's unmatched military might with a preponderance of real power. But American might is likely to be used successfully only against such tiny states as Grenada or Panama or against a major regional aggressor, such as Saddam Hussein. In most conceivable cases of disorder, either force will not be used because the interests are not sufficiently large, the threat is not sufficiently clearcut, or the cost of using force will exceed the probable benefits; or other forms of power, such as financial and technological pressure, will be needed, and the United States is more and more limited in its ability to use both. When it comes to exerting such pressures or to creating fighting forces to deter aggression, we are confronted with a vacuum; yesterday's other superpower has vanished, and the new economic giants, Germany and Japan, are reluctant to commit themselves far beyond their borders. They have learned only too well the lesson the winners of World War II taught them about the perils of *Weltpolitik*. They have been able to disconnect their diplomatic activities from the interests of their private investors, who have managed to succeed brilliantly abroad without much help from Germany's political leaders or foreign ministries.

World leadership also requires money: one can't have order on the cheap. But who can, or will, pay for the almost unimaginable amounts that will be needed for the rehabilitation of Eastern Europe, for preventing convulsions in the former USSR, for narrowing the gap between rich and poor countries so as to prevent famine and huge population flows, for providing debt relief to many of the bankrupt countries, for protecting the environment, and for compensating domestic arms manufacturers deprived of external outlets? The United States is already rejecting demands for aid from Eastern Europe and the former Soviet Union; Germany has been investing more heavily in Central Europe than any other power, but it is absorbed and shaken by the size of the East German disaster; Japan is torn between resentment of "taxation without representation" (as during the Gulf war or in the UN Security Council) and reluctance to be involved beyond its own geopolitical sphere; Britain and France have ambitions but small means.

A final obstacle to any possibility of world order is the ambivalence of the United States. What should its priorities be? Those who, like Bush, call for a policy of "world order" (undefined, beyond Bush's idea of Soviet-American cooperation, which has already been overtaken by events) tend to neglect the domestic repairs that American society urgently needs. If they are not undertaken, the underpinnings of America's capacity to act as a world power will erode or collapse—as they did, behind an impressive military façade, in the Soviet Union. A serious energy policy aimed at reducing American reliance on imported oil would surely be a contribution to world order. On the whole, however, if the United States chooses to concentrate on its domestic crises, there will be little money and attention available or involvement in the world. The recent argument of *Foreign Affairs* editor William Hyland for a "psychological turn inward"[8] is a plea for a withdrawal of resources, not only from traditional entanglements but from international commitments in general. And while it is true that, except in the Middle East, there may be few vital "threats to American interests," a world of diffuse disorder could rapidly become a dangerous place.

Small Steps towards World Order

Small steps, taken as the occasions for dealing with conflict arise, may be all that can be done to promote world order. We ought to think about the ways states can, in specific situations, be impelled to confront or circumvent the obstacles I have described. For instance, while large-scale coercion may usually be unwise, activating the long-dormant Military Staff Committee of the UN under Article 47 of the Charter, and thus putting any UN fighting forces under genuine international control, would be an important change. So would getting the members of the UN to sign agreements allocating forces available for use by the Security Council (as provided in Article 43) and setting up, as a result, standby military units ready for action. This would make possible both limited police operations against minor troublemakers, as the former UN under-secretary-general Brian Urquhart has recommended,[9] and the dispatch of a deterrent military force into a country that feels threatened and asks for it.

As Urquhart also has suggested, in order to prevent aggression such as Saddam Hussein's move across the Kuwaiti border, a new office should be set up under the Security Council to monitor troop movements and threatening deployments of weapons and to call on the Security Council to act quickly when such threats are detected. Peacekeeping forces under Chapter VI or under Chapter VII could be sent to sensitive regions, either before a conflict, when a dispute is unresolved, or after a truce or a settlement. They could be stationed on one side of a border at the request or with the consent of only one party, even if the other party objects. Such forces should be kept there as long as the Security Council has not decided to remove them. This would again require, in conformity with Article 43, the creation of standby (but not fighting) units; and these could be provided not only, as during the cold war, by states other than the permanent members, such as Ireland and India, but also by the permanent members themselves as a guarantee of their willingness to take part in deterrence and prevention.

In the matter of arms control, the case for boldness has been recognized by Boris Yeltsin and Secretary of State James Baker, but they could go further. To prevent the breakup of the Soviet Union from multiplying by four the number of nuclear powers on its former territory, the United States, Russia, Belarus, Ukraine, and Kazakhstan should quickly agree on the elimination of all short-range and tactical nuclear weapons and go on to make drastic cuts in land-based strategic missiles beyond the START limits, with the goal of eliminating them altogether. Since intercontinental ballistic missiles formed the main part of the Soviet arsenal, the United States, in exchange, should accept a reduction in the number of bombers and sea-launched ballistic missiles. Most important of all, a comprehensive test ban should finally be signed. If the major powers were to decide on deep reductions of their own military budgets and forces, they would be in a far better position to impose, through a cartel of suppliers, limits on the sale of all types of arms. They would also be in a position to establish, through regional arms control agreements, a network of confidence-building measures aimed at providing all parties with as much information as possible about each other's forces.

The long-range goal, which should be formally announced, is to reduce each state's forces and arms to the lowest levels compatible with its security needs. In exchange for stopping their own production and testing of such categories of weapons as long-range missiles, the major powers would request that the same curbs apply elsewhere and that the safeguards and inspection system of the nuclear nonproliferation treaty of 1968 be reenforced. Regular and intrusive inspections under UN auspices or under the auspices of regional equivalents of the CSCE could then be instituted. A state's refusal to allow such inspections or violations detected early enough could put into effect sanctions such as withdrawal of credits that would have a less deleterious effect on civilians than an all-out blockade at the last minute. If a state's refusal or violation put the security of an entire region at stake, the Security Council, under Chapter VII, could also threaten to take military action, a threat that might have a powerful deterrent effect; this might ultimately be the most effective policy to follow in dealing with North Korea if it is about to produce atomic weapons.

All the truly dangerous arms buildups in the world—in South Africa, in the Korean peninsula, in the Indian peninsula, in the Middle East—are linked to unresolved disputes. Nowhere is a solution more important—because of the implications of a rotting status quo—than in the Arab-Israeli case, and no solution is likely to be achieved by mere procedural suggestions. In 1991, the Bush administration finally seemed to understand that it had to push the parties toward the goal of provisional autonomy and to insist that Palestinians be the principal Arab negotiators; and in 1992 it has taken the unprecedented step of linking economic aid to a freeze on settlements. Much more pressure will be needed to narrow the differences between the parties' conceptions of autonomy if the current negotiations are to have any success.

A central question is how to get international consent on lifting the immunity conferred by "domestic jurisdiction," an immunity that can have deadly consequences. A new standard worth working for would justify collective intervention by international or regional organizations, or by states with these agencies' consent, whenever domestic disorders or policies threaten a region's peace or security and when fundamental human rights are violated on a large scale. We must remember that when states are in conflict, preventing war through diplomacy is possible, whereas when the troubles are domestic, under present international law, nothing can be done, as with Yugoslavia's slide into civil war.

Four kinds of measures could limit such domestic violence. The boldest would be a treaty, open to (but unlikely to be signed by) all states, that would define rigorously the circumstances in which collective intervention for humanitarian purposes could be undertaken, for a limited period, by a group of states whose action would be authorized by a strong majority of the treaty's signers. The nations would act through a secretariat set up under the treaty and would report all plans for action to the UN Security Council, which could at any time order the end of sanctions taken under the treaty. Such interventions could take place either when entire groups are subjected to violence, when weapons of mass destruction are used against domestic enemies, or when a state remains indifferent to natural or man-made disasters on its territory. No doubt such a treaty might result in interventions that would be called "imperialist"; but this risk—which should not be exaggerated, given the requirement of collective authorization and the cost of military interventions—has to be weighed against the price of indifference.

Second, we should learn from the Yugoslav tragedy. When a civil war threatens to occur that is likely to have disastrous external effects or to cause extensive violations of rights, the Security Council should quickly assimilate such a case to the threats to peace and security among states covered by Chapter VII of the Charter and not delay for months, as was the case in Yugoslavia. It would then be able to send peacekeeping forces to the region even if it has not had the prior agreement of all parties to do so; and if it should decide that one of the parties is the aggressor or blocks the return to peace, it could send a fighting force, as in cases of aggression among states. (In the Yugoslav case, the secretary-general and the Security Council have remained pragmatically elusive about the legal basis of their intervention, first for a cease-fire, later for the dispatch of a peacekeeping force; but the consent of all parties was deemed necessary.) Under Chapter VI, the UN should also be ready to sponsor negotiations between the parties to a civil war, just as it does between quarreling states. The recent Security Council efforts to promote a cease-fire in Somalia are a step in this direction.

A more modest measure would be an attempt to revive, at the request and under the auspices of the UN and of regional organizations (perhaps the CSCE in Europe), the kinds of treaties protecting minorities that were set up after World War I, mainly in eastern and southeastern Europe. Under such treaties minorities could have extensive cultural and administrative autonomy that would be monitored by a system of inspections and reports; violations would be considered as threats to peace. To be sure, such arrangements could not be made without the consent of the states whose minorities demand protection. But these states—Romania, Czechoslovakia, or an independent Croatia and Serbia, in Europe; Turkey, Iraq, and Iran, in the Middle East; Ukraine and Azerbaijan, in the new post-Soviet Commonwealth—might be given a choice between signing such agreements and (as, for instance, Italy and Spain have done) granting on their own to their minorities the rights such treaties would provide. States refusing to accept either formula would forfeit the credits and other economic benefits from international and regional organizations or banks that are so much in demand. In this way, mistreated ethnic or religious groups might be protected, while destructive secessionist movements would be avoided or contained.

A fourth step would be a reinforced system for monitoring human rights violations, beyond the reports provided by UN and regional committees or by private organizations such as Amnesty International. The secretary-general of the UN himself should be asked to draw the attention of the members to domestic acts that, in his opinion, either appear to be steps toward committing genocide (as with past Iraqi policies toward the Kurds) or could have dangerous effects internationally, particularly by inciting interventions by neighbors (as with Cambodia under the Khmer Rouge) or cause large numbers of people to flee the country (as with Haiti). He could also point to the dangers of human-rights violations that accompany preparations for aggressive expansion abroad. In all such instances, the Security Council could request, at a minimum, that all members of the UN cease to provide economic and military aid to the delinquent state (such as the weapons and technology provided by the United States to Saddam Hussein in 1989–1990, before the invasion of Kuwait).

Among the difficulties that may arise in carrying out such proposals, the most important may well be a lack of money. If the cuts in military expenses I have advocated can be made, this would, year by year, liberate resources that could be available for the strengthening of international and regional organizations as well as for the economic missions of world order. Indeed, as Brian Urquhart argues, money spent for peacekeeping should be seen as the most economical form of defense.

If the emphasis is put more on prevention and deterrence than on enforcement, a kind world concert of the major powers—including the current reluctant giants—and of key regional countries (such as Brazil and India) could gradually emerge. One condition for nations aspiring to join such a club would be progress toward democracy and toward allowing autonomy or self-determination, within reasonable limits, for restive nationalities inside their borders.

As for the United States, it is certainly in no position to play the role of sole guardian of world order, which the Pentagon now claims for it, because it cannot postpone the domestic reconstruction that is widely seen as necessary. Nor can it withdraw from the cooperative quest for world order. In order to be able to do both, however, the United States must have a government capable of dealing with more than one crisis at a time and of planning beyond the next congressional election. The ability of the American political system to redirect expenditures toward internal needs as well as toward even a modest system of international peacekeeping is very much in doubt. The same can be said about the ability of American leaders to foster a conception of citizenship that does not equate patriotism with the refusal to pay more taxes. Such questions about American political culture make it difficult to be optimistic about U.S. leadership in the years to come.

The depressed mood following the Gulf war should teach us at least two lessons. Large-scale wars, even those widely deemed necessary and just, may not contribute to a decent world order. As long as statesmen put more energy into the logistics of war than into efforts to anticipate and prevent violence, whatever semblance of international order emerges will more likely be the result of accident than of design.

9

The Price of War

What Role for the UN?

Thanks to the end of the cold war, the society of states finds itself in the condition that had been mistakenly expected by the drafters of the United Nations Charter. For forty-five years, the paralysis of the Security Council prevented the Charter provisions on collective security from being carried out. In the Gulf crisis provoked by Iraq's invasion of Kuwait, the Security Council has at last performed exactly as it had been designed to do. Indeed, the Bush administration has repeatedly presented the crisis as a test whose outcome will shape the future of collective security and determine whether the UN will be able to play the important role that Mikhail Gorbachev, in his famous speech before the General Assembly in December 1988, had requested for the world organization. But we should have no illusions about how easy or rosy that future will be, even if the current coalition prevails over Saddam Hussein; and American policy in the Gulf crisis may well make the task of the UN in years to come much more difficult.

In the world as it has emerged from the cold war, the restraining influence of the superpowers over their respective clients is gone. Old rivalries among states remain explosive: in Kashmir, in Cyprus, and, of course, in the Middle East. Domestic turmoil caused by ethnic or religious minorities will provoke external interventions. Disruptions caused by economic hardships, famines, poverty, tyranny, and civil war may result in colossal migrations and flights of refugees. No single nation will be capable of playing world policeman—hence, the importance of the UN.

But will the UN be able to police the globe? There are two reasons for skepticism. One is that some of the factors that led to the fiasco of collective security in the past have not disappeared along with the cold war. The UN has never found it easy to cope with violent internal conflicts. No doubt the Soviet-American rivalry made the crisis of the former Belgian Congo in 1960 more dangerous, but its complexities and factional battles would have been too much for the organization, in any case. The Charter's Chapter VII on collective security was drafted by people who had the 1930s in mind. They wanted the Security Council to be able to deal firmly and promptly with aggressors who sent forces across well-established borders in order to violate the territorial integrity and political independence of their neighbors. But it turned out that the model of aggression did not fit the realities of the postwar world, and in this respect, the Iraq case may be atypical. For there are many instances (as in Kashmir, or in the Arab-Israeli dispute) where it is the border that is at stake in the conflict or where there has been such a succession of crises that it is hard to identify who violated whose border first or to distinguish the defender from the aggressor. In several of these instances, the Security Council has preferred to use the much "softer" procedure of conflict resolution of Chapter VI—procedures of negotiations and mediation that tend to treat the parties as equals, instead of treating one side as criminal and the other as victim. But these procedures are inevitably slow and frequently ineffectual, since the Security Council, in such cases, merely makes recommendations and does not back them with collective force.

The second reason is that if the main powers, including the United States and the USSR, decide to allow the Security Council to play a much more active part in resolving disputes, and especially if they should want it to resort more frequently to the provisions of the Charter that ban the use and threat of force and organize collective action against the violators, these great powers will have to stop behaving as they have behaved in the past. During the Security Council's long paralysis, they have tolerated a large number of aggressions, either by not dealing with them at all (for example, China's invasion of Tibet), by merely denouncing them without taking any collective action, or by simply calling for a cease-fire (as in Iraq's war of aggression against Iran). To be sure, many states that sent their armies across borders had grievances, as the United States argued in the cases of Grenada and Panama. But the violator usually has some plausible complaints, and the very purpose of the Charter was and remains to prevent those complaints from serving as pretexts for aggression. The observance of a double standard—a lenient or permissive one when aggression is committed by oneself or one's friends, a strict one when it is committed by a foe or by a pariah—will have to cease.

This double standard may have been obnoxious from the viewpoint of morality, but it had the political merit of simplifying the great powers' task and of providing them with a compass. The problem with taking the Charter seriously is that each conflict, and especially each aggression, will require the forging of a new coalition. States used to shift alliances and reshuffle alignments in order to preserve a balance of power. Doing so in order to assure world order and the triumph of principle would amount to a diplomatic revolution. It would, at a minimum, require far more political consultation and coordination than has ever been the case except among close allies, and it will require activating the Military Staff Committee of the Security Council (as the Soviets have suggested) in order to plan collective resistance to aggression; this, in turn, may require a world police force in readiness. Such events as the invasions of Tibet by China, of Timor by Indonesia, of Lebanon by Syria and Israel, and of Cyprus by the Turks could not be passed over as they have been. We would no longer be able to rely, as we have for so many years, on the interplay of unilateral moves and of alliances. Are the major powers ready for such a leap? The remarkably effective coalition put together by the United States in the Gulf crisis against a state whose resort to naked aggression is undeniable may not be easily reproduced in cases that are less clear cut or in parts of the world that are less obviously vital to the security of most states.

The Gulf Crisis

Moreover, the Gulf crisis may still lead to a disaster for the future of world order. The Bush administration has emphasized, rightly, that appeasing Saddam Hussein or stopping short of the restoration of Kuwait's independence would be such a disaster. But its own policy carries risks that are just as serious.

The Gulf crisis obliges us to face for the first time the fact that collective security may mean war. The resort to force in order to punish a crime—instead of being considered as the free choice of any sovereign state—may change the moral basis of war. It does not change its nature. In the past, even the most ambitious attempts at collective security never went beyond economic sanctions and arms embargoes. But against states that can thwart sanctions or are unwilling to retreat unless forced to, the threat of war would have to be employed as in the present case.

However, while collective security expresses the idea that aggression anywhere is a legitimate and essential concern of the international community, this does not mean that unconditional surrender is the only way of rolling back aggression. To take such a stand would, most probably, only harden the determination of aggressors who were tough enough to have been undeterred by the threat of collective force in the first place. A policy of unconditional surrender would also severely strain whatever coalition serves as the secular arm of collective security.

It is only in the twentieth century that unconditional surrender has become the preferred way of ending major conflicts—with highly debatable results. Earlier, many conflicts, even those pitting the "good" side against the "bad" one, have ended by negotiation. Of course, it is not easy without retreating from the principles of the Charter to find a middle ground between a threat of force that shows an unambiguous determination to roll back aggression and one that indicates a preference for a nonviolent resolution; or between a negotiation that results in a tangible material reward for an aggressor willing to remove his forces from the territory he seized and one that ends with the restoration of the victim yet allows the aggressor to save face.

But the principle of international concern should not be interpreted to require potentially bloody and destructive wars leading to unpredictable political catastrophes. It is the function of diplomacy to try to reconcile conflicting considerations. Giving a free reign to aggression would turn the world into a jungle. But so would the equation of collective security with the kind of all-out war that rules out diplomacy. The more serious we are about the future of collective security, the more we need to avoid a course that would compromise this notion, both by making it much more difficult to bring a coalition together the next time and by undermining domestic support for it.

What diplomatic alternatives to war can be developed depends on the nature of each case. The Kuwait crisis occurred in a uniquely contentious part of the world. Nowhere else are there so many interlocking grievances, so many ruthless leaders, so much jockeying for predominance, so many dangerous weapons, such vital resources, such fiercely disputed borders, such intense religious and ideological conflicts. This suggests that even a total victory over Saddam Hussein is likely to unleash forces that the American-led coalition would find hard to control, especially if a desperate Saddam Hussein, in an attempt to divide the coalition opposing him, turns the war into one that embroils Israel and fans the fires of anti-Americanism in an already inflamed subcontinent. Just as in 1950 the temptation to unify Korea by force, after the armies under General

Douglas MacArthur had pushed back the North Koreans behind the thirty-eighth parallel, ought to have been resisted, the temptation to "resolve" the issue of Saddam Hussein by destroying both his arsenal and his rule should be resisted now, because even their destruction and his elimination would not miraculously resolve the fundamental issues in the region.

There are other ways—containment and arms control—with which the threat he represents can be addressed, while a war's cost in American and other lives, military and civilian, could be horrendous, far disproportionate to what is gained. The best strategy is to keep the military pressure on Saddam Hussein, to give economic sanctions time to take their toll, while continuing to make it clear to him that he must withdraw from Kuwait. The administration should be spending at least as much time preparing a diplomatic settlement (for discussion at the meetings that are now being planned in Washington and Baghdad) as it has spent on keeping the coalition together and on preparing it for war.

Pros and Cons of a War

The substance of such a settlement has been plausibly outlined by George Ball[1] and before the Senate Committee on Foreign Relations, on December 5, 1990, by Zbigniew Brzezinski. It would be based on the sensible notion that the issues that make the Middle East such a dangerous place are interconnected and that the Kuwait crisis shows that the time has come to deal with them systematically—after years of pretending that they weren't ripe for settlement. If overt linkage would look like a reward for aggression, we should resort to what could be called unlinked or implicit linkage. Just as we did not formally "reward" the Soviets for removing their missiles from Cuba by linking their retreat to the removal of American missiles in Turkey, yet we removed them afterward, we could suggest to Iraq that we would be willing to initiate (1) an international conference on the Arab-Israeli conflict; (2) an arms-control conference aimed at ending the shipment to the region of certain categories of weapons and at inspecting the nuclear and chemical facilities of all the Middle Eastern states; and (3) arbitration between Iraq and Kuwait, but only after Iraq's evacuation of its neighbor.[2] And we could, subsequently, establish a system of regional security against any future aggression to protect the militarily weak states of the region against their neighbors under UN auspices and with the participation of UN forces, in which the United States would not be an overwhelmingly dominant member.

The reason for taking up the Palestinian issue through such a conference is not merely related to Saddam Hussein's "saving face." The contrast between the West's reaction to his aggression and its leniency toward Israeli's transgressions and occupation of Arab lands will continue to serve both as a justification and as excuse for attacks on Western interests and as a source of troubles for Arab governments friendly to the United States.

There are, however, reasons to fear that such a course will not be taken. As George Ball and others have warned, the very size of the American deployment risks pushing the policy toward an early war, whereas a negotiation leading to a settlement that is neither appeasement of Saddam Hussein nor unconditional surrender by Saddam Hussein is likely to take time. The UN resolution that demands a withdrawal by January 15, instead of merely authorizing an eventual resort to force, and the administration's eagerness to play down the effectiveness of economic sanctions (in a case in which they are quite likely to have deep effects on the economy and the army of the targeted country) are likely to make war highly probable if on January 15 no settlement is yet in sight—because a decision to wait and to rely primarily on the sanctions would then look like a retreat. To "do nothing" after January 15 would, at best, make it clear that we are, in fact, negotiating—and this too would look like a retreat, since the administration has somewhat rashly proclaimed that the conversations we have proposed will not amount to a negotiation.

We have put ourselves in a position that is exposed and unwise. If we want to avoid a war without abandoning our objective, the restoration of Kuwait, we have to negotiate. If we actually prefer war to a negotiation, the hopes raised by the announcement of the "conversations" will make domestic unity even more difficult to reach unless we can prove that Iraq rejected all chances for a settlement and refused to get out of Kuwait unless forced to do so by war.

A war would be a good precedent for the future of collective security if it could be quick, easy, and lead to the kind of peace that chastises the aggressor country but gives it a chance to play a more modest and constructive role in world affairs. The trouble is that nobody can be sure that the war will be easy, and some highly qualified experts fear it may be very costly indeed. Moreover, a quick war would be one that inflicts such destruction on Iraq that it is likely to wreck not only Saddam Hussein but Iraq itself, with incalculable consequences for the balance of power in the Middle East and in other regions as well.

Statesmen are more obsessed with the past than concerned with the pattern their acts may set for the future. The Bush administration seems to want to exorcise both Munich and Vietnam. But, as Brzezinski put it, "to speak of Saddam Hussein as a Hitler is to trivialize Hitler and to elevate Saddam." He added that Iraq is not Germany but a regional threat "we can contain, deter, or repel, as the situation dictates."[3] Nobody has suggested that Kuwait should suffer the fate inflicted by Britain and France on Czechoslovakia at Munich, and the nature and size of the coalition against Iraq shows the irrelevance of the Munich analogy. To argue that any policy short of war would lead to Iraq's domination of the Middle East or create a mortal threat for Israel is to ignore the many measures that could be taken to limit Iraq's future power and to rely on a crude and unconvincing version of the domino theory.

The administration also explains that it does not want to repeat the error made in Vietnam, where we did not use all the force at our disposal, or we used it only gradually. But if it is our intention to use all our might in one huge spasm, there exists an enormous disproportion between our ends and our means, a contradiction between our stated objective, which is the restoration of Kuwait, and our enormous forces, whose engagement is likely, as in so many modern wars, to lead to an escalation of goals and therefore to serious strains for the coalition, to discord at home, and to unforeseen upheavals. The same disproportion exists between the respective contributions of America and its partners.

Vietnam, alas, remains a more relevant analogy than Munich, and—given the Americanization of the conflict both in Vietnam and in the Gulf—it cannot be exorcised so easily. Of course, the terrain is not the same, the enemy can't move and hide in jungles, and Saddam Hussein has no friendly suppliers abroad (another reason, incidentally, for relying on sanctions). But he has more lethal weapons than the Vietcong and the North Vietnamese, in a more combustible part of the world. As in the case of Vietnam, the administration seems to minimize the possible bad effects of military action and to exaggerate the costs of alternative courses. As with Vietnam, the obsession with the Gulf crisis distorts American perspectives and priorities with regard to other parts of the world. It strains relations with allies accused of not fully sharing a "burden" we deem common (but whose size and direction we haven't been willing to set in common); and it concentrates on admittedly important region resources that are needed for dealing with problems of at least equal importance in Eastern Europe, Central America, and at home. As in Vietnam, we may, if the war is not quickly over (and even if it is, but only through the annihilation of the enemy), be trapped in a quagmire of our own making.

Collective security will be the casualty, not the winner, if we lose a sense of proportion, if we launch a war that will divide the coalition and the public far more than a protracted reliance on sanctions, if we interpret the Security Council's authorization of force as a green light for presidential action without congressional endorsement. (Surely the UN Charter did not annul the Congress's constitutional power to declare war.) Only a miraculously successful war—a swift victory through a limited resort to force—would dispel all these dangers. Miracles rarely happen; in international affairs, all good things do not come in a neat package. War may well be unavoidable, if a serious negotiation fails, but the most plausible chance for such war to be brief and limited would be if it occurred after sanctions had had the time to weaken and disrupt Iraq's forces. Any other kind of war risks pushing states away from collective security and—with predominantly American losses on the UN side—almost ensures that the United States will not again provide the leadership—not to be confused with preponderance—required to make it work. There are, to be sure, excellent reasons why one would like Saddam Hussein to lose not only Kuwait but his position and his prestige. But on balance, the cost of allowing him to save face if he leaves Kuwait may be far less than that of blowing him away, and of blowing away in the process the future of collective security.

10

◆———◆

In Defense of Mother Teresa
Morality in Foreign Policy

As a supporter of the Carter administration's ideals who quickly became disillusioned with its performance and denounced the gap between its good intentions and contradictory policies, I appreciate the pithy and pugnacious prosecutor's brief that Michael Mandelbaum, a courageous supporter of Bill Clinton during the 1992 campaign, has drafted.[1] Much of what Mandelbaum says about the Clinton team's policies toward the other major powers and its failures or deficiencies in handling the crises in Haiti, Somalia, and Bosnia is convincing. But the central argument of his essay is, in my opinion, wrong.

Mandelbaum believes that an American foreign policy concerned not with interests but with values, not with relations with countries that have the capacity to affect these interests but with "small, poor, weak," and peripheral countries, is foolish. More than that, it is doomed, both for lack of public support and because turning foreign policy "into a branch of social work" is a recipe for "deep, protracted, and costly engagement in the tangled political life of each country" in which the United States intervenes, in a world "filled with distressed people." I believe, however, that the distinction between interests and values is largely fallacious, and that a policy that would ignore the domestic crises that affect so many states and pseudostates today would have disastrous consequences.

Morality as National Interest

The national interest is not a self-evident guide, it is a construct. It is the sum of the objectives that the policymakers have set. Some of these are

147

indeed imperatives, imposed by the nation's location on the map of power or by clear threats and needs. But many of the goals that states, and especially the major powers among them, pursue go beyond such imperatives and result from preferences and choices. These goals are usually controversial. Those who support them cover them with the mantle of the national interest, and those who do not back them argue, like Mandelbaum, that they deal with developments that "could [not] affect the lives of . . . citizens" (p. 17) and thus are not in the national interest. Even during the cold war, the United States pursued goals that could be connected only remotely to the imperatives of national security and deterrence of the Soviet threat. Mandelbaum presents the invasion of Grenada as part of the cold war but does not mention the intervention in Panama, which, of course, took place after the Soviet threat had crumbled. At the other end of the spectrum, the human rights policies that American administrations pursued, in their different ways, in the late 1970s and in the 1980s cannot be explained away as mere tactical moves in the battle against communism.

Great powers pursue both what Arnold Wolfers has called possession goals and what he terms milieu goals. National security deals essentially with the former. But much of foreign policy is concerned with shaping an international milieu that will provide a modicum of order (i.e., reduce the inevitable loads of violence and chaos that an anarchic international system carries) and in which the nation's citizens will feel not only safe from attack or economic strangulation but, so to speak, morally at home. Among the reasons the opposition between interests and values is a sham are that a great power has an "interest" in world order that goes beyond strict national security concerns and that its definition of order is largely shaped by its values. Many of America's policies during the cold war—especially in relations with allies and so-called Third World countries—and many of the institutions and international regimes it helped establish resulted from preferences that could not be reduced purely and simply to the need to resist the Soviet menace or communism.

In the post–cold war world, there is, in addition to all the classical interstate conflicts that could disrupt world order, a whole new series of dangers arising from the weaknesses or disintegration of many states, ethnic and religious strife within states, and dangerous policies that certain states pursue within their borders.[2] Not all interstate conflicts "could affect the lives of American citizens." But does this mean that these conflicts could not disrupt the balance of power and provoke chaos in many parts of the world and that the United States should be indifferent to them? Conversely, not every domestic crisis is susceptible to a resolution imported from abroad or sufficiently grave to have serious external repercussions (in the form of, say, flows of refugees). Does this mean that a world of generalized internal chaos, in which neighbors of the countries in crisis would be tempted to intervene, would be tolerable from the standpoint of order and of our values? Societies and economies are too interdependent today for us to be sure that what happens in "small, poor, weak" countries will not affect the lives of American citizens, or at least the quality of their lives.

Mandelbaum lives in what scholars have called the Westphalian system, in which relations are between sovereign states of unequal power. But today's world is post-Westphalian: myriad normative restraints and a huge loss of autonomy resulting from transnational forces are eroding state sovereignty generally, and the sovereign state itself, the very floor of the Westphalian construction, is collapsing in many parts of the world. Any U.S. foreign policy that would concentrate exclusively on the traditional agenda would expose the world, and the nation, to intolerable horrors and disorder. (In this respect, even though Sarajevo 1992–1996 is not Sarajevo 1914, Mandelbaum's dismissal of the dangers of an expanding conflict in the Balkans is more than a little rash.)

To Judge a Crisis

Three major qualifications must be attached to my argument. First, not all crises are of equal importance to world order. Two criteria could help us decide when to intervene. Is the crisis, the domestic conflict, or the policy pursued within the borders of the state, we would ask in each case, likely to threaten regional or international peace and security? Are there massive violations of human rights, even in the absence of such a threat? These criteria correspond to the two sides of the coin of world order: the reduction of violence and chaos and the creation or maintenance of a morally acceptable state of affairs. Whether it is in our "interest" to intervene to stop genocide or war crimes on a colossal scale I will let the sophists of national security argue among themselves; what I know is that it is our moral duty to act, whenever there is a chance of success.

That brings me to the second qualification. Even when the criteria are met, not every kind of "social work" can succeed, and there are cases in which outsiders are incapable of dealing with the causes of the crisis. In those cases it may still be a good idea to provide a modicum of humanitarian relief, as in Somalia, or to try to limit the number of victims, as the French did, belatedly, in Rwanda. But when the capacity to get at the problem's roots exists, it is a grave mistake to do too little, by putting crippling limits on the mission or by stopping too soon (as may well have happened in Haiti) or starting too late (as in the Bosnian tragedy, which was caused by Serb aggression and where a much earlier show of NATO force might have preserved the integrity of the multiethnic state of Bosnia and prevented some of the atrocities we are now lamenting). Here I agree with Mandelbaum: when exit becomes strategy, there is something rotten in the realm of foreign policy. There is also something rotten when the blame for failures is dumped on the United Nations, not only because UN fiascoes largely result from the failures, ambivalences, and confusions of member states but also because serious efforts at addressing the sources of crises will always necessitate collective interventions and coordinated efforts.

A third qualification concerns the need for public support. Mandelbaum offers two explanations for the lack of support for Clinton administration policies. One is that the interventions he deplores merely responded to the wishes of particular pressure groups in American society. This seems to me quite inaccurate, especially with regard to Somalia and Bosnia. Far more convincing is his argument that the public remained hostile (or in the Somalia affair, became hostile after the deaths of eighteen American soldiers) because the administration never provided a clear and persuasive account of American purposes. This charge is true. Although it has made some vague statements about expanding democracy, the Clinton administration has been much too timid in defining and defending a foreign policy based on values and other requirements of world order. American officials contradicted each other and themselves endlessly on Bosnia and never made the case for the Haitian intervention that Mandelbaum eloquently presents—an appeal to values and a reminder of responsibility.

Mandelbaum, however, would limit American purposes to two broad security interests (military presence in Europe and in the Asia-Pacific region and prevention of nuclear proliferation) and to trade. He does not seem to notice that the campaign against nuclear proliferation is at least as much about a world order as about protecting American lives; many potential proliferators are in no condition to threaten the United States, but they could create regional chaos and terror. Nor does he note that the drive for free trade reflects American values and beliefs—he himself assumes that "liberal economic policies . . . create wealth and expand freedom" (p. 29)—at least as much as American material interests.

My argument is that a foreign policy adapted to the world after the cold war must go beyond the purposes to which Mandelbaum wants to restrict it. It must include, on the grounds that they will maintain or restore world order, certain carefully selected interventions in foreign domestic crises. This is not a plea for foreign policy as "social work," a struggle against distress everywhere in the world. It is a reminder that certain levels and kinds of distress are morally unacceptable and certain political, economic, and social breakdowns too dangerous to world order to be ignored. That is what the administration has failed to explain. Perhaps it failed to do so because of its internal divisions between those, especially in the Pentagon, who think like Mandelbaum and those who think more like me. Perhaps it refrained because it sensed the public's reluctance to become involved abroad after forty-five years of cold war. But this only increased American's reluctance, which in turn drove the administration's obsession with exit dates and the avoidance of "mission creep." And since such restrictions on difficult missions are almost guarantees that the missions will fail, the end result is likely to be a retreat into the traditional foreign policy realm that Mandelbaum defends—at the cost of spreading chaos and misery abroad. For we live in a world in which apathy about what happens in "far away countries of which we know nothing" can all too easily lead—through contagion, through the message such moral passivity sends to troublemakers, would-be tyrants, and ethnic cleansers elsewhere—not to the kind of Armageddon we feared during the cold war but to a creeping escalation of disorder and beastliness that will, sooner or later, reach the shores of the complacent, the rich, and the indifferent.

11

<hr />

The Politics and Ethics
of Military Intervention

T he issue of military intervention in the internal affairs of states is central in a post–cold war international system characterized by the presence of many dangerous, troubled, failed, and even murderous states. Opponents of intervention stress the functions of sovereignty, while defenders rely on a mix of moral and pragmatic arguments. This chapter argues that military intervention is ethically justified when domestic turmoil threatens regional or international security and when massive violations of human rights occur. In most, but not necessarily all, cases the intervention should be organized or at least authorized by the UN Security Council, which should be given autonomous means and reorganized to enhance both its legitimacy and its capacity for action. The concept of the "national interest," most often cited by opponents of intervention as grounds for inaction, should be widened to incorporate ethical concerns.

Ethical arguments about political issues must, of course, take into account the realities of the political context and the "rules of the game" of the domestic or international political milieu. Since "ought implies can," a deontological ethic in which the definition of what is right is not derived from a calculation of what is possible condemns itself to irrelevance if its commands cannot be carried out in the world as it is.[1] But while we must admit that there is a huge gap between what is ethical and what is likely with regard to military interventions, we should not resign ourselves to the consequences of inaction but should rather take every opportunity to narrow that gap.

This chapter discusses the political and ethical issues raised by military interventions. It does not distinguish between cases in which intervention occurs with the formal consent of a government and those in which it does not, mainly because consent is not always voluntary or genuine. Initial consent may turn into resentment and hostility later on. Nor does it fully separate the political from the ethical aspects of intervention, because political actions, even when they are not preceded by any explicit discussion of moral concerns, always raise such issues. Even actions that seem to aim only at the establishment or restoration of order have implications for justice.

The Political Context

It is wrong to assume that the problem of intervention—which is as old as international relations—has become particularly salient only, or mainly, in the post–cold war world. The issue of intervention in domestic affairs was central during the cold war, when both superpowers tried to take advantage of the revolt against colonialism and of the rising tide of self-determination—as in the Belgian Congo and in Angola—and to export to other countries their very different conceptions of democracy, or to exploit domestic revolutions for their own purposes—as in Vietnam or Cuba. Both the Brezhnev doctrine and the Reagan doctrine proclaimed a highly nonhumanitarian *droit d'ingérence* (right to intervene), in order to crush emancipatory revolts among satellites (such as Hungary, Czechoslovakia, and Afghanistan) and in order to support anticommunist insurgents (such as in Nicaragua, Angola, and Afghanistan), respectively. Moreover, already in that era, civil strife among communities of multiethnic or multireligious states led to foreign intrusions—as in Cyprus, Lebanon, and Sri Lanka—or to bloody civil wars—as in Yemen and Nigeria. Three of the most successful interventions had little to do with the cold war: those of India in Bangladesh, Tanzania in Uganda, and Vietnam in Cambodia—three cases in which the intervener put an end to massive assaults on human rights.

What, then, has changed in the 1990s? First, with the end of the cold war, the emphasis has shifted from unilateral interventions—by the superpowers, by former colonial states like France or Belgium in their erstwhile colonies, or by countries such as the three mentioned above, taking advantage of the paralysis of a Security Council plagued by East-West rivalry—to collective interventions, mainly by the UN, now that the Security Council is no longer the victim of this contest.

Second, the world is discovering the dark side of the kind of order that was built, partly deliberately, partly by trial and error, during the cold war. This dark side had remained largely invisible while the cold war lasted. On the one hand, a tense and armed peace was preserved between the rival superpowers. But the weight and cost of the "military-industrial complex" became one of the major factors of stagnation and ossification of the Soviet Union and its empire. Former Soviet president Mikhail Gorbachev's attempt at reform led to the disintegration of the Soviet system. This, in turn, resulted in an overflow of ethnic conflicts over which the communist regime had for so long clamped a heavy lid—in Georgia, Azerbaijan, Moldova, the newly liberated Baltic states, and Chechnya. Similar conflicts broke out peacefully in Czechoslovakia and violently in Yugoslavia. Some of these conflicts resulted from old grievances. Moreover, both in Yugoslavia and in the former Soviet Union, communist leaders turned themselves into nationalist champions in order to keep, in their ethnic bailiwicks, the power that no longer functioned in a challenged or collapsing center.

On the other hand, the wave of decolonization that had brought about the formal independence of far more than one hundred new states was found to have led to something quite different from a mere extension of the so-called Westphalian system of sovereign states to the whole planet, through the destruction of colonial empires. Many of these states are remote indeed from the model of unitary and rational players that realists from Karl von Clausewitz and Max Weber to Hans Morgenthau and Raymond Aron had described as the basic units of the international system. Many are racked or wrecked by tribal, religious, or ethnic conflicts; many never managed to erect stable and effective state structures and have become the theater of battling gangs competing for power; some have become the preserves of satraps or autocrats ready to use the worst forms of repression in order to stay in office. The new states were often states in name only and, within borders artificially drawn by colonial masters, certainly not nation-states. We now face a large number of failed states, like Somalia or Liberia; troubled states, like Sudan, Sri Lanka, or Rwanda; and murderous states, like Libya, Iraq, or Haiti under the military regime of 1991–1994.

Thus, the system of sovereign states analyzed by students of world affairs is being undermined both from above and from below. It is threatened from above by two "revolutions" that affect sovereignty. There is the empirical revolution of interdependence and globalization that both deprives states of much of their "operational," that is, effective, sovereignty and transfers many of their previous functions to a largely private world capitalist economy that is beyond national control and under meager interstate control. The other is the normative revolution that erodes the content of sovereignty and restricts the rights, derived from sovereignty, that states were free to exercise at home—that is the human-rights part of the revolution—or both at home and abroad, in the case of the European Union's experiment in integration. The attack from below results from the multitude of totally or partially failed, troubled, and murderous states whose claims to sovereignty are either unsustainable or unacceptable. It results also from international terrorism.

As of 1995, the post–cold war international system is remarkable above all for two features. One is noticeable at the top of the hierarchy of sates, the other at the bottom. The latter we have just discussed: it is the crisis of the state in so many parts of the world. The former is the peculiar configuration (or is it the absence?) of that "society" of great powers Hedley Bull discussed.[2] While the system may be "unipolar," if power is defined in military terms, this is not the only important form of power today, nor does it tell us anything beyond the availability of abundant might: a dominant state must also have the will to use it, and this is conspicuously lacking in the United States today.[3] China is still only a potential great military and economic power; Japan and the European Union are major economic powers only; and Russia's crisis is far from over.

Thus, the political context for the 1990s is nebulous and is dominated by two large questions. First, is the present anomie on top a purely temporary state of affairs—a post–cold war withdrawal fling by the United States, a transitional muddle and turmoil in Russia, the tail end of Maoism combined with the beginning of capitalism in China, a gradual shift in Japan and in Europe from merely "civilian" toward all forms of power? If so, will, at the end of the transition, the system again be bipolar, with renewed tensions between the two largest nuclear states, or will it be a global multipolar one? Will the "top of the hierarchy" shape up, so to speak, and act as a kind of steering group of the sort that existed in the days of the European Concert or that was assumed by the drafters of the UN Charter? If not, will the absence of such a steering group lead to a kind of global fragmentation and to the emergence of regional powers dominating regional subsystems? These are only some of the possibilities. The only two that seem thoroughly improbable are Francis Fukuyama's "end of history" (even in a purely Hegelian sense) and Samuel Huntington's "clash of civilization" (a mushy amalgam, a bundle of unexplored and dubious connections between religion, culture, civilization, state, and strife).[4]

Second, will the "floor" of states be repaired so that out of the present turbulence new, workable states will emerge, either along ethnic or religious lines or in the form of carefully balanced multiethnic or multireligious enterprises? Or will there be even more failed, troubled, and murderous states (one can think of quite a number of candidates in Africa, Asia, and the Balkans)? It is clear only that, should the second alternative prevail, the opportunities for successful mastery of chaos by the society of states will be few, and the risks of external, uncontrolled interventions, as well as the cost in innocent lives, will be high. Moreover, given the power of and interests engaged in the ever more integrated, cosmopolitan capitalist economy, the spread of chaos in the state system might lead to a two-tier international milieu produced by the dialectic of globalization and fragmentation:[5] at one level, all the effective states engaged in the ups and downs, the gains and losses, of world capitalism and at the other, a set of poor and either disintegrating or isolated societies left to fend—and to feud—for themselves.

One of the reasons such a gloomy form of triage might occur is the change in what it would be a bit inaccurate to call world public opinion but could be called the prevailing mood, especially in the West. Between 1991 and 1993—from the end of the 1991 Gulf war to the misfortunes of the UN in Somalia and Yugoslavia—a kind of euphoria about collective action for good causes, leading to a new and better world order, built up around what the French champion of humanitarian intervention Bernard Kouchner had called the *droit d'ingérence*—a right to intervention for humanitarian reasons that overrides sovereignty. Traditional interpretations of international law and of the UN Charter that denied the legality of such forcible intrusions were declared obsolete, partly because of the new salience of human rights, partly because the newly favored intrusions were presented as collective ones, authorized by the UN, rather than unilateral resorts to force. The expansion of UN peacekeeping activities, particularly in areas where the cold war was being liquidated (Angola, Mozambique, El Salvador, Nicaragua, Afghanistan, and Cambodia) fed this new enthusiasm for the world organization, whose prestige had also been boosted by success in the Gulf war. The media played an important role, both in shifting their attention from the superpower rivalry that had been their main focus for so long to the long neglected scene of nationalism, ethnic strife, and humanitarian disasters and in emphasizing the potential of the UN. But the tide has turned since 1993–

1994. The successes of the UN now loom less large than the failures—or at least the perceived failures: Somalia (where the record is complex); Rwanda (where indeed the UN did not cover itself with glory); and above all Yugoslavia (where, as Michael Ignatieff has argued, the better may well have been the enemy of the best: "the strategies we chose made it impossible to adopt ones that could have done better").[6] In the earlier phase, the opponents of even a collective *droit d'ingérence* seemed to lose the debate with the enthusiasts. Now, the opposite appears to be the case. It is as if the motto "we should, therefore we must" had been replaced with "we can't, therefore we ought not"; or as if the imperative of doing good had yielded to a far more pessimistic appraisal: "there is little good we can do, and some of the good we try to do produces more harm than good—so let us above all not do harm, even if it means caring less about doing good."

The Intervention Debate

The debate on the ethics and legitimacy of intervention is complex, not only because the moral and political stakes are high but also because interventions in domestic affairs comprise a multiplicity of forms (from bribes, financial incentives, and gentle pressures to the use of force) and (even when they consist of only of military operations) can cover a wide range of cases. So far we have emphasized failed, troubled, and murderous states, but the crumbling of the wall that used to separate—conceptually at least—domestic from international affairs has also raised another tricky issue.[7] This is the problem of states, not necessarily "evil" or disorderly, that pursue, as sovereigns, dangerous domestic policies that could lead to international catastrophes, either for the environment (a subject for which military interventions are not directly relevant) or for the security of neighbors or whole regions, through the production or acquisition of nuclear weapons and other weapons of mass destruction (a danger against which the use of force may well appear as the last resort, should persuasion, pressures, guarantees, and sanctions fail). The arguments for and against intervention vary depending on the issue at stake.

The case against military interventions has a hard core: it is the defense of the norm of sovereignty, cornerstone of the interstate order since the seventeenth century. Sovereignty is seen by its champions not as a license for excesses or atrocities at home or abroad but as a protection of a society's individuals and groups from external control—benevolent, perhaps, but alien and imposed. The sovereign state is deemed to be the protector of the security and property of its subjects, as in Hobbes's *Leviathan*; or the guardian of their rights, as in John Locke and John Stuart Mill; or the expression of their collective will, as in Rousseau. Even if, in practice, the state is one that violates some of these rights, assaults the security and property of some of its subjects, and lacks a "general will" because of a clash of antagonistic group wills that tear the society apart, foreign intrusion is still seen as a greater evil.

Two of the three great theories of international politics—realism, Marxism, and liberalism—have supported this stance. Realism, in Reverend Bryan Hehir's words, argues that "expanding the frequency of intervention, cutting it off from a national-interest foundation, and undertaking broadly defined tasks in unstable political settings will yield the combination of good intentions and bad consequences (for ourselves and for others) that have so often doomed Liberal policies."[8] Realists also warn that interventions in domestic affairs multiply and amplify the factors of turmoil (instead of insulating them), whereas in a world of competing, self-interested actors, moderation or restraint provide the only chance for order. (Note, however, that on an issue like weapons of mass destruction in the hands of dangerous states, the calculus of "bad consequences" may lead to a plea for intervention, for instance, against North Korea, Iraq, or Iran, and that in this case intervention is seen as resting solidly on a national-interest foundation.)

Marxism and its offspring, dependency theory, have also taken a dim view of intervention, not because of a concern for order or out of love for sovereignty but because of the likelihood that intervention, whether unilateral or collective, will mean, in practice, the triumph of the powerful over the poor and powerless and the exploitation of the latter by the capitalist interests that dominate many of the major powers. It is an argument that still finds approval among the leaders of many former colonized states—including very large ones such as India—where the fear of neocolonialism is widespread. This fear is reinforced not only by the fact that many former colonies have become troubled states, with deep internal rifts and minority conflicts that might invite outside interference, but also by evidence that most interventions carefully respect the sovereignty of the great powers, or at least avoid raising the specter of a resort to force insofar as they are concerned.

Liberalism, in contrast, has always been divided over the issue of intervention.[9] The debate about whether such liberal goods as self-government and self-determination—two forms of emancipation from autocracy and arbitrariness—are to be exported, especially by force (an instrument of power that liberalism aims at curbing) has been raging for two centuries. Such prominent and thoughtful liberals as Mill and Michael Walzer have attempted to find a middle ground—in Walzer's case, intervention is justified when self-determination is at stake, when genocide is being committed, and, more broadly (and recently), in order "to put a stop to actions that, to use an old-fashioned but accurate phrase, shock the conscience of humankind."[10]

Indeed, it is liberals who have been the most fervent champions of intervention, or rather critics of the dogmas of sovereignty and nonintervention. One can summarize their case in three points.

First, sovereignty is not an absolute good. While it has great value in protecting a people from outside arbitrariness and rule, the state that claims sovereignty deserves respect only as long as it protects the basic rights of its subjects. It is from their rights that it derives its own. When it violates them, what Walzer calls "the presumption of fit" between the government and the governed vanishes, and the state's claim to full sovereignty falls with it.

Second, the central moral issue is not the defense of a people constituted as a state against outside predators but the weighing of conflicting ethical claims: there are circumstances in which the moral good of sovereignty must yield to superior imperatives, those of "global humanity"—the protection of human beings from intolerable evils such as the violation of their fundamental rights to life and security.[11] The risks of abuses of power by the intervener and of imperialism operating under the mass of benevolence are not ignored, but they should be neutralized by a process of collective intervention, or collective authorization and control of unilateral action. As Hehir has noted, the liberal position tries to find a compromise between the "legal tradition" of the post-Westphalian order, based on sovereignty and the state's right to use force, and the old moral tradition of the just-war doctrine, which vindicated intervention as the expression of "solidarity with those who had been victims of an injustice"—as "a morally prescribed duty, not an offense against a ruler's right." While the old Christian doctrine looked for just causes of war in the relations *among* states, a modern version needs to define such causes for interventions *in* states—a more difficult task, because just causes of war protect states from aggression and hence defend "the system of sovereign states," whereas intervention "threatens an already fragile system by challenging the one principle of authority (the state) in the system."[12] Another way of putting it is that the just-war doctrine traditionally tried to reconcile order and justice, whereas a theory of just intervention risks putting justice (to individuals and groups within a state) above order (which the states presumably ensure).

The third argument is squarely about order. Liberals defend intervention as a necessary means against chaos in a world in which domestic strife and violence risk spreading rapidly beyond borders, if only in the form of masses of pitiful refugees crossing into reluctant neighboring states, and also in a world of conflicting and dangerous unilateral interventions supporting different factions. Insofar as the phenomenon of failed, troubled, and murderous states is a disease of the Westphalian system, interventions can be interpreted as attempts at restoring a modified Westphalian state system—modified insofar as sovereignty can be curbed or overridden in certain circumstances. The argument for overriding it in the name of order is even stronger in cases of what I have termed "dangerous" states, whose domestic policies create mortal threats for regional or global security (as well as for the basic rights of people threatened by such states).

Realists have attacked the case for intervention because, in their opinion, it requires of "normal" states that they no longer base their policies on the national interest. This is obviously not true when there is a threat posed by a dangerous state. Actually, the liberal case for intervention requires that realists give a new, broader, and more farsighted definition of the national interest. The "national interest" is an expression that cries out for deconstruction. It covers two sorts of goals. Some can be called *imperatives* that result from the nature of international society: the need to provide for survival, for security against attack, and for basic economic security in a world of scarcity. But states—and not only the big ones—have always aimed at more: there is a vast category of *chosen preferences* (for instance, for the United States, free trade, or encouragement to democratic institutions, or the promotion of freedom of information). This is close to Arnold Wolfers's old distinction between possession goals and milieu goals.[13] The case for intervention is a case for the importance of milieu goals: our preferences for an international society in which neither the injustices nor the disorders associated with domestic strife and violations of basic rights will run wild should make it clear that certain interventions, even in crises that do not affect our physical or economic security directly and visibly, are in the "national interest." To quote Walzer again:

> All states have an interest in global stability and even in global humanity, and in the case of wealthy and powerful states like ours, this interest is

seconded by obligation. . . . Grossly uncivilised behavior . . . unchallenged, tends to spread, to be imitated or reiterated. Pay the moral price for silence and callousness, and you will soon have to pay the political price of turmoil and lawlessness nearer home. . . . Now obligation is seconded by interest.[14]

For democratic states especially, the "national interest" has an ethical component.

This unresolved debate has been going on for several years. Opponents of intervention have rarely argued that interference in domestic affairs (even apart from the issue of dangerous states) is never justified; several Third World states that are, in principle, hostile to intervention because of their fear of great-power imperialism have either intervened at times themselves (India in Bangladesh and Sri Lanka, for example) or advocated intervention in select cases (Muslim states for Bosnia). Often the opponents have relied more on arguments about feasibility and consequences than on principles. As for the advocates of intervention, they are the ones who have relied above all on a moral stance of doing good or of preventing such harm as famine and ethnic cleansing. But they have often been vague about the criteria for legitimate intervention, as well as about settling the question of who should be entitled to intervene legitimately and what purposes and methods are desirable and likely to succeed. It may well be that none of the "currently leading moral theories inside the academic community can really help us decide when we should rescue . . . (and whom first), and how."[15] And yet this is the essential task.

Intervention: When, Who, What For, and How?

When?

The first question is this: When is intervention in a domestic crisis, or against a state that pursues dangerous policies, right? When should it be permissible to push aside claims of sovereignty? The UN has proceeded case by case and avoided any general statement listing criteria for future actions. But from this cautious approach and from the arguments of academic specialists, two quite different criteria have emerged, and they deserve to be endorsed, even though they provide only partial guidance.[16] One is the case of domestic situations that are deemed to constitute threats to international peace and security, that is, crises and policies whose external repercussions are severe enough to take them out of the "sacred domain" of purely domestic jurisdiction. The UN Security Council has often invoked this argument in recent years, in cases such as the plight of the Kurds in northern Iraq, the Bosnian tragedy, the collapse of law and order in Somalia, and the fight against the military gang that overthrew President Jean-Bertrand Aristide in Haiti. The danger lies in the possible arbitrariness of the Security Council, which might apply this criterion capriciously, either by invoking threats to international security when they are not at all obvious or by failing to recognize such threats in cases where, for whatever reason, intervention is deemed unwise (one may ask: Why Somalia but not the Sudan? Why the Kurds in Iraq but not the Shiites in Iraq or the Kurds in Turkey?).

The second criterion has not been expressly acknowledged by the UN, but it has been proposed by many authors; it is a return to the traditional concept of humanitarian intervention in cases of "massive and systematic suffering,"[17] a repudiation of the view that the UN Charter rules out any resort to force except in cases of individual and collective self-defense against armed attack. The UN has preferred to bring such cases under the umbrella of "threats to peace," because the Charter declares that only "enforcement measures under Chapter VII," which deals with such threats, can override the principle of nonintervention in internal affairs. But a case can be made for considering that instances of "gross abuse of the security of people"[18] should be seen as ipso facto threats to peace and international security. All that is required is the view that the peace of the graveyard is not true peace and that it is in the long-term "interest" of all not to settle for a world "order" in which such abuses are overlooked; and the idea that these should be treated as calling for intervention, given the development of the international law of human rights, even when (as, say, in East Timor) it would be difficult to argue that the terror inflicted on the population has immediate repercussions on the neighbors, for instance, through flows of refugees or the peril of a wider war.[19]

The problem with this criterion is the difficulty of defining the scope of the evil that would justify intervention. Should it be only genocide, as Walzer had originally argued? (The Genocide Convention states that signatories can bring such cases before the organs of the UN.) The scope and nature of recent atrocities, and the rather narrow definition of genocide in this convention, make it necessary to go further and include such acts as deliberate and brutal "ethnic cleansing." My own criterion would be massive violations of human rights, which would encompass genocide, ethnic cleansing, brutal and large-scale repression to force a population into submission, including deliberate policies of barbarism, as well as the kinds of famines, massive breakdowns of law and order, epidemics, and flights of refugees that occur when a "failed state" collapses. A recent international report suggests that such a criterion would require an amendment to the UN Charter.[20] Given the difficulty of changing this document, especially in an area as sensitive as this one, it would be better to resort to the interpretation suggested above: a broader milieu-goal-oriented definition of peace and security. To be sure, the weakness of this criterion is that it fails to specify what constitutes a "massive violation." But, as in the case of the definition of aggression, no attempt at providing a list could ever be complete, and some leeway is politically necessary, anyway. There will always be arguments about whether some situation, act, or policy belongs in a certain category or not, but this does not make categorization any less useful as the trigger for specific kinds of moves.[21]

There is a second meaning to the question "when?": not only under what conditions, but also at what moment, if those conditions exist? Much has been written recently about the imperative of prevention. The record, in this respect, is tragically bad, as recent studies of Somalia, Rwanda, and Yugoslavia have shown.[22] The problem lies both in the resistance of governments, which, when their country is in trouble, tend to fear that outside meddling will further weaken their authority, and in the "myopia" of the outside governments, which are usually too busy with crises that have already broken out elsewhere and reluctant to indulge in the cost-intensive investment of energy and imagination that prevention would require.[23] Nongovernmental organizations (NGOs) may provide excellent monitoring services and send out warning signals—but these still need to be picked up. In his *Agenda for Peace*, UN Secretary-General Boutros Boutros-Ghali argued strongly for "preventive deployment" even in the case of a crisis within a country, accompanying efforts ranging from humanitarian assistance to conciliation. But the necessity of consent by the government may well limit the possibilities for such "deployments," and there may be, in practice, a conflict between respect of the state's sovereignty, which he stresses, and the duty of neutrality and impartiality, which he also states:[24] being neutral between a minority that wants a special status, or even secession, and the country's government may not be quite what either this government or the rebels desire from outsiders. Nor is it likely that a failed state will be easily persuaded to consent to a kind of preventive international receivership and reconstruction formula. And yet, there may be cases when the government of a failed state calls in an international force to prevent the breakdown of law and order (and such a force will be effective only if it is mandated and ready to impose its authority). Indeed, prevention is so obviously preferable to action once a crisis has already provoked extensive misery that coordinated efforts by NGOs, regional organizations, and the UN should be given maximum attention and resources. Precisely because of the political delicacy and explosiveness of domestic crises, this is a field in which the UN Secretary-General—backed up by the informal diplomatic mechanism of "Friends of the Secretary-General"—should concentrate his efforts. Indicators of breakdown and impending strike are necessary and easy to devise. But they have to be plugged in to alerted and active diplomatic mechanisms—private, national, regional, and international.

If, as in the past, prevention fails, intervention may have to become coercive and resort to diplomatic, economic, or financial sanctions or to force. Should such intervention, as a UN official has argued, be only "a measure of last resort, to be applied only when all other remedies or means of pressure have been exhausted"?[25] While in principle this guidance appears sensible, in reality things are not so clear cut. By the time those other remedies have demonstrably failed, the kind of coercive intervention necessary may be much larger and burdensome—or else quite ineffective and too late to stop troublemakers and to save those who could have been rescued by an earlier action. In Somalia, Rwanda, and Haiti this seems to have been the case. There will always be some who argue that all peaceful or diplomatic remedies have not been exhausted. It is impossible to prescribe a course in the abstract, but the idea of the last resort should not be endorsed uncritically.

Who?

The second question is this: Who is entitled to intervene? The defenders of sovereignty have built their case largely against unilateral (and therefore, in all likelihood, self-interested) interventions. The presumption against these needs to be maintained. But it should not be an absolute prohibition. As I have suggested elsewhere, unilateral interventions in crises meeting the two criteria described above (threats to international peace and massive humanitarian violations of human rights) should be deemed legitimate in the following cases.[26]

- when they are authorized by the UN or by a regional organization operating at the request or with the consent of the UN (for example, the Security Council's "licensing" of France in Rwanda or the UN and the Organization of American States [OAS]'s more circumscribed consent to the United States in Haiti). In such instances, the intervening power should allow for its actions to be monitored by, and report to, the UN or the regional organization involved.

- when the UN has been incapable of dealing with such a case, either because of paralysis of its political organs or because the action it took has failed to reach its objectives, and when whatever regional organization competent to deal with the case has also been inactive or impotent. Such a unilateral intervention would be legitimate whenever it is "calculated to cause less damage to the target society than would inaction,"[27] and the intervening state should explain and report its moves to the UN and to the relevant regional organization and try to obtain an endorsement. This is the procedure that should have been followed in the cases of Bangladesh, Uganda, and Cambodia (in which the interveners chose to argue that they were acting in self-defense).

- when the intervener provides help to a democratically elected government that fights a rebellion supported from abroad or moves to prevent a foreign-backed force from imposing its will on a resisting or hostile population (such as U.S. support to the resistance in Afghanistan). Here again, reporting to the UN or the relevant regional organization would be necessary.

The trickiest case is that of "dangerous states," whose policies could threaten the peace and security of an area or the world. Nuclear proliferation and the proliferation of means of mass destruction undoubtedly constitute a "threat to the international system as such"; as a result, as Bryan Hehir has pointed out, states with the capacity to destroy the nuclear installations or the plants that produce other weapons of mass destruction in such states could be tempted to assert their power to intervene unilaterally. Hehir insists that in these cases "the desired norm should be multilateral authorization prior to any miliary action."[28] This is desirable in principle. But one can imagine cases in which the UN or the relevant regional grouping has failed to deal with the issue, and the state (say, the United States) that presses for action (against, say, Iraq or Iran) has made a strong case to show (1) that there is not just a potential and general distant danger but a clear, specific, and present one, resulting not only from the nature of the dangerous state's regime and from the explosive character of the region but also from evidence about its programs and activities; and (2) that nonmilitary means of persuasion and pressure have failed. One should not rule out unilateral action as a last resort in such circumstances.

As for collective interventions, they would be legitimate as long as one of the two criteria discussed above has been met and the operations have been duly mandated by the UN or by a regional organization it calls upon or approves. From the viewpoint of global legitimacy, despite all the reservations that the present composition of the Security Council provokes, the UN remains the main source of authority. Regional organizations are too often either embroiled in or neutralized by disputes among or within states of the region, or else lacking in means of enforcement.

What For? and How?

The third set of questions concerns legitimate intervention: What for and how? What methods should be used? The methods and means depend largely on the goals, and it is those that need to be examined first. Leaving aside the question of the dangerous states—where the goal of intervention is obviously to get them to desist from provocative and threatening or harmful policies, and, depending on what these are, a whole range of measures, from rewards to sanctions, from deals and guarantees to military actions (overt or covert) could be used—and concentrating on the failed, troubled, and murderous states, three strategies are conceivable.

The minimalist one would restrict intervention strictly to *humanitarian policies*, to relief for the victims of man-made disasters (or natural disasters, such as droughts or famines, aggravated by a government's refusal to accept outside assistance or by the government's or the feuding factions' looting of such assistance), the delivery of food and medical aid, and care for refugees and displaced persons. This is the original case and scope for humanitarian intervention—what might be called the Red Cross approach. It needs to be a bit more muscular, insofar as the international rescuers might be authorized to use force to protect their operations from such interferences as hostile raids or blockades.

A second position would go further and follow Rosalyn Higgins's argument, according to which humanitarian operations can function only within a secure environment.[29] The first task would thus be to provide one, which in the case of troubled and failed states would require an end to violence—through truces and cease-fires—and also, in the case of failed states, at least a temporary international supervision of the country. In the case of murderous states, the minimum would be (as in Iraq) a prohibition imposed on the government to refrain from any further repression of its enemies. This second strategy could be called *peace enforcement* (understood simply as the end of violence). It is clear that it entails not only "peaceful" and impartial peacekeeping activities (such as may be required for the preservation of cease-fires) but also the need for and risk of far greater resorts to force than in the "minimalist" approach, for instance, in order to oblige a party, faction, or gang to stop fighting or murdering, or to prevent one side from violating a cease-fire, or to protect the victims of domestic repression from renewed governmental attack. When "safe havens" aimed at protecting people from assault are not defended by the interveners who have established them, as has been the case for years in Bosnia, this approach becomes an obvious sham.

The third strategy is far more ambitious. It is based on a critique of the other two. Humanitarian intervention is deemed to be well meaning but fundamentally insufficient, often naive and self-defeating. As long as the causes of the humanitarian disasters have not been addressed, very little will be accomplished. On the one hand, treating these cases according to the "natural disaster model"—equating massacres with floods or ethnic cleansing with earthquakes—is a form of evasion and may end up prolonging the agony: Sarajevans are kept alive so that snipers can pick them off. On the other hand, even Red Cross–type relief may have political effects, when it helps keep one party or ethnic group fighting or tacitly accepts and assists ethnic cleansing, or provokes the hostility of the forces that caused the disasters.[30]

Even peace enforcement may be too little: in civil wars, cease-fires rarely hold (and when they do, as in Cyprus, they may harden lines of partition that one side deems illegitimate, making a settlement more difficult since it appears less urgent). As long as the contending factions have not given up their weapons (as Boutros-Ghali tried in vain to get the Americans to force them to do in Somalia in early 1993); as long as the failed state has not been able to rebuild both a political process and a set of effective institutions; as long as the tyrant responsible for violations of basic rights has not been removed (as in Iraq), or his democratic successor has not been helped to disband the police and armed forces set up by the fallen tyrant and to establish an impartial judicial system (as in Haiti under Aristide), the intervention will risk being a failure, or a Sisyphean effort that needs to be repeated again and again.

This third position is clearly far more demanding. It requires more diplomacy to achieve political settlements and reconciliation and even more extensive uses of force—to disarm contenders, to oblige a reluctant party to accept a settlement agreed to by its foe and by the international interveners, or to remove a tyrant from power. It may require observers or peacekeepers to monitor elections or to oversee the execution of a political settlement and a willingness to play, in failed states, a role comparable to that which colonial powers played in protectorates or to what the League of Nations and the UN did in mandates and trusteeships. This approach could be called *resolution*.

This analysis leads to two conclusions. First (and this is essential), all three strategies entail a possible resort to force on different scales and for a variety of purposes. Therefore, instead of putting "peacekeeping" forces that are unarmed or only lightly armed into impossible situations (such as protecting safe havens under attack or monitoring a fragile cease-fire or political agreement without having the means to oblige the parties to carry out the promises that accompanied it, as in Croatia and Rwanda), it is necessary

- to invent a new category that could be called peace enforcing and would cover the cases of military action envisaged both by the second and by the third approach. It would consist of a UN capability for limited military operations, provided by the members either ad hoc or on a standby basis, or else by the kind of volunteer force suggested by Brian Urquhart.[31] Such a force would function under Chapter VII of the UN Charter.
- to recognize that enforcement actions under Chapter VII can take two forms: the peace-enforcing forces that would play a role in the domestic affairs of failed, troubled, and murderous states; and the collective security operations aimed at combating aggression, as in the 1991 Gulf war. If the special agreements envisaged by Article 43 of the Charter should ever see the light of day, they, and the Military Staff Committee or Article 47, should have jurisdiction over both.

The second conclusion is that whereas the second and third positions (peace enforcement and resolution) are not incompatible—the second, in a sense, leads to the third—there is a conflict between the first and the other two. Humanitarian action is extremely difficult to carry out when there is no peace, and giving priority to it may be doubly disastrous in such a case: it risks being ineffectual or at the mercy of the combatants, and yet the attempt to carry it out regardless may deter the interveners from taking the forceful actions required by peace enforcement, because they might compromise the relief efforts and threaten the safety of those who deliver the assistance.

This is precisely what happened in Yugoslavia. Indeed, the Yugoslav fiasco combines two huge errors. The first was to treat the conflict between Bosnia and Serbia—two states recognized by international society, two members of the UN—as if it were either a civil war requiring impartiality from the interveners or an interstate dispute requiring no more than mediation of the kind envisaged by Chapter VI, whereas a very strong case can be made that Bosnia was the victim of aggression by Serbia and that even after Serbia formally accepted the Contact Group's peace plan, it continued in fact to support the Bosnian Serbs in their war against the government of Serbia. Under Chapter VII, Bosnia was entitled to international assistance and, of course, to the right of individual and collective self-defense recognized by Article 51.

The second error was to give priority both to humanitarian action and to a political settlement (in both instances, with little or no backing by force). The former had limited good effects as well as large perverse ones. The settlement turned out elusive and ever receding, because the Serbs continued to impose their own "realities" by force: ethnic cleansing and territorial conquests. The UN stance of impartiality left the United Nations Protection Force (UNPROFOR) at the mercy of Serb obstruction and was incompatible with the meager efforts to save parts of Bosnia. In Bosnia, priority ought to have been given to peace enforcement: an end to ethnic atrocities and to land grabs by the Serbs. This would have required the use of force to protect not only UNPROFOR (which soon gave up protecting itself) but also the Bosnians. The quest for a political settlement should have followed—once no side was any longer engaged in imposing its solution—and it would probably have been unsuccessful without threats to use force against the reluctant party—in all likelihood, the Serbs. As for the conflict between Croatia and Serbia, it would also have required a far greater willingness to use force both in order to enforce the terms of the cease-fire set by the 1992 agreement brokered by the former U.S. secretary of state Cyrus Vance and in order to get the parties at least to a partial settlement of the Yugoslav war.[32]

This war has made it clear once more that, among the various forms or means of intervention, the resort of force (which, to repeat, may be needed for all three types of purposes) poses special problems. The timidity of UNPROFOR, NATO, and their political bosses in resorting to force has provoked the resentment of the victimized Bosnians, but the use of force by United Nations Operations in Somalia (UNOSOM II) against one of the main warlords of Somalia, which caused casualties among the civilians UNOSOM was supposed to protect, led to bitterness among Somalians. Two issues deserve a brief discussion.

One is—again—that of timing. Should force be used only as a last resort, after other means of coercion, such as economic sanctions, have failed? One problem with those other means, and with such sanctions in particular, is that they operate very gradually, and, as we have seen in Haiti, former Yugoslavia, and Iraq, they risk being ineffective insofar as they fail to change the behavior of the targeted governments.[33] Sanctions have often turned out to be easily violated—embargoes can be sieves. Not only are they often of dubious political effectiveness (except in circumstances such as Rhodesia and South Africa, where they had the support of the black population as well as nearly universal outside application and thus helped to produce the change of heart and policy of the whites in power), but they also tend to hit the wrong people. They impose heavy costs on the poorer states that apply them, and in the targeted country (which is likely not to be a democracy!) they fall on the under-privileged and the innocent, while the governments, police, and military manage to survive reasonably well. Outside actors who oppose, or are fearful of, military actions because of their brutality and blemishes and their possible cost in lives—of soldiers and civilians—often find it easy to hide, so to speak, behind the argument that more time is needed for the sanctions or the diplomatic pressure to become effective—and during that time many more lives may be lost, both because of the crisis that has provoked the intervention and because of deteriorating conditions of health or nutrition in countries hit by embargoes.

There are situations in which a quick, early use of force may well be the best method, and the only one capable of preventing a further aggravation of the crisis: not, for reasons indicated above, in cases of dangerous states (in which an early resort to force would constitute preventive war—and violate the UN Charter) but in cases where massive violations of rights are being committed (as in Yugoslavia at the time of the Serb shelling of Dubrovnik or in Haiti after the military coup of 1991).

The second issue concerns the amount of force to be applied. Here, we should be wary of the so-called Weinberger and Powell doctrines, which were derived from the (highly debatable) "lessons of Vietnam." The idea that force should be used overwhelmingly or not at all is unacceptable. Many of the purposes for which military means may have to be used require limited amounts of force, which can have a successful deterrent or even compelling effect when they are clear manifestations of a will to reach the objectives set for the operation and to escalate if this turns out to be necessary. Moreover, the model of overwhelming force risks (even in a case of collective security against aggression) violating the old *jus in bello* requirements of proportionality and noncombatant immunity. Indeed, military intervention in failed, troubled, or murderous states, whatever the level of necessary force may be, should take as its basic imperative the protection of civilian lives, even if operations have to be waged against a gang, or a leader, who tries to obstruct, or even is the target of, the operation.

The idea that such military means should be used only when there is a quasi certainty of success and a clear exit strategy needs also to be taken with a pinch of salt. I would rather emphasize specific, well-defined objectives than an "exit strategy" (reaching the former may well require postponing exit). As for chances of success, they depend in part on the nature of the objectives (some may be beyond reach, others not; some may only be reachable at an unreasonable cost) and in part on the skills of the military leaders. Preserving a noncommunist South Vietnam without the massive presence of U.S. forces, and in the absence of an effective South Vietnamese government, was indeed unachievable. Using force against a highly mobilized and resistant population has often turned out to be self-defeating (witness Afghanistan, or Israel versus the Palestinians). But the cases envisaged here are very different from those. While many of them may require only limited uses of force, the chances of success will depend largely on the extent to which the means engaged are adequate for the purposes set by the interveners and these purposes fit the crisis at hand.

Prospects

We have, so far, dealt with what ought to be done. But in few areas is the gap between what is ethically desirable and what is politically likely and possible so large as in the area of military intervention. Thus, what is likely to happen is very different from my prescriptions.

First, it is far from obvious that the presumption against unilateral interventions will be observed and that the conditions suggested above for such interventions will be respected. Would the United States do nothing, for example, if a crisis in Cuba provoked huge flows of refuges trying to reach U.S. shores and resulted in a power struggle or civil strife of such proportions as to tempt Washington into intervening in the name of democracy? Can one expect France—especially under its present, activist president—to refrain from interfering in its former African colonies' affairs, should some of these become failed or troubled states; or even into an Algerian civil war, if it created vast flows of refugees and threatened French lives and property in Algeria on a large scale? Above all, will Russia give up its claim to protect the twenty-five million Russians in the "near abroad," despite the evidence, produced by the war in Chechnya, of the physical, psychological, and political costs of such operations? Would Israel remain passive if a power struggle in post-Hussein Jordan, or in a Lebanon no longer controlled by Syria, or in a Palestinian state, led to the victory of violently anti-Israeli Islamists? Would Iran, Turkey, or Syria remain passive if Iraq went into political, ethical, or religious convulsions? The potential for unilateral interventions based on claims of self-defense (more or less loosely defined) is great—even though some states have found out how unrewarding or exhausting such exercises may be (India in Sri Lanka, Vietnam in Cambodia, and Cuba in Angola).

Second, the recent past teaches us, if not to despair, at least to worry about the capacity of collective (and especially UN-sponsored) intervention to cope with the troubles that plague so many states. There are three sets of reasons for pessimism.

The first concerns the state of domestic opinion in many countries. In the democratic countries of Western Europe and North America, as well as in Japan, enthusiasm for military intervention is missing. Humanitarian operations are often the maximum the public accepts (indeed, it tends to demand them), and peacekeeping in situations where peace exists is tolerated or welcomed, but even in countries (such as France) that are not in thrall to what I once called America's new doctrine of (American) combatant immunity, the willingness to put one's soldiers at risk except in self-defense, or in cases in which there is no immediate and visible connection to national security, when narrowly and traditionally defined, is anemic. In the United States, both the Clinton administration's Presidential Decision Directive (PDD) 25, which sharply restricts U.S. participation in collective interventions, and the Republicans' hostility to the UN show how little political support there is for activist multilateralism. As for many of the formerly colonized, nonaligned, or developing countries, they remain suspicious even of collective interventions, both because of the prominent role played by the major powers, with their imperialist past, in promoting such enterprises and because most of the cases of intervention in domestic wars have occurred in Africa, Asia, or Latin America and affected small and poor states. This is why Boutros-Ghali once referred to the situation in former Yugoslavia as a conflict of the rich.

Second, disagreements among states about the purposes that international intervention ought to seek tend to result either in the avoidance of hard cases or hard choices or in minimalist or fuzzy UN resolutions. The desire of the great powers to maintain close relations among themselves—especially between the United States and Russia—has led to a kind of continuous dilution of the UN undertaking in former Yugoslavia. There simply is, at present, no international consensus on the need to act preventively against states that use their sovereign rights to pursue policies dangerous for humanity. While a consensus has developed, case by case, around UN actions (based on consent) for the monitoring of elections or for brokering reconciliation among factions, there is no agreement on either the goal of establishing democracy or the means necessary to do so and to nurture it. Saving the victimized subjects of a tyrannical and evil government remains a highly controversial issue, perhaps because so many governments fear that licensing interventions against one may boomerang at their own expense; the Organization of African Unity has been particularly insistent on nonintervention, and the OAS, despite the recent Santiago commitment to democracy, remains hesitant to sponsor operations in which the United States would be likely to provide most of the means and influence.

In civil wars, the fear of entrapment has led many members of the UN (backed by the secretary-general) to emphasize the duty of impartiality and neutrality, which inhibits a resort to force even when it would help the UN operation reach its goals (as was the case during the 1960–1961 Congo crisis). And when the cause of a civil conflict or of the failure of a state is ethnic or religious strife, despite the ritual and quasi-universal commitment to the "people's right to self-determination," deep divisions exist between those who believe that this norm must lead to borders based on ethnic or religious demarcation lines and those who think that formulas of "consociationalism" or federalism or schemes for the protection of minorities might save multicultural or multiethnic societies. Discussions in the Contact Group about the future of Bosnia have been marked by acrobatic and so far fruitless attempts at reconciling these two conflicting points of view.

The lessons of Somalia may be important for the future handling of failed states: the Security Council's resolutions remained very vague in prescribing the methods of political settlement and for the "re-establishment of national and regional institutions and civil administration." As a result, the operation was plagued by a rift between those who (like the United States—some of the time) wanted to rebuild political life "from the bottom up" (according to the model some authors have called "encouraging new institutions")[34] and those (particularly in the UN bureaucracy) who preferred the model of "accommodating existing forces" and of working with the factional leaders, from the top down. This rift did much to reduce the UN's capacity to reach a political solution, which would, in any case, have required the disarmament—never enforced—and the demobilization of the gang's militias—never requested—by the Security Council.

Third, there is a gap—some would call it an abyss—between the magnitude of the problems discussed here and the collective capabilities at the disposal of the UN and regional organizations. The UN has neither the financial resources (witness the plight of the admirable and overburdened United Nations High Commissioner for Refugees) nor the military means that would be required, and the number of cases and crises exceeds the diplomatic capacity of the secretary-general. As a result, there may often be a discrepancy between a vaguely but ambitiously defined mission and the tools available to carry it out: in Somalia, UNOSOM II was given a much broader mandate than the American force it was replacing, but it was much weaker. Nor was the meager force sent (belatedly) to Rwanda capable of helping many of the victims of the genocide perpetrated by the Hutu extremists. Nor was UNPROFOR at any time provided with the means that could have made it successful in enforcing the 1992 cease-fire between Croatia and Serbia.

Moreover, collective operations, even when they are reasonably well financed and equipped, tend to be plagued not only by disagreements among the participants—as in former Yugoslavia—but also by tensions between some of them and the UN "establishment" (this happened frequently both in former Yugoslavia and in Somalia) and by disagreements and inefficiencies within the UN bureaucracy (like those that plagued UNOSOM I).

The combined effects of all these factors are likely to be the following. First, as in the past, the great powers will be immune from collective interventions in what they deem their domestic affairs; it is hard to imagine the UN going beyond verbal expressions of dismay and disapproval should large-scale repression take place in China (as with Tibet) or Russia (as with Chechnya).

Second, the UN and other organizations will probably become more selective (and therefore more inconsistent) in their interventions and more modest in the setting of purposes. Lea Brilmayer has argued that selectivity is ethically acceptable if there is a principle, or a set or principles, that explains and justifies choice.[35] In reality, the cases of nonengagement risk being determined by purely political and pragmatic considerations, such as excessive scope of the crisis, insufficient media attention to prod states into action, disagreement among members, or a desire on their part to put what they deem their vital imperatives and preferences ahead of the more unselfish and long-term considerations that justify intervention in distant places.

Third, even in cases that meet the criteria for justified collective (or, if necessary, unilateral) intervention, recent experience teaches two bitter lessons. One is that some nuts are too hard to crack. Some crises create so much violent turmoil that the only short-term action outsiders can sensibly undertake—for all its limitations—is humanitarian relief (as in Rwanda). Civil wars of genocidal proportions cannot be either terminated or resolved before the contenders themselves are ready for a truce or reconciliation or before the triumph of one side. In such cases, when the combatants' fury risks jeopardizing the safety and effectiveness of outside humanitarian efforts, it may sometimes be wiser to rely primarily on NGOs rather than mounting frustrating and necessarily circumscribed operations. Some failed states may be too large, and too far gone, for a UN quasi protectorate to be successful. Sponsoring talks among factions may be the maximum that can be done. Removing tyrannical leaders or murderous regimes may prove equally difficult (despite the precedent of Haiti), either because too much force would have to be used or because no political consensus would emerge either about such a removal or about what to do next (as in the case of Saddam Hussein).

The other lesson is that, especially in cases where the purposes are ambitious (peace restoration and resolution), collective enterprises simply will not succeed unless there is a clear political will behind them, which must be provided either by a major state (such as the United States in Haiti) or by a coalition (the United States, Britain, and France for the protection of the Kurds in Iraq). When such will vanishes (as was the case in Somalia, where the United States, after its unilateral intervention, which led to UNOSOM II, lost heart as its casualties mounted) or is absent (former Yugoslavia), the record is likely to be sad and disappointing.

Fourth, there may be more instances in which the UN, either in order not to lose face or because of its own limited resources, will endorse or license great power interventions (without necessarily monitoring them adequately). In some cases, this may be much better than inaction. In others, this may be no more than a fig leaf covering a classical case of great-power arbitrariness or neo-imperialism.

Thus, if we look ahead to the twenty-first century, we find—unsurprisingly—that some of the domestic travail that is likely to occur is simply too unmanageable from the outside and beyond the possibilities of even a "well-ordered" international society (to use John Rawls's expression). Moreover, this society, even in the absence of a major fault line comparable to the cold war, is in any case not well ordered enough to endow its collective institutions with the financial, military, and administrative capacities that would allow it to cope effectively and consistently with all that is both manageable and essential to any just and moderate world order. Anomie and chaos may well be with us for a long time.

Should we resign ourselves to this? No, because it would be politically nefarious and ethically scandalous. Every opportunity for a morally justified intervention—whether it is created by the media or by atrocities that shake the public out of its complacency (as in Bosnia at the end of August 1995 after the latest massacre in Sarajevo)—needs to be seized and pushed as far as it can be so that the gap between what we ought to do and what is politically feasible will narrow. This means, for instance, that states, especially democratic ones, should exploit every formal and informal opening for prevention; that they should provide humanitarian operations with an explicit mandate, and with the military means, to protect the victims they try to help. It means setting up, in the UN, a peace-enforcing potential provided, initially, perhaps only by a handful of states motivated by a sense of duty or an expectation of prestige; making sure that Security Council resolutions always match the means to well-considered ends and aim at settlements that protect human rights, punish the guilty, and safeguard chances of reconciliation; trying to reform the council's composition so as both to increase the legitimacy of its edicts and to reduce the risks of its paralysis; and providing the UN with resources at least partly independent of the whims of governments and parliaments. Also, given the indispensable nature of domestic political and financial support, statesmen should remember that they have been elected to persuade and to lead, and not just to accept as fixed the momentary moods and pernicious prejudices of the public.

Even a small number of successful cases of restoration of internal peace or of radical healing may help contain or even roll back chaos and anomie and thereby build into the new and volatile world system we now face a capacity for collective management it desperately needs.

12

◆══════◆

Thoughts on the UN at Fifty

S tudies of the United Nations seem to have come full circle. In the years that followed the adoption of the Charter in San Francisco, most of them dealt with the functions that were stressed in the Charter—the maintenance of peace and security, which the League of Nations had signally failed to ensure. The outbreak of the cold war and its effects on an organization whose most important body, the Security Council, could only function if the permanent members—the victors of World War II—remained in agreement inspired many works that examined the ways in which the UN was managing to avoid total paralysis. Gradually, after the Korean War, the Suez crisis, and the protracted drama of decolonization in the Belgian Congo, scholars' attention moved away from the rather unrewarding scene of Chapters VI and VII toward the other activities of the UN. This shift coincided with the vast increase in membership that resulted from decolonization and with the growing importance of the developing and nonaligned countries that now made up the majority of the General Assembly.

In the 1970s, scholarly explorations of international economic interdependence and of the "regimes" which were being set up to regulate and manage it thus led to a view of the UN in which the central "peace and security" functions had dwindled almost to the point of disappearance. It is as if the study of world affairs had been split into two halves. The dark half was accounted for by a realist (or neorealist) theory that emphasized the inescapable security dilemma faced by states competing in an anarchic system where the distribution of power largely determined their strategies and where international and regional organizations other than military alliances were of little significance, except as arenas and echo chambers for the major contests. The light or more cheerful half was the domain of a theory that called itself institutionalism (or, sometimes, liberal institutionalism). It stressed the services that international and regional institutions and regimes could perform even for the states defined as self-interested actors, in areas in which the satisfaction of state needs and preferences required cooperation and common solutions and in the absence of any rational possibility of using force. It also tried to show how the resort, by states, to the institutions that provided such services could gradually affect the way in which states saw and defined their preferences. Thus, the specialized agencies of the UN were often studied as important actors in this process, and the debates in the General Assembly over the nature of the global economic order were seen as attempts to define, so to speak, the terms and rules of "interdependence" in a world of highly unequal states with profoundly different views about the best economic system and the priorities for economic development.

After the fading away of the cold war, the collapse of the Soviet empire in Europe, and the disintegration of the Soviet Union itself, there was a brief moment of hope and great expectations for the UN. It appeared to many statesmen and academics that the optimistic vision of liberal institutionalism might perhaps at last cross the great divide that had separated the realm of economic interdependence from that of strategic and diplomatic interaction, and also that the UN could now at last perform, in the latter, the mission that had been entrusted to it by the Charter for the preservation and defense of peace and security. Gorbachev's "new thinking," which seemed to convert Soviet foreign policy to the key concepts of American institutionalists, the Gulf war, which came pretty close to the collective security model of the Charter (despite certain departures but mainly because of the relative harmony of the permanent members), the American hope that the "Big Five" would (as in FDR's scheme) remain united under American leadership, all this allowed for talk about a new world order. Four years after the Gulf war, a new disillusionment prevails.

As in the 1950s and early 1960s, we have seen a mass of symposiums, books, and articles that examine the performance of the post-1989 UN in the political-military realm, the role played by the secretary-general and the Security Council in conflict resolution, peacekeeping, and enforcement. But for reasons that are no longer the superpowers' bipolar conflict and the violence it engendered, the conclusions often tend to be gloomy and to highlight the new obstacles encountered by the UN in its current activist phase. They tend to emphasize the responsibility of the

UN's own institutions, or the misuse of Charter provisions, or mistaken strategies adopted by the political organs. They are right to do so; but it is necessary to step outside the UN. For many of the flaws that are deplored here result from the nature of the current international system, so radically different from the one both the realists and the liberal institutionalists had in mind.[1] It has always been a problem that specialists of international politics dealing primarily with the diplomatic and strategic scene dismissed the UN from their analyses, whereas lawyers and political scientists specialized in the study of the UN's political functions tended to lock themselves up, so to speak, within the UN and to look at the world outside only dimly, as it was filtered into and through the UN.

Attempts to deal with the distinction between interstate conflicts and domestic turbulence or civil wars have dominated the UN agenda in recent years. And when one examines what is at stake in such internal crises, one realizes that the customary distinction between order and justice is untenable. Even in interstate relations, while "anarchy"—the absence of a world center of power—obliges states to deal first with order (or disorder), every scheme of order incorporates certain conceptions of justice (or injustice), or at least certain forms of justice or injustice emerge from it; and the Charter makes of the Security Council not only a policeman but a "good officer" or mediator: one cannot resolve disputes without being concerned with justice (especially because the Security Council is not bound to offer only terms of settlement proposed or accepted in advance by the parties). One cannot be in charge of "peace" without worrying about the justice of that peace. In intrastate disorders, rival conceptions of both order and justice are almost always at stake; and while the very *cause* (in the *jus ad bellum* meaning) that the Council has invoked to justify its interventions in domestic affairs despite the principle of state sovereignty—that is, the notion that the (internal) trouble constitutes a threat to international peace and security—appears to stress only order, the *cases* in which interventions have occurred are all instances in which disorder provoked massive violations of justice (ethnic cleansing, famine, refugees) or else massive violations of human rights, the supreme form of injustice, constituted the disruption of order.

Functions and Flexibility

During its fifty years, the UN has been remarkable for two reasons in particular. The first is the variety of the functions it has carried out. One is the promotion of cooperation in the vast realm of economic, social, and ecological interdependence. This may well form the most valuable part of the UN's activities. A second function is of the highest importance: the production of norms of international legitimacy, a task that has been carried out through a large number of treaties and declarations as well as through such policies as the drive for decolonization and against apartheid. The relation between this function of legitimization and the cornerstone of the international order, sovereignty, is especially interesting—and ambiguous. Decolonization has led to the multiplication of states formally endowed with all the trappings of sovereignty. The emphasis put by the UN on the principle of self-determination has resulted both in encouraging the disintegration of empires and multiethnic states and in promoting new, successor "sovereign" states. The norms proclaimed in the realm of human rights impose sharp limitations on the internal sovereignty of states and establish a set of standards for the treatment of individuals that all states are supposed to observe.

A third function is the settlement of disputes among states. In this area the UN has encountered difficulties, partly because of the cold war, partly because of the intractable character of some of these disputes (India-Pakistan, Israel and the Arabs, Cyprus, etc.), and partly because the UN has often been preempted, as a mediating agency, by some of its members or by other organizations. The secretary-general has found, in this area, one of his main opportunities for influence.

The fourth key function is the legitimate collective resort to force against threats to peace, breaches of peace, and acts of aggression, as provided for by Article 2(4) and by Chapter VII. There have been only two instances of collective security: Korea and the Gulf war; and in the absence of the agreements for military enforcement called for by Article 43, neither operation was fully in conformity with the prescriptions of the Charter: the UN merely provided its authorization of "coalition forces."

And yet, Chapter VII has been invoked with increasing frequency, especially since the end of the cold war. This points to the second characteristic of the UN: its flexibility. The UN has been extraordinarily creative both in avoiding the paralysis to which the bipolar conflict seemed to condemn it and in finding new techniques for dealing with situations unforeseen by the drafters of the Charter (like almost every international or regional organization the UN was set up to cope with the problems that had defeated "international society" in the recent past). Thus, at the time of the Korean War, the Uniting for Peace resolution transferred in fact some of the deadlocked Security Council's powers to the General Assembly. During the Belgian Congo crisis, Dag Hammarskjöld, Ralph Bunche, and the General Assembly gradually established some principles for dealing with a civil war, as Brian Urquhart has reminded us in his very fine biography of Bunche.[2] The greatest mark of flexibility, in the realm of peace and security, has been the development of "peacekeeping": both after the political settlement of a dispute and in the (frequent) absence of such a resolution but after a cease-fire (often brokered by the UN), UN observers or peacekeepers have been sent all over the world to try to use the prestige of the organization as a deterrent against a breakdown of peace—often successfully, often not (as in the Sinai in 1967 or in Croatia in 1995), and sometimes the very success of peacekeeping has made the ultimate resolution of a dispute even more remote (Cyprus, Kashmir). There have now been two "generations" of peacekeeping, the second one entailing a variety of new executive responsibilities for the UN. Much of this goes beyond what was envisaged by Chapter VI.

Is such flexibility an unmitigated blessing? Admittedly, there are drawbacks: excessive flexibility, indifference to categorization, and a "pragmatic," case-by-case approach can lead to "operational uncertainty" and noncompliance. Above all, the blurring of the border between peacekeeping and enforcement action, the resort to "interpositional peacekeeping" in a conflict in which there is no cease-fire at all (as in Bosnia) or a very shaky one (Croatia) or when there are no organized parties (Somalia), and the removal of "the condition of prior agreements firmly in place" for these new, ambitious forms of peacekeeping risk precipitating the UN into fiascos such as its Yugoslav conundrum, where what should have been a case of collective security (to protect one of the UN's members—Bosnia—from aggression) was treated by a mix of diplomatic procedures for the settlement of ordinary disputes, peacekeeping (in the absence of peace), and ill-advised, limited, and unenforced enforcement measures. Of course, the reason for the frequent resort to Chapter VII in recent years was the felt need for the UN to deal with a variety of often horrendous civil conflicts: given the barrier constituted by sovereignty or domestic jurisdiction, a finding that domestic strife threatened peace and security in the whole region or in the world was necessary. But the fact is that Chapter VII-type enforcement measures are often inadvisable in civil wars (one of the principles established in the Congo crisis was the nonchoosing of sides) and unlikely to receive much support from the members. Although Chapter VII may remain necessary as a *basis* for action, it is Chapter VI that ought to be "stretched" so as to allow the UN to deal, through preventive good offices, mediation, or the provision of humanitarian aid, with the avoidance, the resolution, or at least the mitigation of civil war. The distinction between enforcement action and the settlement of disputes ought to be maintained. It is the distinction between international and internal disputes that ought to be softened or even abolished—whenever the latter are, or should be, of general concern. Here, as I have suggested elsewhere,[3] two norms for collective intervention are needed; one, already in place, deals with order and concerns domestic strife that is a genuine threat to peace and security across borders; the other, which is painfully and slowly emerging, deals with justice and concerns massive violations of human rights; these ought to be seen ipso facto as a legitimate cause for collective intervention in a civil war.

Limits and Liabilities

Failures often attract more attention than successes—both because the media feed on fiascoes and because the triumphs are usually modest or unspectacular. It is true, however, that some fiascoes seriously affect the reputation and future effectiveness of the UN—the Yugoslav debacle may be a sinister turning point—and that the difficulty of reforming the UN, lamented by several scholars, is a cause of dismay.

And yet one always has to remember that many of the UN's problems result not from a top-heavy bureaucracy, inadequate international public servants, or stuffy procedures but from the behavior of the members. It is they who are responsible for the financial plight of the UN, for the absence of military forces at its disposal. How can there be an effective international tribunal dealing with war crimes in Yugoslavia and Rwanda, or a pool of trained conflict managers, without adequate resources? How can the UN strive for "sustainable developments" without some international taxation? How can it succeed in Yugoslavia, given the division and flickering concern of its key members? (In the Congo crisis, as in the Gulf war, the United States was a prime mover). In the United States, at present, there is a kind of obscene convergence between an administration whose retreat from multilateralism in peace and security matters was signaled by its directive on peacekeeping in May 1994 and a Republican majority in Congress whose foreign policy consists largely of denouncing, hampering, and financially starving the UN. An international or regional organization's impotence is always the result of its members' policies.

The difficulties and failures of the UN can be explained by two sets of factors. First, strict limits on its possibilities are imposed by the anarchical structure of interstate society. Success, for the UN, depends on the convergence of its members' preferences and imperatives, especially those of its more powerful members, and on their willingness to let long-term considerations of order and justice prevail over short-run calculations of gains and losses. It is therefore not surprising to find that the UN can do little or nothing to affect the domestic policies of its major powers (Chechnya, Tibet); that it is seriously handicapped, despite torrents of well-meaning suggestions in recent years, in preventing the outbreak of domestic conflicts, given the principle of sovereignty; that this same principle makes it difficult for the UN to prevent states from pursuing within their borders policies (such as disastrous environmental ones, or the production of weapons of mass destruction, or policies of racial discrimination) that could ultimately result in international violence and calamity. It is not surprising that collective security is a rare occurrence and is anything but the quasi-automatic or axiomatic response to aggression that the theory of collective security requires—indeed, it has often been stated that this theory is quite incompatible with the logic of the states' competition. It is not surprising that international criminal justice remains embryonic, given the number of skeletons states have in their closets and their determined resistance to handing over state criminals voluntarily; that states remain reluctant to grant extensive competences to the International Court of Justice; that disputes are very difficult to settle when the stakes for the parties are high, and in particular when the self-image of a state is involved in a conflict (see the importance of Kashmir both for the Muslim state of Pakistan and for the multiethnic and secular state of India), when old ethnic hostilities are in collision (as in Cyprus), or when there are conflicting claims on the same territory (Jerusalem). Nor is it surprising that in a world in which different conceptions of the rights and duties of subjects vis-à-vis their governments coexist, it should be difficult to agree on the execution even of those provisions on human rights that almost all states have pretended to endorse; or that the different conceptions of distributive justice, and the conflicting economic systems advocated by the champions of these conceptions, should make agreement on the nature, mutual obligations, practices, and institutions of global economic order difficult—and should lead, at the end of the day, to the preponderance of the most rich and powerful. All of this is true, whether the interstate system is bipolar, multipolar, or, as today, pretty indeterminate.

Secondly, the UN suffers also from a grave discrepancy between its own structure, defined in a fifty-year-old charter, and the structure of the international system (or, to be more accurate, the world political system). The Charter is a scheme of cooperation, a (weak) regime for a "Westphalian" interstate system. But even though the states remain the most visible agents in the global system, they are neither the only ones nor always—despite their monopoly of the use of legitimate force—the most powerful. There are two other sets of agents (besides the various international and regional bodies). On the one hand, there are all the actors in the global capitalist economy, other than the states that have set it up by providing it both with a huge deregulated sphere of free movement for goods, services, and capital and with a framework of rules for trade, monetary transactions, and so on. These actors are either corporations, banks, firms, or the millions of investors and speculators who can move funds almost instantaneously across borders. Their effects are often profoundly disruptive: capital flows capable of overwhelming the reserves of central banks and of forcing governments to devalue their currencies, investment flows that aggravate inequalities both between advanced and less advanced countries and within each country, illicit but prospering traffics of drugs and weapons, and so forth. This global economy raises a formidable problem of accountability, which governments and international agencies have so far dodged, partly out of fear of killing the golden goose of capitalism by strangulating rules, partly because of powerful domestic pressure groups whose interest is *not* to be accountable at the national or the world level.

On the other hand, there are—again—individuals and groups operating not across and, so to speak, above borders but within and under them: all the forces that disrupt the existing states, either because they deny the legitimacy of these states for ethnic or religious reasons or because they revolt against leaders they deem oppressive or illegitimate. These phenomena existed even while the cold war went on, but they received less attention than they should have, partly because the rival superpowers interfered with, provoked, or exploited those trends, partly because they tended to be equated with decolonization. Now we can see them unobstructed, and we face a world in which many states are "failed states," in a situation of chaos, anarchy, or permanent strife, either because of disintegration along ethnic or religious lines, or because of the flimsiness and corruption of their institutions, or because of the artificiality both of their borders (arbitrarily traced by colonial rulers) and of the Western-based notion of the state when it is imposed on parts of Africa and Asia. Many of the UN's current difficulties result from the multiplication of these cases, but we must remember that less recent examples already showed how little the UN could do when the "floor" of states on which it is established crumbles: it stayed away from the Nigerian civil war, it averted its eyes from the plight of the Kurds, it left behind, in Zaire, a nightmarish one-man show. The UN is simply not equipped to deal with collapsing states or with rulers who systematically violate human rights. (It is true that there have been some successes here, too—in Central America, Cambodia, Namibia, Mozambique; but they have been connected with the liquidation of the cold war, and fragile).

One needs, ideally, a world organization capable of coping with all three dimensions of the global system—the world economy, currently out of control, the interstate system, and the groups and peoples trying to reshape their fates at the expense of the status quo. This does not mean that we have to be satisfied with the UN as it is. A control of the legality of Security Council and General Assembly resolutions might be useful (there are strong grounds for believing that the arms embargo on Bosnia violates this state's right to self-defense). Such a task might be entrusted to the International Court of Justice and provide it with much-needed new business. Indeed, the whole issue of the legal and political accountability of international agencies deserves imaginative study (only in the case of the European Union has there been a genuine debate, because it is more than a regional organization, albeit less than a federation). One should think of some body that would have to be less than a "parliament of peoples," in a world where democracies are still only an endangered minority, but more than an assemblage of official representatives. Could this be a task for the next fifty years?

Part Three

Ethnicity, Nationalism, and World Order

13

The Passion of Modernity

O f all the secular ideologies that have moved men and women to action in the past couple of centuries, nationalism now appears to be the most widespread—and the toughest survivor. It has led to the unification of peoples who had been living under a variety of rulers but felt that they belonged in a single state, such as the citizens of nineteenth-century Germany and Italy. More frequently, nationalism has resulted in the disintegration of multiethnic states and empires, such as the Ottoman Empire, Austria-Hungary, and, today, Yugoslavia and the Soviet Union. It has also provoked the collapse of colonial empires, once the colonizing powers found themselves too weak to resist the onslaught of peoples who had never in the past formed nations but now caught the contagion of the nation-state and became determined to obtain their independence and sovereignty. The demand for national self-determination had been endorsed by liberals: in France during the French Revolution, in England by John Stuart Mill, in the United States by Woodrow Wilson. Today liberals are beginning to recoil, because at the same time that economic interdependence is emptying sovereignty of substance, demands for sovereignty are multiplying—leading to a proliferation of conflicts and the risk of endless challenges to existing borders in a futile quest for the perfect "pure" nation-state. Meanwhile, migrations old and new have made it almost impossible to avoid the presence of minorities on the soil of any conceivable unit (unless it succeeds in closing off its borders completely and in expelling all such minorities—another recipe for disorder and tragedy).

Attempts at transcending nationalism and the nation-state have been far less effective than the ideology itself. The United Nations and other international organizations have limited resources and powers and can only try to cope with the conflicts that the quest for self-determination constantly provokes. Communism, which pretended to transcend nationalism and to reorganize the political universe on the basis of class alone, did not ultimately succumb because of nationalism, but it began to split because of it: remember Marshal Tito's defection in 1948, the USSR-China split a dozen years later, and the war between China and Vietnam in 1979. And once communism collapsed in the USSR and Eastern Europe under the weight of its economic and political rigidities, national quarrels reemerged with a vengeance. The attempt by the European Community (EC) to move the peoples of Western Europe beyond the nation-state has been only partly successful. It has integrated their economies and made war among them inconceivable, but their polities remain distinct, and the EC's own ideologues have never been able to explain how one could create a truly unified Europe without simultaneously creating a new European nationalism to replace the nationalisms of its members. No such European nationalism exists, and many of the champions of a united Europe do not want to see it anyhow, because they are afraid of the ugly aspects of nationalism. But in its absence the EC remains above all a utilitarian arrangement that serves the interests of the member states and can go only as far as the national governments and their citizenries allow it to go.

The literature on nationalism is not as impressive as one would expect, given the importance of the phenomenon. For a long time, before and just after World War II, what flourished was principally the study of the idea of nationalism: the intellectual history of the concept and of the writers, poets, historians, and geographers who celebrated it. This told us little about its appeal, about the reasons for its spread or for its hold on the imaginations of millions of people. Later came the sociologists, who analyzed nationalism as a process of social communications and interactions (rather than as an idea)—a part of the sweeping advance of "modernity," of which capitalism was seen as the most important manifestation. Lost in this shift was the rich texture and diversity of the nationalist phenomenon; we got taxonomies, instead. We also got books, usually by Marxist historians, that looked at this phenomenon as something irrational, an atavistic anachronism that was bound to disappear sooner or later in a rationally organized universe.

These days social scientists often thirst for general theories, grand testable hypotheses, structural analyses, and quantifiable results. Nationalism does not lend itself to these. One of its strengths, and the reason for its durability and resilience, is its diversity. It may well be true that nationalism has played, and continues to play, a vital role as a kind of substitute for religion in parts of the world where religious faith has declined, but it can also ally itself with religious surges, as in the case of Islamic fundamentalism. And since nationalism responds to local circumstances, feeds on the peculiarities of a multitude of social and political systems, colors authoritarian as well as liberal ideologies, and can be promoted by any class or coalition of interests, it is too elusive to be easily captured and dissected by modern social scientists. They are often more interested in the evolution and operation of structures (such as class systems or capitalism) than in the feelings, desires, and needs of human beings, and when they gingerly approach social psychology, they do so with highly rudimentary concepts and hypotheses. As a result, our understanding of the appeal of nationalism and of its multiple manifestations and perversions leaves a great deal to be desired.

Liah Greenfeld, in *Nationalism: Five Roads to Modernity*, deals with five enormous cases: England, France, Russia, Germany, and the United States.[1] She is curious about the interplay of ideas and interests and tries to identify the groups in whose interest it was to adopt the idea of the nation. But—unlike many present-day social scientists who see passions as a kind of overflow of interests and ideologies as the rationalization of interests—she does not believe that history is the product of rational decisions by people and groups engaged in a cool calculation of benefits and losses.

A key factor in Greenfeld's analysis is *ressentiment*, "a psychological state resulting from suppressed feelings of envy and hatred . . . and the impossibility of satisfying these feelings"; she sees nationalism as often growing out of the resentment that certain groups feel toward a society that deprives them of or undermines the status to which they feel entitled. She also sees the idea of the nation as "the constitutive element of modernity": "Rather than define nationalism by its modernity, I see modernity as defined by nationalism." She points out the initial link between nationalism and democracy: "Democracy was born with the sense of nationality"; both locate sovereignty in the people and proclaim "the fundamental equality among [the people's] various strata." But this connection does not always prevail, and Greenfeld divides nationalism into two categories: "individualistic-libertarian" nationalism, a form of civic nationalism that stresses the rights of individuals and conceives of the nation as an association of equal and free individuals; and "collectivistic-authoritarian" nationalism, which celebrates not the "actual sovereignty of individuals" but a collective being, the Nation, endowed with a will of its own. This kind of nationalism can be either civic, when "nationality is at least in principle open and voluntaristic; it can and sometimes must be acquired," or ethnic, the more usual case, when only members of the dominant ethnic group constitute the Nation.

To study her five cases, Greenfeld has read voraciously, in four languages, memoirs, diaries, private correspondence, "laws and official proclamations, . . . works of literature" and political philosophy, and a vast number of secondary works. She covers a period of five centuries, from the beginning of the sixteenth century to the present, although her focus is on the formative period of national identity and consciousness in each case. Some of the most stimulating passages are set pieces—not digressions, for they are important to her study, but stories that can be read almost independently of it: the role of science and empirical knowledge in seventeenth-century England. German romanticism, American attitudes toward intellectuals. The book is thought provoking, and one can only pay tribute to the author's ambition, erudition, and stamina. At a time when much of social science either reduces the most profound human experiences to equations or tell us more and more about less and less, Greenfeld's intellectual audacity and her civic concern (she does not conceal her preference for "individualistic-libertarian" nationalism) must be applauded.

And yet this is a flawed book. Two kinds of flaws have to be distinguished: those of her design and those of the specific case studies. The main weakness in design is displayed on the very first page, where Greenfeld tells us

> The word "nationalism" is used here as an umbrella term under which are subsumed the related phenomena of national identity (or nationality) and consciousness, and collectivities based on them—nations; occasionally, it is employed to refer to the articulate ideology on which national identity and consciousness rest, though not—unless specified—to the politically activist, xenophobic variety of national patriotism, which it frequently designates.

This is a real mess. On the one hand, Greenfeld lumps together such different concepts as *nation*, which *The Oxford English Dictionary* defines as "an extensive aggregate of persons, so closely associated with each other by common descent, language, or history, as to form a distinct race or people, usually organized as a separate political state and occupying a definite territory" (a definition full of inevitable hedges); *national identity*, the material and spiritual, physical and behavioral, features that are characteristics of a given nation and distinguish it from all others; *national consciousness*, the subjective self-image that citizens have of their nation, which often selects only some features of the national identity, or distorts them, or invents new ones; *patriotism*, which is a sense of attachment and loyalty to one's nation; *nationality*, which is a legal concept; and *nationalism*, which is an ideology, a program of action that sets goals (and, more often than not, defines and defies enemies).

Much of the trouble with the book results from the blending of these quite distinct notions, and readers would do well to ask themselves at every moment which of them the author is actually discussing. The most interesting object of study is the relationship between national consciousness and nationalism—between the way in which different groups in the population conceive of the nation and the specific programs, propaganda efforts, campaigns, and so forth that leading intellectuals, political activists, and agitators put forward. National consciousness may grow in the absence of any nationalist ideology; nationalism as an ideology can foster national consciousness and modify it; yet a strong national self-image can limit the appeal of, or neutralize, nationalistic ideologies incompatible with it. In order to study these connections, one has to begin by disentangling the two notions, and this Greenfeld fails to do.

On the other hand, insofar as she focuses on the ideology of nationalism, primarily in the chapters on Russia and Germany, and insofar as her distaste for the "collectivistic-authoritarian" model of the nation is one of the most powerful foundations of her whole enterprise, leaving out the "xenophobic variety" means excluding a major part of the story (and, indeed, she finds she cannot leave it out completely). If "nationalism" today evokes the horrible images of rape and murder in Bosnia, of turmoil in Nagorno-Karabakh, and of the destruction of Muslim mosques in India rather than the serene vision of Jules Michelet, Giuseppe Mazzini, and John Stuart Mill, who dreamed of a harmonious world of nation-states, it is because the xenophobic version of nationalism has tended to shape national consciousness more often than the liberal version.

A second flaw of design lies in the author's decision to focus on the beginnings of national identity and consciousness in each case. This means that she dwells on England in the sixteenth and seventeenth centuries, on France from 1715 to 1789, and on Russia, Germany, and the United States during the second half of the eighteenth century and the beginning of the nineteenth. If the book had been called *The Origins of*

National Consciousness in Five Cases, this would have been fine. But Greenfeld herself recognizes that "the origins of a nationalism which define its nature" do not completely "shape its social and political expressions," and I would add that the nature of national consciousness is not determined or defined exclusively by its origins. The book is profoundly disappointing, especially if we are interested both in the later forms of national consciousness and in nationalist ideologies, because it leaves us on the threshold of the era in which international relations ceased to be merely the game of states and became the clash of nations—a clash that resulted in two world wars—with rival nationalist ideologies often clashing at home. For instance, Greenfeld abandons French nationalism at the beginning of the Revolution, just as it became the dominant force inside France and abroad, and she has nothing much to say about American national consciousness and nationalism in the twentieth century. Only in the cases of Russia and Germany does she go beyond origins, but the study of the later developments in Russia is very thin, and in the passionate chapter on Germany she tends to read what is going to be the evil future into the past on which she concentrates; indeed, it is as if this future explained her interpretation of the past. Also, since the formative period for some nationalisms was later than for others, when we are learning about, say, Germany and the United States in the early parts of the nineteenth century, nothing is said about developments in Britain or France that occurred at the same time and may have influenced or paralleled what happened in the United States and Germany.

This brings me to the problems of the specific chapters. In the case of England one might ask whether the emergence of a national sentiment that Greenfeld calls "English" national consciousness ought not to have been called British. For, as the Yale historian Linda Colley has shown in her brilliant book on this subject, *Britons* (1992), what developed was a sense of nationhood that was superimposed on and coexisted with English, Scottish, and Welsh loyalties. Colley, who focuses on the eighteenth century, and Greenfeld, who discusses the sixteenth and seventeenth centuries, both stress the importance of Protestantism in that development. Greenfeld sees in the British brand of national consciousness the consciousness of one's dignity as an individual, and she connects it to the principles of individual liberty and political equality. She shows how struggles with the anti-Protestant Queen Mary, the early Stuarts, and other monarchs, in which the growing middle classes and a new aristocracy based on merit took part, shaped these liberal ideas and the ideal of the rational, empirical intellect. Since Greenfeld admires England, *ressen-*

timent has no place in her story. But Colley shows how in the eighteenth century Francophobia and war played important roles in the development of a British national sense, and she pays far more attention than Greenfeld to economic progress (profits as a source of patriotism) and to a focus on the monarchy, after the Glorious Revolution, as the source of pride and loyalty. Only in the chapter on the United States does Greenfeld tell us that the "idealistic" national consciousness she analyzed in the chapter on England had not been the only one, that there had also been a more conservative, concrete, and materialistic one, "the emotional attachment to the land, government, and ways of England . . . an updated particularism, clothed in nationalistic rhetoric." It is the idealistic national consciousness she sees blooming in the United States, whereas "Englishmen in England tended toward the concrete or materialistic variety." One would never have guessed it from her chapter on England, although a reader of Colley's richly textured book would have known it.

Greenfeld's treatment of the French case is, to be blunt, far more wrong than right. She is right in pointing out (though she does so at excessive length) that "a narrow elite circle" had for centuries "the consciousness of being *French*" but that this was not yet a national consciousness. France was first seen as a Christian country; not until the seventeenth century did the polity become equated with the king. Only the Huguenots, in their bitter struggles with Catholics in the sixteenth century and with Louis XIV in the seventeenth, appealed to all the oppressed in modern terms, by calling for popular resistance. But the bulk of Greenfeld's story is the development of national consciousness by the eighteenth-century aristocracy, the truly revolutionary class. The aristocracy had lost its political power to the absolute and centralizing monarchy; it was losing its economic power to the rising bourgeoisie. It reacted by incorporating the intellectuals, rejecting and despising capitalism, and embracing the ideas that there was a French nation and that "the nobility was the bearer of the sovereignty of the polity." These ideas were imported from England, but anti-British *ressentiment* gave to concepts such as liberty, equality, and nation a very different meaning, one both collectivist and undemocratic.

Take the word *nation*. "From . . . a name for the association of free, rational individuals, it turned into a super-human collective person. . . . In England, it was the dignity of the individuals who composed it that dignified the collective body. . . . But in France it was the dignity of the whole that restored dignity to those who claimed membership in it." Two things are wrong with this account. First, Greenfeld distorts the role of the aristocracy. Yes, the Revolution began as an aristocratic reaction against an absolute monarchy that had deprived the privileged castes of any power to block unwelcome changes in taxation and in the social order. But insofar as the modern idea of the nation is concerned, it was the bourgeoisie and the intellectuals who used it as a war machine against both the absolute monarchy and the privileged orders (church and nobility). Second, she misreads Montesquieu, who was not merely a champion of the *thèse nobiliaire* (the idea of the nobility as the "legitimate, governing part of the sovereign nation") but also the great exponent of the British system of government, with its lower House representing the middle classes. And she misreads Rousseau, turning him into a Hegelian. It is true that Rousseau's conception of the general will, which captured the imagination of the French revolutionaries, sharply differs from the liberal emphasis on individual rights and limited government. But the sovereign nation *is* a democratic concept: the general will is not a force imposed on individuals, it is the will of all of us when we think, as citizens, about the common good.

What makes Rousseau's idea dangerous is its utopian assumption that citizens will, if properly enlightened, always agree on what is the common good. It can be all too easily diverted and distorted by clever demagogues, but the conception is neither authoritarian nor truly collectivistic. The community is seen as an association of free and rational individuals, who, unlike the citizens of a liberal state, transfer all their rights as social beings to it and gain citizenship in exchange. If one wants to find a really authoritarian and collectivistic French nationalism, one has to wait for the end of the nineteenth century, with Maurice Barrès and Charles Maurras. Only then did a major part of the French nobility finally convert to nationalism, adopting that rather ugly ideology after a whole century of having rejected and despised the revolutionary, Rousseauian nationalism of the Republicans and of having devoted its loyalty to the absent king and the pope in Rome.

The chapter on Russia dwells on the ambivalence of Russian thinkers toward the West—on the split between admirers of the West, who wanted Russia to use it as a model, and Slavophiles, who denied that Russian society and culture were inferior and that the West had anything good to offer. Both groups, Greenfeld tells us, were steeped in *ressentiment*. "In Slavophilism, this revulsion [against Russian reality] was transformed into excessive self-admiration. In Westernism, the very same sentiment led to the generalized revulsion against the existing world and to the desire to destroy it." This is the Westernism that she sees in Leninism and the Russian Revolution. Admirers of the West, in her eyes, shared the Slavophiles' view of Russia as the anti-West but "still accepted the direction in which the West developed as the only way." I find this hard to follow. It is a curiously schematic and bloodless chapter, in which social and political realities barely figure, and here the absence of most of the past two centuries is particularly regrettable.

There is nothing bloodless about the chapter on Germany. Greenfeld's profound dislike of German nationalism animates every page. She sees it as a belated creation of "unattached" intellectuals who were resentful of their inferior and often miserable situation in a society dominated by aristocrats, divided into many authoritarian states, and endowed with a very small reading public. These intellectuals were attracted first by a form of religious mysticism called Pietism, which was egalitarian and emotional, stressed individual salvation rather than dogma, and associated beauty with blood. Later the intellectuals invented romanticism, which demoted reason, exalted the irrational and unthinking feeling, and denounced the "unnatural" view of society propagated by the Enlightenment. The cult of action, the emphasis on the importance of geniuses and artists and on "the never-never land of the perfect Community"—all this resulted in "a new and sinister ideal of political leadership." Romantic philosophy is analyzed here entirely as the product of "the intellectuals' dissatisfaction with their personal situation" and German national consciousness as the direct product of another *ressentiment*: French invasion and occupation during the wars of the Revolution and of Napoleon. According to Greenfeld, "German nationalism is Romantic nationalism," with its view of Germany as the only pure and perfect nation and of the West as the "antimodel." She makes a long, brilliant, and highly questionable digression into Marxism, which she describes as a kind of inversion of nationalism involving simple substitutions of class for nation, the proletariat for Germany, and capitalism for the West, still the embodiment of evil.

Quite apart from the issue of whether Marx was really, as she thinks, a German nationalist, there are many problems with this chapter. Why did romanticism in Germany lead to a political philosophy and a kind of nationalism so profoundly different from those that it fostered in France? Why did the view of Germany as the nation that expressed humanity most fully lead to results far more "sinister" than the quite similar view of France held by Michelet? Is it fair to read Hegel as a totalitarian? Greenfeld would have been well inspired to read the late political theorist Judith Shklar's books, *After Utopia* (1957), on romanticism, and *Free-*

dom and Independence (1976), on Hegel. How did German hatred of the West settle on an "Asiatic" race, the Jews, and how did they become "the principal embodiment of Western degeneracy"? How did the old Christian anti-Semitism become the modern hatred of the Jews as a race? In order to understand German nationalism and why "German national identity was from the outset defined as a racial identity," one needs answers to all these questions, but they are not provided, nor are the questions even asked by Greenfeld. Her main concern seems to be to show that "Germany was ready for the Holocaust from the moment German national identity existed." Providing answers would have required, here again, moving much further into the nineteenth century and examining both the pseudoscientific forms and the social appeals of modern racism. Moreover, no reader of this chapter would guess that there were also German defenders of a conception of the nation derived from the Enlightenment and steeped in liberalism.

The chapter on the United States presents American national sentiment as the blossoming of the idealistic British conception, imported by the immigrants who came to this country with a preexisting (English) national identity. The revolt against British violations of their rights transformed it into an American national identity, which was later adopted by immigrants who came with no preexisting national feelings. "They embraced American identity eagerly," Greenfeld writes, "because only as Americans were they elevated to the status of men." She spends only a few pages on the Civil War (she sees the South as having had a nascent ideology that would, like Germany's and Russia's, have been racial, anticapitalist, and authoritarian). She is more interested in refuting Richard Hofstadter's thesis about anti-intellecutalism in America. Citing Ralph Waldo Emerson, she stresses the individual American's enthusiasm for knowledge and culture and dismisses the intellectuals' lament as mere annoyance at the refusal of Americans to pay special respect to professional thinkers, as a result of which the intelligentsia has eschewed "patriotic effusions" and retreated into universities, to become an aristocracy of merit within the larger democracy. This, in turn, has produced a cultural vacuum in the society at large, which mass culture fills; but the removal of intellectuals to the ivory tower has probably been good for social and political stability.

Again, much is left out, and much is questionable. Hofstadter was talking not about Emerson but about manifestations of a refusal to take seriously ideas devoid of obvious practical application and about various forms of evangelism and primitivism. These have almost no place in

Greenfeld's one-dimensional celebration of America's cult of liberty, equality, and reason. That a nation of free individuals can also suffer from the pressure of social conformity and from what Alexis de Tocqueville called the tyranny of the majority—despite, as Greenfeld writes, the "plurality of tastes, views, attachments, aspirations, and self-definitions within the shared national framework"—is neither mentioned nor accounted for. Nor does the time span Greenfeld selected allow her to consider recurrent forms of anti-immigrant nationalism. "Americanism" in its uglier guises is never treated here. I am no fan of systematic debunking and revisionism, but the idyllic image offered by Greenfeld seems a bit too close for comfort to the kind of cultural propaganda offered by the *Voice of America* during the cold war. One can admire American national sentiment without concealing its blemishes or the fact (also analyzed by Judith Shklar in her last book, *American Citizenship* [1991]) that the battle for inclusion has been constant and isn't over yet.

Greenfeld's enormous effort is serious and impressive. But a satisfactory study of national consciousness would require a far deeper look into the minds of people in a variety of social groups and settings and into the ways in which highbrow intellectuals, popular culture, the media, the economic elites, and the politicians who pull all the levers of power inculcate such consciousness into citizens—or even, as Eugen Weber has shown in his classic *Peasants into Frenchmen* (1976), turn subjects into citizens of a nation. And a satisfactory study of nationalism as an ideology would require a much closer examination of political doctrines and programs and of the reasons why they were embraced by a variety of groups. *Ressentiment* is certainly one of the springs of social action. But how it leads to a particular brand of nationalism, and how it can be redirected against scapegoats, is a far more complicated story than what we are told here. Politics in its broadest sense—not merely what goes on in the political system but its interaction with the society at large—is, unfortunately, absent from the book.

The development of national consciousness is more than a product of "the structural contradictions of the society of orders." It is, as Greenfeld also says, "fundamentally, a matter of dignity." National consciousness arises in large part as a democratic demand. Every society is hierarchical, whether or not it is a society of orders, and many of the groups in which we live and work—family, profession, church—are also inegalitarian. If nations are imagined communities, as in Benedict Anderson's celebrated 1983 title, it is because we can indeed imagine a community different from the ones we experience daily, one in which we are all alike and equal, no longer separated by rank and by division of labor. In addition, national consciousness arises from a powerful desire to protect what we see as common to "us" from "others"; enemies, invaders, or intruders. (The "other" need not even be a foreigner: to the revolutionaries of 1789, the resented "other" was the privileged orders.) Nationalist projects have been built on both of these foundations.

Even more significant than the distinctions between liberal and authoritarian national self-images and between civic and ethnic conceptions of the nation is the distinction between inclusive and exclusive ones. Ethnic conceptions are by definition exclusive. Nonethnic ones can be exclusive, too, as the case of right-wing French nationalism from Barrès to Jean-Marie Le Pen shows. Moreover, there is rarely a single national self-image or a single form of nationalism. Rival conceptions usually fight it out—as we see today in India, where an inclusive and secular idea, symbolized by Nehru, stands against the religious and exclusive conception embodied by Hinduism. Making different conceptions and programs coexist peacefully within a country is often as hard as making different ethnic groups coexist within a state.

Both the virtues and the flaws of Greenfeld's book force one to think more about a phenomenon whose importance is as profound as its complexity and diversity. This is no mean achievement. Greenfeld has written mostly about ideas and ideals. She should now turn to societies and politics and thus yield to what she herself calls "the irresistibly fascinating nature of social processes," which in this book she has resisted only too well.

14

Nationalism and World Order

The resurgence of nationalism after the cold war, in a world in which states are increasingly interdependent, incapable of providing by themselves the services their citizens expect, and dependent on international cooperation, gives rise to two kinds of intellectual inquiries. We have seen a remarkable flourishing of normative works that discuss the ethical implications of nationalism and cosmopolitanism, the claims of multiculturalism, and the rights and duties of immigrants and refugees versus the rights and duties of host countries and their citizens. This chapter belongs to the second type of inquiry: the empirical analysis of this protean phenomenon, nationalism, as an expression of the limits and possibilities of internationalism in a world of leaking, or melting, or shrinking, or diffuse, and sometimes shared or pooled sovereignty. My purpose is to examine the extent to which and the conditions under which nationalism is compatible with world order.

Defining Terms

Unlike national consciousness, or patriotism (sentiment national), nationalism is an ideology. Patriotism means loyalty to one's nation. Nationalism is, in my opinion, more than "a belief held by a group of people that they ought to constitute a nation or that they are already one."[1] In the first place, nationalism, like other ideologies, addresses a problem: what is the secular community that deserves the individuals' highest allegiance and that will provide its members with a common social identity? Second, it provides an answer, an explanation: we are not merely the

members of a nation (whatever the way in which the distinctive characteristics of the nation are defined); our identity is constituted by our membership in a nation; all other memberships are partial, or weaker. Third,
like all ideologies, nationalism offers a program. At a minimum, it is the
promotion and protection of the nation's integrity and uniqueness.
Often, it goes beyond this and proclaims not only the nation's singularity
but also its mission in the world, or its superiority over others.

Nationalism made its appearance at a time when two social phenomena transformed human consciousness and behavior. One was the demise
of the monarchic and religious conception of the polity, replaced by an
emphasis on the people and its collective will or on individuals bound to
one another by the cement of the nation. The other, emphasized by Ernst
Gellner, is the "delocalization" of the individual in the new economic
order of capitalism, the opening or even the destruction of the small and
relatively closed communities that had absorbed human lives for centuries.

The question remains why these "delocalized" individuals, these
groups that were being told that they were entitled to the mastery of their
fates, chose to give their highest allegiance to the nation and not to the
competing claimant, class. Why did the "imagined community" become
the nation? A historical answer emphasizes the fact that in several cases
(e.g., the United Kingdom and France), the state had already established
institutions and promoted ideas that created a nation out of a galaxy of
ethnic and cultural groups. In other cases, the nation appeared in resistance to foreign aggression or domination: in the Netherlands, in Spain
under Napoleon, in Fichte's Germany or Mazzini's Italy, and of course
in Poland, Ireland, and the rebellious colonies that became the United
States. Despite Marx's conviction, class could not compete. Industrializa-
tion and the formation of a proletariat took place within the borders of
national states: in Britain, France, Bismarck's Germany, the United
States, and Japan and in empires dominated by one nation, such as Russia. The transnational solidarity of class provided symbolic satisfactions
to workers embroiled in battles against capitalists and poverty within the
confines of the nation-state. But this solidarity, as the tragic history of
the Second Internationale demonstrated, never transcended national differences sufficiently, and the workers themselves found in the nation a
way of escaping from the constraints and humiliations of their lives as
alienated producers. The community of labor was their daily condition.
The "imagined community" they needed was the nation—not only be-

cause it transcended class but because it corresponded to an aspiration to become "citoyens à part entière" in the nation in which they lived.

Ideologies need mobilized believers who will propagate them and do battle for them. Few ideologies have been so resourceful in their choice of vehicles of propagation. Nationalism has sometimes surged from below, with the help of intellectuals and students, and sometimes—as in Hungary and Japan—from above. It has sometimes been locked in battle with the church, as in France, and sometimes been carried and supported by the church, as in Poland. In some instances, it proved to be a powerful instrument of change of the existing class system, as in revolutionary France. Elsewhere, it contributed to the preservation of the existing class system—as in Britain, or Hungary, or Germany before World War I. It often was a force of modernization, as Gellner and Ernst Haas have chosen to emphasize. But it could also buttress resistance to important elements of modernization, as in the case of Gandhi's nationalism and in several aspects of Nazi ideology and policies (I am sorry to bring Hitler and Gandhi into the same sentence). It comes in all the forms—four "revolutionary" and three "syncretist"—that Haas distinguishes in his elaborate typology.[2] The problem with most of the typologies of nationalism I have seen is that each one refers to only one of nationalism's many dimensions (in Haas's case, it is the attitude toward traditional values; in the famous and overworked distinction between civic and ethnic nationalism, it is the basis of national identity, i.e., the characteristics that differentiate "nationals" from "foreigners"). Nationalism, as an ideology, has managed to be compatible with, parasitic on, or destructive of all other ideologies.

Let us turn to the concept of world order. Hedley Bull's definition of world order is a condition or situation (I would prefer "a construct and a condition") in which the basic requirements of the units that constitute the international system are satisfied: survival, a reasonable degree of security, and a low level of interunit violence, that is, a condition of relative stability or moderation.[3] The term also refers to the set of procedures (established both among the major powers and in hierarchical relations) that ensure this condition. They vary, depending on the nature of the units, the number of great powers, the composition of what might be called relevant power (neorealists tend to focus excessively on military power), and the main ideologies that exist in the system.

World order can be a deliberate goal of states—a policy aimed at producing an international milieu favorable to the material interests and the values of a given actor—or simply the product of policies that are not directly aimed at establishing a certain kind of order. We need also to distinguish between a minimalist conception of it (i.e., the one entailed by Bull's definition) and a maximalist one, which adds to the focus on moderation a focus on fairness in the relations among the units and even in the relations between governments and people within the units. Such a definition introduces considerations of justice and humanity into the analysis of world order. Bull himself did so at the end of his lamentably short life.[4]

Political Philosophies and Nationalism

Among the many reasons political scientists who study international relations should concern themselves with something as apparently nonscientific as political philosophy is the fact that many of the philosophical theories, and especially those of the last two centuries, have provided us with images of world order; and they have shown the ways in which several features of the international system (such as its structure) or of the units (such as the domestic political or economic regime) shape, or misshape, world order. Yet one cannot avoid being surprised at how little attention the main doctrines have paid to nationalism. It is as if nationalism, one of the central social phenomena since the French Revolution—and one which has given to the link between the individual and the state a wholly new substance and intensity, thus profoundly affecting the "game of states"—had been merely tangential or incidental to these philosophies, or unassimilable to them.

For modern realists and neorealists, basically, nationalism does not matter much. In a system of distinct and competing units, be they empires, nation-states, dynastic states, or city-states, anarchy (the absence of central power and the frequently violent conflicts that result from it) is a permanent and defining feature. Realists and neorealists emphasize the rationality of behavior such a feature engenders: the need for each actor to calculate his forces, the interest of prudent actors in establishing and preserving a balance of power so as to moderate the ambitions of troublemakers, the interest of even an ambitious actor not to behave in such a way as to provoke a coalition of threatened units that could bring it losses instead of gains, and so forth. It is true that Hans Morgenthau wrote about "nationalistic universalism" in referring to this century's totalitarian regimes, but even here nationalism was seen mainly as a rationalization and aggravation of state expansionism. The one realist who did take the force of modern nationalism into account was Max Weber, with his gloomy view of international relations as a contest among national cultures—almost national essences—and as a Darwinian universe in which the bigger ones were bound to swallow the smaller ones.[5] This was a view, derived from but far more pessimistic and less "rational" than Hegel's, that left one with no illusion about the possibility of world order. But the other members of these vast and amorphous schools, German, Swiss, British, American, or French, all subscribed, explicitly or implicitly, to the view that insofar as nationalism prevents or distorts a reasonable definition of the national interest—by prodding the state into acting beyond its power or into building up its power in a way that would backfire—it is to be curbed or excommunicated. Realist nationalists such as Michel Debré and his great mentor Charles de Gaulle tried to separate a good and necessary nationalism that gives a sense of identity, cohesion, and purpose to the unit in the global "state of war" (as well as to its citizens in their daily lives) and a wicked nationalism that, in Debré's words, "was to national feeling what Inquisition had been to faith, a degradation and a disease."[6] The realist vision of a moderate interstate order made such a delicate distinction necessary.[7] For realists à la Kennan or Kissinger—or Walter Lippmann—the intrusion of excess and incompetence into the difficult game of states, resulting from nationalist passions relayed by democratic institutions, breeds only chaos; cool expertise respectful of tradition is needed for world order to be possible in an anarchic world.

Marxism, in essence, tends to deny the significance of nationalism. In international as well as in domestic affairs the relevant actor is class, and nationalism is an ideology that the dominant class uses in order to consolidate its hegemony over the proletariat. The international system is the scene of the dominant elites' rivalries, fueled by uneven economic development. Revolution, when it comes—and whether it begins, as in the orthodox version, among the most advanced capitalist countries or, as in Lenin's, among more backward ones—will be a worldwide phenomenon. Thus, the nation is either the arbitrary arena in which class conflict is played out or a basis for the chauvinistic propaganda elites concoct in order to divert the working class from its duty and to delay the revolution. Insofar as it was a nefarious nuisance, the range of options for dealing with it went from outright, uncompromising hostility to the federalist constructions of Otto Bauer. But the fundamental attitude remained one of distaste for an irrational secular faith that took the exploited away from the realities of capitalist exploitation and from the truly significant engines of history: the mode of production and the relations of production. This attitude pervades Eric Hobsbawm's book on nationalism.[8]

Liberalism is the philosophy that has most to say on our subject. John Stuart Mill came to national self-determination from his perspective as an advocate of liberal self-government, the former being necessary for the solidity and survival of the latter. Conversely, Mazzini and Michelet, celebrators of a popular nationalism, embraced broadly representative institutions as well. What is clear is that, for post-1776 or post-1789 liberals, self-government and self-determination were two sides of the same coin. One could conceive of a national state in which representative government was pushed aside either in an authoritarian (say, Bismarckian) or in a Jacobin fashion; but this was not a liberal state. One could also imagine representative institutions for a multinational community. But then, as Mill argued, unless the different national components had consented (in some kind of federal or consociational formula) to these common institutions, one national group was likely, over time, to oppress the others (or else paralysis would prevail).

Liberalism, like realism, addresses itself to one kind of nationalism only, for two reasons. One is the individualistic basis of liberalism, economic as well as political. The fundamental actor is the individual, not the group. Among their many rights, modern individuals have a right to a nationality and to be free citizens of (free) nations; but the nation is conceived as a community of citizens, bound both to their nation and to its institutions by consent, not by ascriptive features. This, of course, leaves out not only "ethnic" nationalisms but the "integral" nationalisms that use Burkean arguments to establish the priority of the nation over the individual. Second, liberalism offers a vision of a world order based on moderate, democratic, representative nation-states. This was both Kant's ideal of a peace of national "republican" regimes, a classic revived by Michael Doyle (and controversially received by skeptics), and Mazzini's vision of harmonious nation-states as a stage toward a finally united mankind. In Kant's and in Jeremy Bentham's versions, this world order of the satisfied entails some international regimes, in the form of common norms (Kant) or institutions. In all the versions, the taming of state power by public opinion and by trade across borders would make such a world order possible, by defanging, so to speak, the more aggressive potential of nationalism.

As I have suggested in chapter 5, above, liberalism never entirely overcame its original inspiration—which was to emancipate individuals from arbitrary and authoritarian institutions and to build new ones based on their capacity for reason. The founding fathers of liberalism—Locke and Montesquieu—wrote before the age of nationalism. In that age, which is still and more than ever ours, liberalism's problem has been an uneasy relation to reality. It describes only one path to and one form of nationalism (Mazzini lamented that Italy's path turned out not to be the one he had advocated, and Germany switched from the liberals' fiasco of 1848 to Bismarck's expeditious reliance on force). Liberalism's own conception of the individual and of the nation based on consent was only very selectively applied by liberals: the individual tended to be a white male, and "inferior" or "barbaric" peoples were to receive neither self-government nor self-determination soon—Mill and Tocqueville agreed on this. Liberalism à la Mill and Woodrow Wilson underestimated the turmoil that so often accompanies self-determination: what is the unit that is "entitled" to it? What happens to hapless minorities? Unscrambling multinational omelettes—from the Balkans to Quebec—has turned out to be a highly frustrating and frequently bloody Sisyphean task. After 1945, granting self-determination to units artificially carved out by the colonizers, in which the intellectuals' nationalism was less a commitment to nation building than a declaration of war on colonialism, has created big headaches both for the "liberated" peoples and for world order. Finally, strong national governments have found many ways to keep public opinion national and to put the free market at the service of national concerns and ambitions.

Thus, of the three main ideologies, one evaded our issue (and this, along with the mismanagement command economies fostered, ultimately caused the death of the communist creed). The other two, whose visions of world order are very different—one centered on states, one on individuals—proved capable of incorporating only a small part of the phenomenon of nationalism: a somewhat castrated nationalism, in the realist universe, a highly partial sanitized and idealized one in the liberal world. The challenge nationalism throws to political philosophy has not received an adequate response.

Is Nationalism the Enemy of World Order?

The case against nationalism has been made often—and rarely better than by Lord Acton. It is the opposite of the liberal case. It argues that a world in which nationalism is the dominant ideology of states is not "merely" one of ordinary anarchy, as in the seventeenth or eighteenth centuries. Then, the game of power was a competition of dynastic and mercantilistic interests, a struggle for supremacy among sovereigns. Nationalism, like religion earlier, added a number of poisonous elements to the contest. From the perspective of the unit, nationalism affected both the definition of ends and the available means. It introduced into the preferences of actors such goals as the "recuperation," through annexation, of nationals living beyond the current borders of the state (Nazi Germany, Slobodan Milosevic's Serbia) and the propagation abroad of what might be called the "national formula"—the institutions and values of the actor (the French Revolution and, despite its denegations, the United States after 1945; the Soviet case was one in which the forcible export of a so-called socialist formula became an instrument of Russian control). The old considerations of honor, glory, and reputation were given a new, far more potent and explosive content: tests of will and strength became tests of national merit and virility. Above all, a new set of means was put at the actor's disposal: the mobilization of the population. Social mobilization, which so many theorists of nationalism have presented as a precondition for or a key feature of it, thus becomes a prelude to national mobilization against a designated enemy. The age of nationalism becomes the age of mass propaganda, universal conscription, general mobilization for the war effort; it turns interstate conflict into the kind of total war that devastated Europe twice in this century and led to its downfall.

From the perspective of the international system, nationalism crippled one of the main requirements for an effective balance of power: the possibility of flexible alignments. After 1871, there was no chance for Franco-German accommodation, and a factor of permanent hostility was introduced into the rigidifying system. Nationalism also affected the system through contagion. French revolutionary nationalism rudely awakened a dormant German "national feeling" and gave it a virulent anti-French component; Napoleon kindled nationalism from Spain to Russia. Nationalism provided states with new pretexts for intervening in the affairs of others, in order either to crush or to assist movements of national emancipation; the policies of Russia and of Austria-Hungary in the pre-1914 Balkans, with the help of Serbian nationalism, resulted in the first world war. As self-determination gradually became a norm of the system, not only did it qualify the norm of sovereignty as it had been understood before 1789, but it also served to undermine sovereignty whenever self-determination affected the integrity of multinational states. It injected a permanent stream of trouble and conflict, either in the form of often bloody secessions (the Ottoman Empire shrank at regular intervals, the Austro-Hungarian one perished in defeat) or in the form of turbulent and bellicose regroupings, successful (Germany, Italy, Poland after 1918) or attempted (Arab post-1945 nationalism, present-day Serbia).

The case for the prosecution thus concludes that a world in which nationalism is both all-pervasive and sanctified is doubly disastrous. First, it is disastrous because of the fundamental contradiction between two constitutive principles, or *Grundnormen*, of the international system, the principle of inviolable territorial integrity and that of national self-determination—a conflict that has, in recent years, led to the tragedy of former Yugoslavia. Second, it is calamitous because of the clash not of civilizations (a very murky concept) but of definitions of what constitutes a nation. Sometimes, this clash remains confined to the domestic arena. Thus, the battle between "republican" and integral nationalism in modern France, and the battle between a territorial and secular definition of the Indian nation and a Hindu one, did not spill over into the international scene. But Alsace-Lorraine, Kashmir, Jerusalem, Bosnia, and the Falklands show the international dimension of the ambiguities of national self-determination.

How solid is the prosecutor's case? Its weak point is the underlying assumption of a single and malevolent kind of nationalism. The reality is a blooming confusion and a bewildering complexity. How dangerous nationalism is for world order may depend on what brand we are talking about. As always in social science, we need distinctions. Nationalisms can be analyzed according to four factors: their origins, their bases, their intellectual formulas, and their behavior.

When we examine origins we find that nationalism can be a reaction either to domestic conditions or to external oppression. The classic cases of the former are Britain and France. Linda Colley has admirably documented the development of a British nationalism of pride, Protestantism, and prosperity.[9] The French case is completely different: French nationalism grew as a reaction against absolutism and a society of orders and particularisms. The central role played by the state in the Old Regime meant that in this battle, the key question was going to be, whose state is it, the king's or the nation's, and that those who sided with king and church were expelled from the nation (see Sièyes). Nineteenth-century Russian nationalism also grew in reaction to domestic conditions of political and social oppression, but the nationalists were split between Slavophiles and Westernizers.

Reaction to external oppression, or to conditions experienced as external oppression, is far more frequent. I have already mentioned post-Napoleonic Europe. In this century, anticolonial nationalism led to the breakup of colonial empires and the victory of nationalist elites in India, Vietnam, Algeria, and Egypt. The collapse of communism in the Soviet Union led to the emancipation of the Baltic states and Ukraine and to the astonishing transformation of Soviet officials into nationalist leaders, as in Georgia and in Central Asia. In Yugoslavia, Croat and Slovene nationalisms grew in opposition to what was perceived as Serb exploitation, and Serb nationalism grew in defense of an allegedly global plot against Serbia. Quebec's nationalism (like Ireland's) is fueled by perceived "British" domination.

The first kind of nationalism is less dangerous for world order, although it can be pretty bad at home (British nationalism left little leeway for the Scots and the Welsh and mistreated Ireland; Jacobin nationalism was both xenophobic and murderous toward Vendéens and "aristocrats"). The second kind spells more trouble for world order—especially when, as in former Yugoslavia or in Azerbaijan and Georgia, minorities are caught in the reshuffling. But such generalizations need to be qualified. On the one hand, in the second group of cases, much depends on how accommodating the "oppressor" is: see the contrast between Baltic emancipation—relatively peaceful—and Chechnya; or between most of Britain's decolonization and France's. On the other hand, some of the most interesting cases are those in which nationalism grew out of external as well as domestic conditions. After 1792, French nationalism found a new vigor and turned outward, in reaction to the conservative powers' bumbling aggression. American nationalism, reversing the French pattern, started as a reaction against what was felt as violations by the metropolis and continued to grow as a celebration of American exceptionalism, a kind of self-congratulation so remarkable that not only was it not acknowledged as a form of nationalism, but it was seen as distinguishing America from the nationalisms of all other nations. Contemporary Chinese nationalism developed in reaction both to external humiliations and to domestic degradation. The fact is that in an international system of competing powers, domestic nationalist revolutions rarely fail to produce external effects, either because states threatened by them intervene (1792 in France, 1918 in Russia, U.S. support of Chiang against Mao, the Iraqi attack on Iran) and thereby give a xenophobic twist to the revolution they fight, or because the nationalists, in their drive to modernize their nation, resort to war to test and expand its power (Japan; U.S. expansion to the "frontier").

If origins tell us little, what about bases, that is, the fundamental inspiration of the nationalist creed? Are some more dangerous for world order than others? Let us review them. Ethnic nationalism has a particularly bad press, although it is a far from clear and simple notion (ethnic factors "can be organized an rendered meaningful in various ways, thus become elements of any number of identities").[10] But it often deserves its reputation, in part precisely because it is not easy to define an "ethnie" and conflicts arise out of these discordant definitions (are Croats, Serbs, and Bosnians all South Slavs or members of different ethnicities?), in part because the predominance of one ethnic group in a state can create dangers for, and provoke a revolt by, other ethnic groups (see the Tamils in Sri Lanka, the Hutus in Rwanda, the Ibos in Nigeria) as well as risks of external interventions justified on grounds of ethnic solidarity (Serbia to "protect" Serbs in Croatia, Armenia in Nagorno-Karabakh). A world in which the borders of ethnic groups would be those of nation-states is both inconceivable, given the confusion about what is an "ethnie" and the imbrication of ethnic groups, and also a recipe for permanent conflict, insofar as the emphasis on this single factor magnifies the differences among peoples and transforms each one into what Erik Erikson called a "pseudospecies." When ethnic nationalism turns into a doctrine of racial superiority, the effects abroad can be catastrophic: Hitler's rampages and ravages are unforgettable.

There isn't anything very different to say about religious nationalisms; the combination of religious and secular faiths is highly combustible. The Catholic nationalism in Northern Ireland is fueled by, and in turn reinforces, the Protestant British nationalism of the Unionists. Islamic fundamentalism, spreading within the borders and in response to the unsolved political and social problems of existing states, is turning into a set of such nationalisms, which find both internal and external enemies easily. The case of Muslim Bosnian nationalism is a curious one: it grew as a reaction to the Serbian view of Bosnians (who were often only nominally Muslim) as a separate ethnic group, among people who, prior to the war of 1992, had seen themselves as part of a multireligious and multicultural Slavic community. The religious component of several apparently secular nationalisms cannot be discounted; we have seen Greek opposition to a Muslim state of Macedonia and the integral version of French nationalism in its sorry present-day form—Le Pen—shrilly enouncing the "unassimilability" of Muslims in Christian France. The Hindu version of

Indian nationalism is far more exclusive—and specifically anti-Muslim—
than the secular, official one. Cultural nationalism is usually less bellicose, although, as we see in Quebec, it can lead to demands not just
for special rights aimed at safeguarding a cultural heritage but for full
independence and to the disregard of the rights of "lesser" cultural minorities.

What might be called territorial-traditional nationalism is also a milder
variety. It is the kind of nationalism whose basis is a common attachment
to a given territory and to a history of living together in it; it allows for
the coexistence and interpenetration of several cultural groups, ethnies,
or religions, as in Switzerland. This exposes it to severe strains when
some of these groups produce their own, separatist nationalism based on
ethnicity, religion, or culture, as in the case of the Basques and Catalans
in Spain or the Sikhs in India. But the territorial-traditional foundation
tends to allow for institutional compromises.

I have left for the end the case of two universalist nationalisms—
nationalisms that claim as their basis a common creed consisting of principles of universal relevance: the United States and France, the two products of early liberalism, the two melting pots of individual assimilation.
Their champions like to present this brand as ipso facto good for world
order. Reality is a bit less simple. First, the abstract creed—allegedly a
universally accessible abstract creed—needs to be embodied in specific
groups, and repeatedly, the people who act as guardians of the common
faith decide that certain alien groups are not fit, for reasons of race, color,
or religion, to partake of the common creed: the racial divide is still the
central one in the United States, and Muslim integration in France faces
many obstacles. In the French case, the highly assimilationist Jacobin
doctrine that fuels the melting pot creates tensions with groups that are
reluctant to leave what they deem essential cultural or religious characteristics to the private domain: for instance, Alsatians, Corsicans, and
Jews of North African origin. While a balance between assimilation and
multicultural pluralism has been easier to establish in the United States,
where the general interest is not seen as superior in essence to particular
interests, there are recurrent fears about the divisive effects of multiculturalism, especially when it entails linguistic diversity or different family
or work values; the ideology of the common universal creed does not rule
out regular witchhunts of "un-Americans."

To be sure, what precedes affects internal harmony more than world
order. However, faith in such a creed brings the temptation of external
proselytizing: if our national values are universal, why shouldn't the uni-

verse benefit from them? The imperialism of free institutions has been a recurrent motif in U.S. foreign policy, just as, after 1792, the French indulged in an imperialism of popular sovereignty and later—outside of Europe—in an imperialism of the "civilizing mission."

I distinguish between the basis of nationalism and its intellectual formula in order to focus on two key institutional issues: the mode of acquisition of nationality and the philosophy of the governmental system. On the first point, is the nationalism voluntaristic, the acquisition of nationality based on consent, as in Joseph Renan's famous formulation (but he also mentioned habituation, traditions, a common experience)? Is nationality imposed on the individual by race, religion, language, or culture? Many states try to produce a rather uneasy mix. When the voluntaristic element predominates, nationalism tends to see itself as more peace loving, more attuned to world order, than when the alternative conception prevails. But as we have just seen, there are many lapses. Either formula can lead to turbulence and conflict, and neither guarantees that aliens will be well treated.

Three philosophies of the governmental system can be distinguished. One is liberal and is usually connected to a voluntaristic conception of nationality. As suggested earlier, it is, in principle, less war prone, at least against other liberal nations. A second philosophy is, like liberalism, individualistic (government rests on the individuals' consent) and voluntaristic; but it departs from liberalism in adopting the Rousseauian and Jacobin formula of the general will, which assumes the superiority of that will over particular wills and interests; it is therefore suspicious of multiculturalism and willing to override individual rights if they clash with the common good defined by the general will (France, Quebécois nationalism). It is easy to see why this formula could push the balance between passion and reason in the direction of the former, if only by placing common will ahead of deliberation and separation of powers. Finally, there are authoritarian nationalist polities, and they usually are the ascriptive ones; a good liberal has learned to see them, therefore, as doubly dangerous.

What about a fourth factor, the actual behavior of nationalist states? The late French historian Jean-Baptiste Duroselle liked to distinguish inward-looking and outward-looking policies. Many small powers—especially Switzerland—are indeed satisfied with protecting their independence and integrity, but not all, especially not when they also want to protect their kin abroad. And outward-looking policies can be defensive and conservative. What history shows is that the same nation-state can behave in different ways at different moments.

This long review of nationalist features leads to a conclusion that is different from the prosecutor's but only in degree. Not all nationalisms are evil. On paper, some appear beneficial, insofar as they provide spiritual and material goods for their people. But while some characteristics are more worrisome than others, each feature carries its own load of dangers for world order; and much depends on the circumstances provided by the international system. As we have seen, even peace and world-order-oriented nationalisms can go to war, either defensively or offensively, in certain moments of crisis. And much depends on the degree of homogeneity that exists within the nation's borders: is there community or cacophony? The one variable that appears less ambiguous than the others, the nature of the political regime, introduces a significant exception into the prosecutor's case: liberal democracies haven't fought each other, are rather reluctant to go to war, and are more likely to deal fairly with minorities. But there aren't enough of them, and in the contest with nonliberal enemies, they are perfectly able to overcome their preference for peace, in the name of survival, democratic ideology, or a civilizing mission. Moreover, the process of liberal democratization may be turbulent at home and abroad. In a word: some nationalisms are evil, and all others can become evil. This, at least, is the lesson of the past. At present, nationalism, so often pronounced obsolete, is more than ever rampant in the international system, fueling both interstate and intrastate conflicts. What does this mean for world order?

World Order in a World of Nationalisms

Since the American and French Revolutions, nationalism has been both a principle of organization (national self-determination) and a dissolvent of order—even though the continental victors, at the Congress of Vienna, had tried to exorcise both liberalism and nationalism. The first world war resulted both from the national ambitions of some actors, big (Germany) and small (Serbia), and from the fears of dissolution of one multinational empire (Austria-Hungary). The logic of alliances, enmities, and military timetables did the rest. The nineteenth-century story could be seen as that of a competition between a "cosmopolitan liberal nationalism" (the one that liberal political philosophy proposed and that countries such as Britain, the United States, and republican France tried to approximate) and more particularistic nationalisms, which derailed the former and thwarted the liberal ideal (quite apart from the fact that it was never extended overseas—or to Ireland).

In the interwar period, cosmopolitan liberal nationalism was on the defensive, besieged by another universalistic cosmopolitan theory (communism), by the squabbling particularistic nationalisms of many of the new nation-states of the Europe of Versailles and Sèvres, and by the messianic and imperialistic nationalisms of Fascist Italy, Nazi Germany, and the military's Japan. In the cold-war era—longer than the interwar period but shorter than anyone had foreseen—the collapse of the fascisms resulted in a global collision of two universalisms, a liberal and a communist one, behind which two very different nationalisms, an American and a Russian one, pulled the strings, as de Gaulle used to warn. But decolonization sowed the seeds of new, potentially nonliberal, undemocratic nationalisms (Algeria, Vietnam, and Pakistan; Cuba could also be put into this category). And behind the cosmopolitan facade of communism, nationalism acted—once more—as a dissolvent, leading to the emancipation of Marshal Tito's fragile Yugoslavia (which behaved as a single nation only in its resistance to Moscow), of Red China, and of a Vietnam that didn't want to be anyone's satellite.

At present, the world system bears some resemblance to the nineteenth-century situation. We have seen a new wave of liberal democracies, primarily in Europe but also in Latin America and South Africa. However, it has been accompanied by further nationalist fragmentation: the explosion of the Soviet Union, the divorce between the Czechs and the Slovaks. The liberal democracies are obliged to coexist with a multitude of nonliberal, particularistic nationalisms, from Iraq to Singapore, from Cuba to China. The post–cold war system's originality lies in (1) the importance of a global economy that deprives many of the actors of traditional instruments of control (although some, like the United States, remain more "sovereign" than others), a fact that exacerbates nationalistic reactions of a defensive nature in many countries: we have seen it in France and in Russia, and even in the United States (against NAFTA [North American Free Trade Agreement]); (2) a singular configuration of great powers: a unipolar system in some respects, multipolar in others; and (3) the existence of two spheres of conflict, the traditional one of interstate conflicts, such as India-Pakistan, North and South Korea, Iran-Iraq, Israel and the Palestinians (a state in the making), Turkey-Greece, and a huge sphere of intrastate conflicts, some of which result from the clash of competing nationalisms (Yugoslavia, Chechnya, the Kurds versus the Iraqis, and the Turks), while others are the effects of the disintegration of weak, artificial, or corrupt states (Zaire, Somalia, Liberia, Rwanda, Cambodia).

This situation creates some formidable problems for world order. In that second sphere of troubles, there is always a risk of aggravation through external intervention. China has muddied the Cambodian waters for a long time, Russia has intervened in Georgia and Tajikistan, France in African internal conflicts, Turkey in Cyprus. A second issue is the capacity of the international system to tolerate protracted intrastate turbulence, whether it takes the form of bloody wars for independence or restoration, as in Yugoslavia (or for domination, as in Rwanda) or mistreatment of minorities in new (Croatia, Sudan) or older (Turkey, Iraq) entities. A third issue is the feasibility of the kind of internationalism that represents the maximum achievement of cosmopolitanism so far: a compromise between the cosmopolitan idea that tends toward some form of world governance and the existence, and resistance, of multiple actors that cling to their sovereignty either because they are strong (United States, China—potentially) or because they feel it slipping. I am referring to the difficulties faced by international and regional organizations in the present system.

As I have suggested in chapter 8, the system suffers from a clash, not just between the norms of state sovereignty and national self-determination (already battling the nineteenth century), but among four universally recognized norms (however different the interpretations of each may be): sovereignty, national self-determination, self-government (democracy), and human rights. All four commands are derived from the liberal scriptures, and it is possible to dream of a world that would respect all four. Alas, as they sing in the *Three-Penny Opera*, "nur die Verhältnisse, die sind nicht so": our circumstances are not the right ones.

What is to be done to contain and curb the dangers of nationalism? To the problem of external intervention, there are three conceivable approaches. One is simple indifference, due to the absence of collective will and means. Depending on the region, this could lead to an escalation of violence and to a return of forms of colonialism and domination (the scaling down of French military presence in former black African colonies is welcome news). At the other extreme, one can envisage a collective, and collectively enforced, ban on unilateral interventions—a ban based not on the principle of respect for sovereignty (since these interventions claim that they are aimed either at restoring territorial integrity or at making self-determination possible) but on the threat to peace and security unilateral interventions constitute. But this remains both unlikely and also, in some circumstances, inopportune. The third approach is a kind of halfway solution. It would consist in either the collective licensing of a unilateral intervention, putting it under the control and conditions of the Security Council or of a regional organization, or the launching of a collective intervention wherever the conflict threatens peace and security or crushes fundamental human rights and whenever a unilateral intervention would be likely to make bad matters worse (clearly, a Russian intervention in a conflict that tears apart a former Soviet republic in the Caucasus or in Central Asia would be less threatening for peace and security than in the Balkans).

This halfway approach brings us directly to the issue of what the international society ought to do about turmoil in what I have called the second sphere of conflicts. I have dealt with this issue extensively elsewhere.[11] There is, in this domain, a huge gap between what is likely and what is desirable. What is likely is either collective nonintervention, when the problem appears to be "safely forgettable" (in the Sudan, Sri Lanka, East Timor, Burma) or, at best, a modicum of humanitarian intervention, as in Rwanda. Nonintervention justifies itself by such varied considerations as a conviction of the futility of coping with civil war, the reluctance of major powers to engage forces trained for "real" wars into peacemaking operations, or the difficulty even international policemen have in disarming factions and knocking heads together in faraway countries. This is not very satisfactory, to say the least. My preference is for a collective reinforcement of two sets of norms. Insofar as collective interventions are concerned, I would like to see them undertaken not only when the Security Council determines that international or regional peace and security are threatened but also when fundamental human rights have been violated. And among such violations, I would include not merely genocide but mass killings not covered by the genocide convention (such as those that are aimed at political groups), ethnic cleansing, and mass rape. The protection of human rights also requires a return (with improvements) to the safeguarding of minorities, through internationally guaranteed statuses and treaties. It is difficult to see how this admittedly ambitious program of collective interventions could be carried out without an international police force, or at least earmarked national forces at the disposal of the Security Council. In this respect, internationalism is still in its infancy.

The first traditional sphere of conflicts—interstate clashes, usually between incompatible nationalist claims—requires a more determined and effective use of equally traditional methods: collective diplomacy to prevent, if possible, and resolve disputes (in the Palestinian-Israeli case, the monopoly imposed by the United States has not brought the benefits Washington expected: the main progress came from Norwegian good offices) as well as collective security against aggression. It remains only too obvious that in the latter case, as well as in that of internal conflicts, collective actions are most unlikely to target major powers—a fact that serves, alas, as a legitimizer of the resistance many middle and small powers oppose to collective action.

The respect of both civil and political rights, and of economic and social ones, conceived as rights individuals can legitimately claim, is an obligation that transcends the partly phony debate between so-called Western and so-called Asian conceptions of human rights (there is nothing in Western liberalism that denies the possibility for individuals to form groups that deserve protection or denigrates the importance of the family; and there is a lot in so-called Asian notions that can be used to muzzle and oppress individuals). Democratic self-government is not a norm that can be enforced from abroad, since democracy is both a set of institutions that need roots in a given society and a set of practices and *moeurs* that can only be indigenous.[12] But outsiders can certainly encourage or facilitate the establishment of democratic institutions, and we are witnessing the development of new norms, ranging from the requirement of democratic self-government for membership in certain regional organizations (the Council of Europe, the European Union) to the protection of democracy from coups and the nonrecognition of governments established by such coups, in the case of the OAS.

The norm of sovereignty has been turned from an absolute into a conditional norm. It still deserves to cover security from external aggression and interference and the right of the state to run internal affairs, but only insofar as it respects internationally recognized human rights and the kind of international obligations that a treaty establishing a global system of criminal justice might, one hopes, establish. This revision of the norm would, if enforced, curb many of the external and internal excesses of nationalism. As for the competing norm of self-determination, this battering ram of nationalism also requires restrictions, dictated both by the pervasive problem of interlocked minorities and by considerations of peace and order. Even if, with Daniel Philpott, one endorses a prima facie right to national self-determination,[13] we need new international norms to regulate secessions so as to make them a last resort in cases where there are legitimate claims for secession (the violation of fundamental rights by the existing state, economic discrimination and exploitation, cultural survival) and where such claims rest not on an ascriptive or collective foundation that could lead to continuing or new forms of individual oppression but on a liberal-individualistic one. Such a revision of the norm of self-determination would, in cases of internal conflicts between competing nationalisms, allow for federal, confederal, and minorities-friendly solutions short of full secession.

Nationalism, Liberalism, and World Order

I have few illusions about the likelihood that even the rather nonutopian suggestions presented above will be carried out in the near future. World order remains a fragile construction threatened not only by many forms and implications of nationalism but also by the temptations to which anarchy always exposes the mightier states, whatever their regime or dominant philosophy, by the divagations and inequities of global capitalism, by the availability of weapons of mass destruction, and by the artificiality and weakness of so many nonnational states. Above all, the "national idea" survives, both in old nations and in new ones as well as in those states that haven't become nations yet, not only because it provides the state with a principle of legitimacy and the people with a source of collective identity and social bonds but also because no other focus of allegiance transcending the nation-state has yet appeared. States have done their best to prevent this. Someday, nationalist ideologies may fade, because of the glaring deficiencies of the nation-state—but not before a new institutional kit capable of attracting mass loyalty has succeeded in being more than a set of utilitarian and technocratic correctives to these flaws.

If this is so, doesn't the only hope, both for human rights and for world order, remain the liberal vision, especially in its Kantian version, revived by Wilson, empirically corroborated by Michael Doyle? At the core of this ideal, we find the conviction that democratic, representative government tames the bellicose potential of nationalism (through the combination of the citizens' interest in preserving their lives, rational deliberation, and the separation of powers) and the conviction that liberal self-determination favors harmony rather than conflict—a conviction that inspired Jean Jaurès as well as Mazzini. But much of what I have suggested above tells us that things are not so simple. Even if liberal democracies multiplied, we would be left with a number of major sources of disorder. We would still have all the ambiguities of self-determination and of what constitutes a nation (if the Croats and the Bosnians are entitled to a state of their own, what about the Serbs in Croatia and Bosnia). We would still find liberal democracies having troubles with minorities that feel oppressed by majority rule, from Canada to India. We would still, in all likelihood, face conflicts between liberal democracy and authoritarian pariahs, conflicts that are often clashes of nationalisms. It would still be possible for a "peaceful" liberal democracy to undermine another state without war (see the United States in Chile or Guatemala).

At best, we would achieve two gains: a reduction of violence and some growth in the *ersatz* of world government that is constituted by two networks, that of public international and regional organizations and that of private transnational associations and regulations. They are not negligible, and they certainly point in a direction spurned by the neorealists: progress through the spread of liberal nationalism, the only one compatible, in principle, with internationalism. But liberal nationalism can still be an obstacle to the kind of cosmopolitan cooperation world order requires now. It is so because, as Dominique Schnapper argues, institutions of "a purely civic nature," "founded on abstract principles" and on an "intellectual commitment," do not have the "strength to control passions born from allegiances" to nations. In her view, a modern democratic nation, *pace* Habermas, "cannot be of a purely civic nature," it has to be based on "the specific values, traditions and institutions that define a political nation." "Every organized, democratic society indissolubly carries ethnic elements—cultural, historical, and nationalist—as well as a civic principle." The "affective desire of human society" (Elias), the political space for "choice, arbitrations, obligations, and the desire to exist" remain at the national level, despite all the leakages of sovereignty.[14]

The example of the European Union (EU), which Schnapper mentions, is doubly important in this respect. It shows us how much can be accomplished by liberal democracies, and it shows the limits of cosmopolitanism. On the one hand, the process of European integration since 1950 has almost certainly ruled out war among the EU's members; the recognition of economic interdependence has led not merely to policy coordination but to the creation of a single market of goods, capital, and services, soon to be completed—barring last-minute hitches—by a single currency and European Central Bank. However, we must remember that the enterprise was launched at a time when nationalism had been beaten out of Germany and Italy and when the two leading "integrationist" parties of France, the Socialists and the Christian Democrats, were more internationalist than nationalist. With the persistence or revival of nationalism in several of the current members of the EU, the quasi-federal or suprana-tional dream of Jean Monnet seems way beyond achievement.

As integration proceeds, states tend to cling to those leaves of the arti-choke of sovereignty that are still in their clutches, and to its heart: diplo-macy in the "strategic-political realm," the domestic configuration of governmental institutions, and politics. Key symbols of national identity, bizarre as they may be, benefit from popular attachment: the deutsche mark in Germany, the *force de frappe* in France. It is interesting that resistance to further integration (in the sense of expanded majority rule and a reform of the EU's institutional puzzle) is strongest in a United Kingdom whose nationalism is basically liberal-individualistic, attached to the rights of British citizens and to that focus of national loyalty, Par-liament; and also in France, whose battered nationalism is preserved by the myth of French universalism and bound up with the concept of an indivisible and untransferable general will. In principle, national identity should be able to exist and persist without nationalism. In reality, when national identity is felt to be threatened—by globalization, by American-ization, by Europeanization—nationalism revives and makes new steps toward internationalism and cosmopolitanism more arduous.

At least in the European case, we can observe the coexistence of what Joseph Weiler calls, imaginatively, the national Eros and the civilization of common European citizenship, largely disembodied though the latter may be. We can hope that over time, at least a modicum of Eros will settle on the common institutions and policies. Europe, so full of doubts about itself—for good reasons—can at least be proud of being ahead of other continents in this regard. Here, partly tamed nationalisms allow for and coexist with an innovative if imperfect new European order. How long will it take for international society to reach this stage—and will it?

15

On Ethnic Conflicts and Their Resolution

A World of Ethnic Conflicts?

In the world of the cold war, as had been the case for several centuries, the state was viewed as a coherent entity—Karl von Clausewitz assumed that it could be assimilated to a person endowed with reason and intelligence. The floor of the system was made up of states. Another metaphor, used by realists, was that of states as billiard balls. Between the fundamental norm of state sovereignty (from which was derived the imperative of nonintervention in other states' domestic affairs) and the ideal of national self-determination, endorsed by liberals, there were, obviously, conflicts. Self-determination led to the secession of Belgium from the Netherlands and of Greece from the Ottoman Empire, to the reunification of Germany and Italy at the expense of the many states into which these nationalities had been split, to the recurrent fragmentation of the Ottoman Empire, and to rebellions in partitioned Poland and in Hungary. But successful national self-determination led to the formation of new states, as in central and eastern Europe after World War I; and in the process of decolonization after World War II, emancipation from colonial rule often had little to do with national self-determination: in much of Africa, unlike in India or Palestine, the new states' borders were simply those the colonizers had artificially created. The "floor" of the international system was periodically rearranged; it was not dismantled.

In the cold war system, the main question was ideological. The central conflict was over the legitimacy of the government in the sovereign state; the "Free World" and the Communist countries had radically different conceptions of legitimacy, although both claimed to stand for democracy. And the central risk was that of a violent conflict between the rival blocs, now armed with nuclear weapons. This fundamental danger led to conflicts among lesser states belonging to the two camps, as between the two Koreas or the two Vietnams. It also led to many interventions by the superpowers in the domestic affairs of weaker states, in order to change the character of the government there (the United States in Iran, Guatemala, Santo Domingo, and Nicaragua, the Soviet Union in Hungary in 1956 and in Dubcek's Czechoslovakia in 1968) or in order to prevent a "friendly" government from falling (the United States in El Salvador, the USSR in Afghanistan). To be sure, there were many other interstate conflicts that had little to do with the cold war: in the Indian subcontinent, in the Middle East, in Cyprus, and so on. But even these tended to become, so to speak, hitched to the central conflict.

The present international system, by contrast, is one in which many billiard balls disintegrate, torn by internal conflict or flawed in their construction. The damaged floor of international politics is a heterogeneous collection of sturdy states, of new and often still untested ones produced by the collapse of the Soviet Union, and of failed or corrupt states. The principle of self-determination appears mainly as a factor of fragmentation and turbulence more than as a lever of human liberation, it is a threat to the territorial integrity of states, an engine of secessions and splits, actual (Ukraine, Central Asia, Georgia, Azerbaijan, Eritrea) or potential (Sri Lanka, Quebec). Moreover, it often collides with another norm of contemporary international law: the respect and protection of human rights, individual or, in the case of minorities, collective. The Yugoslav tragedy provides many examples.

In this system, the central question is one that had already troubled nineteenth-century thinkers: what constitutes a nation? Insofar as nationalism is the one universal ideology that, after the collapse of communism, is left to coexist (most uneasily) with liberalism (celebrated a bit too hastily by Fukuyama as having established a kind of intellectual "end of history"), Renan's old question—*qu'est-ce qu'une nation?*—is more pressing than ever. But there is a second central question, in ironical counterpoint to the first: is the sovereign state (national or not) still an effective shelter and provider for its members, in an age of pervasive insecurity where the state cannot defend its subjects either from nuclear attack at the cosmic level, so to speak, or from terrorism at the microscopic one, in an age of economic interdependence in which practically no state is self-sufficient and, furthermore, the global capitalist market, a network of individuals and private corporations, severely constrains and shapes the "operational" sovereignty of the states? The main risks, in this system, are both violence and anomie: the violence of often genocidal conflicts, within or over the ruins of states, and the anomie of chaos, due to the deficiencies of international governance, for whenever state sovereignty has become atrophied or meaningless, the international public and private institutions that have developed remain too weak to provide adequate substitutes or to regulate a global economy whose sudden somersaults shake and shock the states that are at its mercy.

Let us now focus on a few facts. First, many of the interstate or intrastate conflicts in the present system are not ethnic at all. In the Somalia of 1991–1994, in Liberia, in Afghanistan, in Nicaragua, in Albania, in Cambodia, in Zaire, in Angola and Mozambique, and in Korea, violence has been fueled by political gangs, by ideological parties and armies, by tribal rivalries, by personal ambitions, and so on. Prolonged political repression is a powerful breeder of such violence, as in Albania and Algeria. Religious forces and fanaticisms are another major source of bloodshed—in the Sudan, Algeria, and Afghanistan, between Sunnis and Shiites in Iraq, between Sikhs and Hindus in India.

Second, what constitutes an "ethnie" is far from clear. The Yugoslavs were all South Slavs, the Czechs and Slovakians are Slavs (and the Serb- and Croat-based notion that the Yugoslav conflict was a war among Catholics, Orthodox, and Muslims—a notion rashly endorsed by Samuel Huntington in his muddled thesis about the clash of civilizations—is pretty hard to swallow, if one remembers that much of the population was secular and that the leaders were communists reconverted into nationalists). The line between tribalism and ethnicity is thin, or artificial (Rwanda and Burundi, Nigeria). We need to resort to the concept of "subethnies." Each one of them is based on a combination of religious, historical, and cultural factors, and the dubious concept of race is not of much help. What matters most is the self-perception of the group, but we must remember that this is often fabricated by the leaders.

Third, the phenomenon of nationalism is difficult to account for in purely rational terms. What one can show is that the choice of a nationalist strategy may be perfectly rational for an ambitious leader or elite. But the heart of the phenomenon is a human need for social identity in a world in which the traditional and rather static hierarchies have collapsed, in which what Karl Deutsch called social mobilization and others call modernization occurs. This identity, first in Britain, France, and the rebellious British colonies of America, focused on the nation and on the right of the nation to have a state of its own, both for domestic reasons (the provision of security, education, and services) and for external ones (protection from foreign domination and intrusion). The idea of the nation and the nationalist ideologies that it bred thus filled the needs of human emotion and imagination in an otherwise "disenchanted" society of bureaucratic regulations and capitalist calculations. In a world of functional hierarchies, this idea (or ideal) and these ideologies provided human beings with a sense of equality as citizens, of common membership despite and across social divisions. Social scientists, including Marx and Ernst Gellner, have tended to underestimate the powerful nonrational elements that provide the glue of the nation-state or to confuse the (modernizing) function of nationalism with its source and essence.

If we turn to the dimensions of ethnic and subethnic conflict in the present international system, three points stand out. First, we find an extraordinarily widespread occurrence of such explosions: when empires break up, as in the case of the Soviet Union and within some of the units that resulted from its disintegration (in Russia—the war in Chechnya; in Georgia and Azerbaijan); when the state structure was weak (Yugoslavia after Tito; Sudan, Rwanda) or weakened by war (Iraq in 1991, Afghanistan); when repression was ruthless enough to provoke collective resistance but not enough to wipe it out (Kurds in Turkey and Iraq); when an incipient process of democratization fulfilled John Stuart Mill's expectation that democratic self-government would be fatal to multiethnic states (Yugoslavia in 1990–1991, Czechoslovakia after the fall of communism); when a minority receives support from an outside power dominated by the same "ethnie" (Turks in Cyprus, to some extent Albanians in Kosovo, Armenians in Nagorno-Karabakh, Russians in Moldavia, transnational "Pan-Tutsiism" in central and eastern Africa).

Second, ethnic and subethnic conflict has become a major disruptive factor both in international relations and in domestic affairs. In world politics, it destroys the status quo and produces a kind of universal security dilemma: it puts into jeopardy existing borders (for example, the Ibo rebellion in Nigeria); it creates headaches for other states concerning the recognition of new units (see the OAS reluctance to recognize Eritrea, the intra-European squabbles over the recognition of Slovenia and Croatia); it raises questions about the devolution of treaty obligations to successor states. It produces huge masses of refugees, thus provoking frequently hostile and inhumane reactions of closure in "invaded" countries (see the restrictions on asylum in Germany after the Yugoslav war, and the Schengen provisions) and putting an almost unbearable strain both on the international regime for refugees and on the resources of the UN High Commission in Refugees. It fuels lasting conflicts among states, as those between India and Pakistan, Greece and Turkey, Israel and Syria, Israel and the potential Palestinian state. It fosters unilateral external interventions—from within the region (Turkey in Cyprus) or from a faraway power (France in Rwanda). It creates major problems for an international law and a UN Charter still founded on the norms of sovereignty and nonintervention (which includes a ban on humanitarian intervention without the consent of the targeted state).

From the viewpoint of a state in prey to ethnic or subethnic conflict, difficult choices have to be made. Should a secession be allowed, and if so, how? (see the pending Canadian crisis). Should it be averted by a reshaping of domestic institutions in a federal, confederal, or consociational direction or by a grant of extensive rights of autonomy to an ethnic minority—but wouldn't this actually encourage it to escalate its claims? Can it be averted by a policy of assimilation that treats all members as equal citizens—but in the process either erases or relegates to the purely private domain the ethnic or subethnic characteristics of minorities (the French and, to a large extent, the U.S. approaches)?

Third, there is something intractable and often murderous about ethnic conflict. Warlords come and go, gang members melt into jungles and mountains, ideological armies fade or compromise, but ethnic feelings (and often religious ones as well: see Northern Ireland) have a way of surviving even if they go underground for a while. As I have argued elsewhere, nationalism is ubiquitous, polymorphous, parasitic on other ideologies. It can be openly ethnic, singling out "its" ethnie as radically unique, it can be civic and voluntaristic and develop around the sense of superiority of such a democratic formula over ascriptive ones. It can be a means to, or a companion of, liberal, representative institutions; it can also be authoritarian and aggressive. It can graft itself even on a cosmopolitan creed such as communism or on a transnational force such as Islamic fundamentalism, or Pan-Arabism.

Nationalism does not only have multiple faces. It also has multiple parents. It often depends on the determination of elites to triumph over foreign domination or over nonnational rulers (see the role of the Congress Party in the Raj). It certainly depends on intellectuals, who construct a national idea if not ex nihilo at least, often, on the flimsy basis of an imagined past or even an almost vanished language (like Hebrew) and whose all-important role is to provide the myths and the *lieux de mémoire* for national unity. It requires masses willing to fight and suffer for it.

Precisely because so much can be invested into nationalism by so many, it risks degenerating into warfare, in two ways. One is the kind of total war humanity has experienced twice in this century. The horizontal complicity of monarchs and diplomats before 1914 was destroyed by the European nationalisms that grew harder after 1871 and by the fear they inspired in a multinational state such as Austria-Hungary. World War II was initiated by the hideous racist nationalism of Hitler—and revived Russian nationalism after June 1941, as well as the American nationalism that inspired "unconditional surrender" and the dropping of the atomic bombs on Japan. The other form is genocide: the Holocaust was the product of Nazi nationalism. Genocide has reappeared, despite all the pious post-Holocaust promises of never again, both in Yugoslavia and in Rwanda (and, on a somewhat smaller scale, in East Timor). The Cambodian killing fields resulted not from ethnic but from ideological fury. But in all cases of genocide, we find the manipulation of the many (killers) by the few (leaders, political or military—sometimes, as in the Serbian case, with the help of the media).

Ethnic Conflict Resolution

Given the importance and the consequences of the problem, what is to be done? This is not the only conundrum of world politics, because we must also worry about the proliferation of weapons of mass destruction and acts of terrorism (two kinds of tools nationalism can use) as well as about the effects of global capitalism (a form of cosmopolitanism that is both open to national manipulations and a breeder of nationalist reactions and resistance). But it is assuredly the central *casse-tête* of modern diplomacy. I would like to distinguish between the present scene and the long term.

Much has been written recently about the prevention of ethnic violence. It can take two forms. One, already alluded to, is from the inside of a threatened country. The threatened country can decide to give a special status to a minority by law or by agreement with the country that sees itself as the natural protector of the minority (see Hungary's recent agreement with Romania—an agreement in which outside powers were actually involved: France, with Balladur's idea of a stability pact; the EU, which Hungary and Romania wanted to please so as to make future membership easier). This was also the case in South Tirol. But the willingness of a state to concede extensive autonomy to minorities depends not only on the nature of the regime (it is hard to envisage Saddam Hussein granting genuine power to the Kurds or the Turkish military allowing for Kurdish autonomy) but also on its philosophy (French Jacobin assimilationism leaves little room for Corsican or Alsatian assertions of distinctiveness) and on the danger of contagion (these last two factors have made successive Indian governments hostile to a recognition of minority rights). It also depends on the degree to which a state could fear that such a recognition would ignite rather than extinguish foreign meddling of the kind that Hitler practiced in the Sudetenland and in Poland. As for the creation of an institutionalized form of multiethnicity, it has sometimes worked: in the Swiss confederation, in Spain in relation to Catalonia. But sometimes, as in Canada and Belgium, it is shaky, even when (as in India and Canada) there are multiethnic parties cutting across the dividing lines. Here again, we have to look at the state's philosophy. Zionist Israel does not envisage becoming a binational state, and Milosevic's Serbia much preferred a greater Serbia to a revamping of the Yugoslav Federation that would have increased the autonomy of Slovenes, Croats, and Bosnians, hence their power over Serb minorities in the last two cases. We must, of course, look also at the mind-set of the ethnic or subethnic groups fighting against the existing states. The Basques are not willing to settle for what the Catalans obtained. The Québecois nationalists want the principle and symbols of independence.

This means that there are cases in which permanent warfare (as in Sri Lanka) and secession (or partition) are the only alternatives. As in the case of Eritrea, or Chechnya, or, earlier, Bangladesh, secession can be bloody—especially when fostered with outside help (Bangladesh, Cyprus partition). The only contemporary example of voluntary secession is the "velvet divorce" between the Czech Republic and Slovakia, a fascinating case in which the relative indifference of one key negotiator (Vaclav Klaus) to the whole issue of nationalism versus the multiethnic state, because of his preferred emphasis on economic issues, led to an agreement between leaders without popular consultation (a condition most political philosophers writing about secession insist on).

The other kind of prevention, through outside good offices, has known some successes. If many ethnic dogs growled but didn't bark in Eastern Europe or in Macedonia, the efforts of the OSCE and the magnetic pull of the EU are largely to be credited. The OSCE and the Council of Europe have pressed the Baltic states to treat Russian minorities fairly. These successes suggest that regional organizations may be best equipped to provide the diplomatic good offices and, if necessary, the peacekeepers prevention requires. And yet, the record of the Organization of African Unity (OAU)—often paralyzed by the fear that any questioning of existing borders could lead to destabilization all over the continent—has been poor. As for the UN, it has not done much better. Many research institutes have proposed setting up indicators of impending troubles, but the problem lies much more in the willingness of the secretary-general to ring the alarm bell and of the member states to act. International law and the Charter being what they are, this should be easier when the possible conflict is interstate, but in the Arab-Israeli conflict the UN has been increasingly pushed aside by the United States, and in the conflict over Cyprus, NATO plays a more important role. When, as in the majority of cases, the conflict is an internal one, the UN is handicapped by the need to establish that there is a threat to peace and security (something that is easier to find when the conflict has already broken out), by the need to get the consent of the troubled state's government (which may well see UN good offices as legitimizing the minority that agitates against it), and by the reluctance of governments to start on a slippery slope that could lead to military intervention and casualties. Although, in 1994 in Rwanda and in 1996 in the case of the Tutsi revolt in Zaire, small outside forces might, in the opinion of many high officials of the UN, have prevented the massacres that ravaged the area, neither the OAU nor the Security Council decided to raise them—indeed, in the Zairian case, African states such as Uganda intervened to help the Zairian Tutsis and, later, the anti-Mobutu forces. In the Yugoslav drama, even though political developments in Slovenia and Croatia in 1989–1991 made a breakup predictable, the UN did practically nothing (the secretary-general's interest was focused on Africa), and the EU did too little too late. Only in Macedonia was a preventive force sent in time.

The fact is that preventive intervention by the UN or a regional organization is a highly intrusive affair. It may involve interference in and the redrafting of internal constitutional arrangements, a delicate operation indeed. It may necessitate the sending of forces and in that case run either into the reluctance of states (many of whom have ethnic skeletons in their closets) to set a precedent that may boomerang on them or into the preferences some of them may have for a decisive victory by one or the other side in the conflict, rather than for the shaky standstill that a military intervention could ensure (as in Cyprus, where the international force keeps the country divided and the conflict unresolved).

If prevention fails (or isn't even attempted), what about the methods of settlement of a conflict that has turned violent? In ethnic conflicts between states we find a somewhat greater ratio of success when the risks of escalation—in intensity or in geographical scope—are very high. The UN has, with the active help of the major powers, stopped several conflicts between India and Pakistan; it has obtained cease-fires in the 1967, 1973, and 1982 Arab-Israeli wars. But the cost, frequently, has been (as in Cyprus and in southern Lebanon) a freezing of a miserable status quo; and when one of the parties is a major power—China in its wars against India and Vietnam, the Soviets in Afghanistan, the British-Argentinean war over the Falklands—the UN has remained on the sidelines.

In intrastate ethnic conflicts, we find few cases comparable to the settlements achieved in instances of ideological or gang conflicts (as in Liberia, with the help of Nigeria and other West African states, in Angola and Mozambique under the auspices of the United States and the UN, in Cambodia, or in El Salvador). To be ultimately effective, they require either a disarmament of the factions or a willingness to share power; when neither occurs, the settlement comes from the victory of the stronger side, as in Laurent Kabila's case in Zaire. What we find instead in ethnic international conflicts is a mixed record of external unilateral and collective interventions. In the first category, we can place India's intervention in East Bengal, which ensured the partition of Pakistan, that is, the victory of the weaker side, and India's intervention against the weaker side, the Tamils, in Sri Lanka—which ended in a fiasco. We can also place there the misguided intervention of the Greek colonels against Archbishop Makarios in Cyprus, which helped mobilize the Turks, as well as a variety of post-1991 Russian interventions in the "near abroad," which helped Eduard Shevardnadze against his foes in Georgia, and one faction against others in Tajikistan. In none of these cases did the outside intervener facilitate or make possible a negotiated settlement. (The same can be said about French support for the Hutus in Rwanda.)

Collective intervention in internal ethnic conflicts by the UN also presents us with a blurry picture. The criteria legitimizing intervention have remained narrow: the existence of a threat to international or regional peace and security and (only in the case of the Kurds in Iraq) a record of brutal oppression—but only as a kind of appendix to collective security against Iraqi aggression. Those criteria have not been applied consistently (contrast action in Yugoslavia with inaction in the Sudan); and of course great powers, such as China in Tibet or Russia in Chechnya, have not been sanctioned. When the UN Security Council chose to intervene, the burdens created by these operations often seemed doubly disproportionate—too flimsy to be effective tools of settlement, too complex and costly for the meager financial and operational resources of the UN. Humanitarian assistance, both in Yugoslavia and in Rwanda, has run into formidable obstacles: obstruction by some of the parties (the Serbs in Bosnia, both the Tutsis and the Hutu armed gangs in refugee camps in Rwanda and Zaire); the Sisyphean nature of the humanitarian effort as long as war keeps raising the number of the wounded, the hungry, and the exiles; the lack of means at the disposal of relief and refugee agencies to prevent the diversion of their aid for war purposes; and so on. The definition of the political mission, beyond humanitarian assistance, has often been disastrously fuzzy (as in Somalia) or contradictory (as in the Bosnian conflict, where the Security Council had one foot firmly planted in the soil of a political settlement among parties deemed equally good—or bad—and the other gingerly posed on the soil of collective support to the Muslim Bosnians against ethnic cleansing and massacres). Or else, as in the Dayton agreements, after the cease-fire and separation of forces finally achieved through the belated use of NATO force against the Serbs, the mission given to the successors of that hapless hostage, UNPROFOR (UN Protection Force), IFOR (Implementation Force), and now SFOR (Stabilization Force) was both too limited and too handicapped by lack of political will to enforce the peace and to deal with war criminals.

The problem of political support for such collective interventions remains crucial: contrast the Gulf war (up to and including the protection of the Kurds after the coalition's victory) and the Yugoslav tragedy. We can be reasonably sure that a new Iraqi invasion of Kuwait would provoke a new demonstration of collective security. We do not know today what the UN or NATO will do if Dayton fails, war resumes, and the Bosnian Serbs are responsible for that resumption. The reluctance of national armed forces, geared to fighting enemies of their nation, to intervene in police operations among foreign factions fuels the reluctance of states to get engaged too deeply in such adventures. Settlements still elude international society—both in the interstate ethnic conflicts of the Middle East (despite Oslo) and in internal ones, in Yugoslavia and Rwanda. And of course, civil violence not deemed to threaten peace and security goes on: in Sri Lanka, East Timor, Algeria, the Sudan, and elsewhere.

When we turn to the long term, we are reduced to the normative (in the sense that Hegel gave to international law, a law that tells us how we ought to act but says little about how we actually act). Rather than producing a long laundry list of oughts, I will limit myself to three sets of exhortations.

The first, which I have developed elsewhere, concerns international governance. If one is convinced that ethnic conflict is both a threat to peace and security (in part because of the role of contagion in this epidemic phenomenon, nationalism) and a threat to fundamental liberal values of respect for life and diversity, then one must provide mechanisms capable of accomplishing the tasks of prevention and settlement that are so badly carried out at present and that cannot be left to often questionable, fragile, and selfish states. What this requires is, on the one hand, the scrapping of the sacrosanct distinction between interstate and intrastate conflicts, once the latter begin to threaten peace or to violate fundamental human rights. On the other hand, since in human affairs—domestic as well as global—the triumph of reason so often rests on the threat or the use of force, international and regional agencies need to be provided with standby forces specially trained and earmarked by their members, or with the kind of volunteer army Sir Brian Urquhart has suggested for war-preventing, peacekeeping, and peace-enforcing purposes. They would still require the consent of a number of states in order to be legitimately used. But this would amount to a major revolution in world affairs.

The second imperative deals with the tension between the norm of state sovereignty and the principle of national self-determination. Each one, if pushed too far, has unacceptable effects both on international order and on the lives and rights of individuals. Solutions will have to be found through strict limitations on both. Concerning sovereignty, liberal representative government is largely an effort to curb it inside the borders of the polity: it splits the powers of government among many branches and levels and creates a zone of inviolable human rights. External sovereignty is already being eroded by the facts of interdependence, as well as by international norms for the protection of human rights. We need to move to a situation in which it is clearly understood, and enshrined in international law, that sovereignty is justified by and limited to the protection of the polity from outside threats and interference and to the provision of order, justice, welfare, and self-government. Sovereignty should be subject not only to the self-imposed restrictions that result from treaties but also to the authority of international and regional organizations with the right and power to enforce these restrictions, to ensure collective security, and to protect human rights both through collective interventions and through a system of international criminal justice.

As for self-determination, a debate is proceeding among political philosophers, between those who consider it a fundamental human right—the right to a nation and nationality of one's own—and those who reject this view either because they consider it disruptive of world order and dangerous for the vital good of peace or because they are appalled by the injustices self-determination often breeds, through the mistreatment of minorities and the excesses of nationalism—or for both reasons. There is, in my opinion, no way anymore of removing national self-determination from the list of rights granted by international law to individuals and peoples; to revoke it would also be disruptive of world order and peace and license new imperialisms. But there is a need for serious conditions and curbs to be imposed on it. They would concern secession and the recognition of new states. Secession should be a last resort, after all other attempts at reaching a solution that reconciles autonomy for the group claiming it with the territorial integrity of the state in which it resides have failed; and these attempts, if they do not succeed through bilateral negotiations, should continue through the good offices of a regional organization or of the UN. Also, it should occur only if the grievances of the claimants are serious (economic exploitation, legal discrimination, danger of cultural extinction, political oppression) and recognized as such by a regional organization or the UN. It should be accompanied by statutory measures protecting the rights of minorities within the seceding entity. And it should be (despite the Czechoslovak precedent) endorsed by a qualified majority of the people who claim independence.

Recognition of a new state should be denied if such conditions are not met. (If this condition had been observed, the recognition of Croatia would have been refused or delayed.) Beyond recognition, membership in regional organizations should meet an additional condition, already required by the EU, the Council of Europe, and, increasingly, the OAS: the presence of democratic institutions (including free media).

A third imperative, which gets us close to the shores of Utopia, is a gradual decline in the significance of ethnicity in international relations, the prevalence of multiple, overlapping identities over a hierarchy in which ethnic identity and loyalty to one's nation are valued as supreme. This means no less than a decline of nationalism. Patriotism, attachment to one's nation (whether it is defined in ethnic terms or in "civic," "melting pot," or multicultural ones) should be compatible with loyalty to a state composed of several nations and to suprastate institutions whose aim is to provide those services (including peace and security) that states can no longer deliver. This is, in essence, what the European Union tries to accomplish. Its example shows both that it is not an entirely utopian dream and that it is a very difficult task. The creation of "international regimes" in which both ethnicity and state borders are devalued is a worthy goal; what makes it so hard to reach is, of course, the resistance of nations and states, the danger of backlash among citizens who resent the transfer of powers to often technocratic suprastate institutions and continue to see the national cocoon as the condition of their independence, as the shelter of their distinctiveness, and as the framework of their political and democratic autonomy. The conditions that made the launching of European integration possible are hard to replicate in the larger Europe that emerged from the fall of the iron curtain. But in international affairs, we always need to remember the old dictum: it is not necessary to hope in order to undertake, or to succeed in order to persevere.

16

Nation and Nationalism
in America Today

D
ebates about multiculturalism and the persistent tensions between Afro-Americans and the other components of the American population have led to arguments and worries about the
degree of cohesion of the American nation. There seems to have been,
over the last forty years, a sharp shift from the celebration of integration
and consensus, to pessimism about the state of the American national
community, the disintegration of its fabric, the disappearance of the civic
republican spirit, and so on. Is this gloom, are these Jeremiads justified?
I will try to answer by examining four related issues: national identity,
national consciousness, nationalism, and national unity.

National Identity

Two features, a material and an ideological one, make the American nation distinctive. The material one is the composition of this nation. It
is a blend (or a juxtaposition) of immigrants, some of them—African
Americans—captured by force, most of them attracted by the hope of a
better life, from all over the world. Through violence and disease, the
purely native population has been reduced to a tiny component. The fact
that a vast majority of Americans first came here by choice—even when
it was necessity that drove them out of their homelands—distinguishes
the United States from that other melting pot, France, another nation of
immigrants; the ratio of immigrants to the preexisting stock of French
inhabitants is significantly smaller. I don't see much change affecting that

first original feature. There is rising hostility to immigrants, both legal and illegal, in certain quarters, both on the Left and on the Right. But, especially at times of economic slowdown, or when, as today, prosperity is accompanied by job losses, or when the nation goes through one of its scares, such hostility is anything but new. In the beginning of this century, it was aimed at Orientals, now at Latinos. But the flows of immigrants persist.

The ideological feature is the "American creed." American distinctiveness is not based on ethnicity, nor is it based on religion. It is not based, as is the case in France, on a long history and high culture that are supposedly shared by all. It is based, rather, on the principles of the Constitution and the Bill of Rights. In this sense, America is the liberal nation par excellence. In liberal Britain, monarchy and tradition are still essential components of distinctiveness. The combination of the two American features makes of the United States an example rather than a model. Although history has shaped them, a common history is not revered as the common glue, both because of that democratic ambivalence about history so well described by Tocqueville—people come to the United States to leave their past behind and to build their own future, as the story of Secretary of State Madeline Albright and of the Korbels, her parents, has shown once more—and because so many of today's Americans are recent immigrants. Nevertheless, the historical conditions that have produced a nation of immigrants and a nation with a liberal democratic faith remain unique and almost impossible to reproduce elsewhere.

National Consciousness

What makes this last point particularly paradoxical is the fact that Americans perceive their nation as a kind of model for humanity, as a beacon of universal relevance. America and France remain the two nations that have a messianic, universalistic form of patriotism. In France, the so-called republican model fosters the belief that the values carried by French (high) culture and by the French Revolution, and the institutions derived from both—especially the state, seen as the definer and guardian of the common good and thus the necessary provider of education, order, justice, and services—are valid for all humankind. In the United States, where the formula that is deemed universally valid is based not on Rousseau and the Jacobins but on orthodox liberalism, the state is seen more as a threat, and a reminder of human deficiency (if society was perfect, no state would be necessary), than as an indispensable straitjacket and common inspiration. What the American formula offers to the world is the freedom of liberal democracy and the miracles of the invisible hand—the free market and capitalist productivity, competition for wealth.

It is a formula that has, in recent years, spread widely around the globe. We have seen a "third wave" of democracies, and the socialist and communist rivals of capitalism have vanished. The two great advantages of that model over the French one are, first, that the latter is centered on the French language, as the carrier of French culture; it plays in the French melting pot the role the American constitutional creed plays here. But French is much less widely spoken than English, the language of world business and world communications. Second, French was also the language of high culture and what has swept the world, even more than capitalism and certainly more than liberal democracy, is popular culture, which is Anglo-American, and predominantly American. Thus, at the end of this century, there is a remarkable concordance between the American self-perception of the United States as the country of the common, self-reliant person, showing the world what such persons can accomplish, and much of the world scene, whereas French universalism faces a crisis of relevance, made worse by the internal deficiencies of a state-based model at a time of increasing state impotence and rising awareness of the state as actual obstacle to initiative and growth.

Nationalism

Americans continue to impute nationalism to others—partly because there appears to be a contradiction between the universal values of the American creed and the (assumed) self-centeredness of nationalism, partly because for much of their history, Americans have not felt physically threatened from abroad. And yet there have been many kinds of American nationalism, defined as an ideology that proclaims the duty to protect and maintain the nation and occasionally—indeed, very often—its superiority over others.

One form of American nationalism is not so different from what we find in many European countries: the belief that, being both superior to and stronger than others, the United States needs to act unilaterally to promote or to preserve its interests. Flexing one's muscles and exhibiting touches of xenophobia are traits common to the creed of Theodore Roosevelt and to the bluster of Pat Buchanan. A Congress and a Pentagon that look with dismay at the possibility of foreigners commanding American troops, with suspicion at increasing the authority of the UN, with anguish at the risks of sharing command and commands in NATO with America's allies express this kind of nationalism quite strongly. The Clinton administration's swift retreat from its initial endorsement of multilateralism and its policy of aggressive expansion of American economic influence—the neo-imperialism of free trade and services—show how potent this nationalism remains.

The main form of American nationalism, however, is internationalist.[1] It is the expression and extension of the universalism referred to above. Being superior to others because of its creed, its composition, its success, wealth, and power, it has a message for the world—or rather, several messages. Sometimes, it wants the United States to be a model and a beacon but sees no need to shed blood or spend money to spread its formula and its might abroad. Indeed, this seems to be the mood at present: a conviction that we have the best of everything, a willingness to believe that it is so even in areas (such as welfare services or public transportation) where it is obviously not so, a broad confidence that others, seeing where their interest lies, will follow the American example sooner or later, indignation or sarcasm when others, like the French, raise objections to the American model of capitalism or to the scope of capital punishment in the United States and proclaim their own social system to be more humane—but no particular desire to proselytize or to take big risks. At other moments, as in 1917 or during the long era from Pearl Harbor to the Gulf war, mobilized Americans have been quite eager to spread the American model across the map. But this, too, knows several forms. One is the missionary approach: we must do good and through good works raise others to our level. It did wonders in defeated Germany and Japan, it sustained America's foreign aid programs, it inspires public and private programs for democratization and economic free enterprise in the former Soviet empire. Another is the image of the sheriff—the United States as Gary Cooper stopping the bad guys at high noon—or the lone cowboy, in the self-referential metaphor attributed to Henry Kissinger. The missionaries dislike the sheriffs because they believe that force is bad and corrupting, the sheriffs look down on the missionaries as bleeding hearts devoid of guts, but the two types are remarkably complementary. Both are currently napping, but the debate over China provokes stirrings in both groups.

In other countries, where nationalism is of the more usual kind—bigoted and self-centered—the tendency to interpret American internationalism as just a disguise of traditional national self-promotion is, of course, very strong, like the tendency to interpret U.S. policy abroad as far more deliberate and coherent than it really is (after all, an imperious superpower, an "imperial Republic" in Raymond Aron's words, must know what it is doing). This reading of American beliefs and behavior, which challenges American exceptionalism, offends Americans. France, with its own mix of traditional and of universalist nationalism, has been particularly vocal in denouncing American "hypocrisy," the American belief that the United States knows better than the foreigners what is in the interest of the latter and pursues the common good, on the whole, unselfishly. Hence, recurrent crises break out between two offended parties. Current Asian complaints about the United States' (rather pale) insistence on human rights abroad also read U.S. exhortations as imperialistic attempts at imposing American values abroad. Foreigners will believe that American policy is purely self-serving even when it isn't; and Americans will believe they are serving the world even when they are mainly boosting themselves.

National Unity

Will the national creed and the "American dream" of prosperity for all through the efforts of each suffice to preserve American unity? Or will the new immigrants from south of the border, who find the practice of English difficult and whose family and work values appear radically different to many, make the melting pot inoperative? Will the voices for multiculturalism, affirmative action, and group rights shatter a national unity based on the principle of individual assimilation (turning each new American into a citizen) and on the relegation of ethnic and religious communities to the private sphere? Will the frenetic evolution of a global capitalism create a huge fracture between the highly successful and mobile, in the advanced sectors of the economy, and an urban underclass of unskilled, unemployed, (involuntarily) part-time, and unprotected employees dealing with broken families, drugs, and crime? Will the decline of communities and community, assaulted both by modern capitalism and by the "procedural liberalism" that puts an individualistic emphasis on rights far above the concern for common duties and individual choices above collective norms, corrode America's social fabric?

This litany of jeremiads, sung by voices as diverse as Samuel Huntington, Arthur Schlesinger, Robert Putnam, and Michael Sandel, is impressive indeed. But it leaves me somewhat unworried for a variety of reasons. Americans like to scare themselves about the fate of their nation; we've had Red scares, spy scares, moments when the conviction grew that the Soviets were ten feet tall, nightmare scenarios of Soviet nuclear predominance, and terrorism scares; we put Japanese and Japanese Americans in camps in 1941–1942, trembled about Afro-American nationalism in the late 1960s, briefly feared a deliberate policy of Japanese economic domination, are beginning to suspect Chinese expansionism, and we are busy measuring this phlogiston of modern social science, social capital, as if it were a dangerously depleted resource like fish. OK, the Jeremiahs may say, but isn't, this time, crying wolf justified?

I don't believe it. The great strength of this country lies in its pluralism. Unlike the *Titanic* and the *Brittanic*, which sank because water rushed from one compartment of the ship into others, the United States has an extraordinary capacity for absorbing shocks as well as correcting flaws. It is endlessly experimental and practical, willing to learn from occasional disasters and temporary declines. Remember the great debate on decline, initiated by Paul Kennedy? Joseph Nye was right to point out the differences between the United States and early-twentieth-century Britain. American multiculturalism strikes me as a strength more than a threat. The demand for group rights is a means to extend individual possibilities in areas where they have been held down. One advantage of the American "formula" over the French one is this: both relegate ethnic and other groups to the private sphere, but in France the private sphere and private interests are deemed inferior to the common good and the general will, whereas in the United States the common interest is seen as a compromise among the private interests and factions.

Each wave of immigrants was denounced as incompatible with, each new exotic group as unassimilable to, the existing stock. I have no doubt that the United States will integrate its Latino population (and France its North African immigrants) as it has done with other groups in the past. Recent attacks on the rights of immigrants (in Congress, from California) strike me as part of the assault on welfare rather than an attempt at curbing immigration. And I remain to be convinced that community (small and large) is fading. Old forms of association may atrophy, new forms of cooperation multiply; mutation is not the same thing as decay.

This does not mean that there isn't much to worry about. A political system entirely dominated by money, where fund-raising and rewarding the funders eclipse the concern for issues, is obviously a threat to the liberal democratic ideal so important for American distinctiveness and self-image. As for American unity, it remains threatened by the residues of racism that perpetuate, although on a reduced scale, the wall between blacks and other Americans (whatever its excesses, affirmative action has helped to lower and pierce that wall). Above all, the growth of the urban underclass is worrisome, insofar as it is an effect of a national faith in laissez-faire capitalism that is at the heart of the American creed and because a serious attempt to cope with it would require national and state policies aimed at educating and at providing skills and jobs—as well as essential welfare—to those who are currently left behind and ignored, or even blamed for their fate. On occasion, as in FDR's days, disaster has led the pragmatic Americans to turn to the state, or states, for help, despite the basic creed. In a period of skewed prosperity, it is harder to expect something comparable—especially given the present nature of political parties and legislatures.

Thus, the problem does not lie, as is being suggested, in the impossibility of keeping an increasingly diverse nation together—in the absence of a common enemy—simply by the virtue of a common faith, creed, or dream. Increasing diversity has been the American dynamic since the beginning. It is the creed itself that needs attention: insofar as the creed—liberal democracy—is valid, are American institutions and practices still serving it? Insofar as it has deleterious social effects—the creation, and perpetuation, of the underclass, the unprotected, that is, the dark side of capitalism—can it be corrected and supplemented rather than turned into a hard faith any departure from which would be a heresy? Above all, the problem of the American nation is the problem of its political system—and of American abstention from dealing with it.

17

———◆———

Conclusion:
Principles of a Liberal Ethics for
International Relations:
A Normative Outline

L iberalism is concerned with the individual's capacity to lead "a life that is good" and to formulate his or her own definition of the good life. Recently, the communitarian critique of contemporary formulations of liberalism has centered on Rawls's argument that liberalism gives priority to the right over the good: it aims, he says, at ensuring equal liberty and a fair scheme of distribution so that individuals will be able to pursue a great variety of conceptions of the good and to revise these conceptions or projects as they see fit. In my opinion, the idea of the priority of the right over the good is misleading.[1] Liberalism embodies a conception of the good, which is precisely the establishment of conditions in which individuals will be able to fulfill themselves and their projects while respecting the personality and projects of others. This means that there are liberal virtues—tolerance is obviously an important one— and also that there are limits to so-called liberal neutrality among projects or conceptions of the good; insofar as "the variegated quest for 'neutrality' is basically the endeavor to define a form of social life free of moral coercion . . . in circumstances of deep social disagreement,"[2] it is fully entitled to place limits on projects that would impose moral coercion and hamper the ability of individuals to define and pursue their own ideas of the good.

Liberalism is obviously concerned with individual rights, conceived as legally defined and protected capacities and claims.[3] As I have argued elsewhere,[4] individuals, to pursue their concerns, require a combination

242

of "negative" rights (such as the protection of their physical and mental integrity) and "positive" rights (such as participation in collective decisions) and also a combination of civil and political rights and of economic and social ones. (This does not prevent one from endorsing Amartya Sen's powerful argument about the supreme importance of political and civil rights, because only their exercise makes possible "the comprehension and the conceptualization of economic needs" that are the foundations of economic and social rights.)[5] But liberalism is also a system of duties. Kant distinguished between negative duties, which he called narrow, such as the duty not to refuse to help others in need, and positive duties, which he called wide because they allow for some latitude in application, such as the duty of beneficence (or the political obligations entailed by life in a well-ordered and fair political society).[6] The view of liberalism as primarily a system of rights, and of litigation about rights, is a truncated one.

I am concerned with one particular aspect of liberal ethics: the ethics of political life. It is therefore important to explain my conception of the political. It, too, is inspired by Kant and also by the writings of John Rawls, despite the differences he sees between his "political constructivism" and Kant's moral constructivism.[7] "Political constructivism views the person as belonging to political society understood as a fair system of social cooperation" (93). Like Rawls, I understand political society as neither a community nor an association: it has many more aims that the latter but is not "governed by a shared comprehensive religious philosophy, or moral doctrine" (42), at least not usually. It is a combined product of history (with its vast share of accidents, upheavals, and manipulations) and human choice. But whatever its origins, its moral standing rests on its ability to respect and protect the rights of its members and on their consent, explicit or implicit, to its rules and institutions. Both the nation—defined as a group that provides individuals with a sense of social identity that transcends other secular, and often also religious, cleavages—and the state—defined as a set of institutions that aim at providing individuals on a certain territory with order, justice, and a variety of services—derive their moral standing and their rights from the will and the rights of the individuals who constitute the nation and over which the state rules.

My conception of individuals, for all its Kantianism, is not disembodied or sparse. I see them as possessing, as Rawls puts it, "a capacity for a sense of justice and for a conception of the good"[8], as needing both a sense of social identity (or of multiple social identities, among which they must establish a hierarchy) and a framework of order and justice within which they can seek happiness and fulfillment according to their conception of the good. Political life as a whole is a ceaseless process of accommodation among individual rights and duties, the rights and duties of groups within a nation, those of the national group, and those of the state. But neither a group, nor the nation, nor the state can be seen as possessing inherent rights; the rights they can claim derive from those of the individuals, and when they define their rights and duties in a way that tramples the basic rights of individuals, they forfeit their legitimacy.

This variety of liberalism recognizes that persons are social beings and that society, including the state, cannot therefore be seen as existing only for the protection of private lives and activities from anarchy. Individuals often want to get together in order to achieve common purposes, to carry out grand designs, to build a common civic culture, and so on. Political society is not simply a market for free private enterprises. But from the moral point of view, the social groupings formed by persons are derivative and constructed, and they draw their legitimacy from the will and consent of these persons. In addressing international relations, I therefore argue from a position that looks at the notion of a "morality of states" with some suspicion and at cosmopolitanism as a political ethic that may be desirable as a goal but does not correspond yet to the choice of highest social identity made by the great majority of individuals.

Individual Human Rights

A first issue is that of the international or regional protection of individual human rights, defined by a variety of international covenants or regional treaties. This international or regional protection is important because the state is at least as often the violator as it is the defender of these rights. Two questions are addressed here.

The first is that of the universal value of such rights. Those who affirm it had to face, at a recent international conference on human rights in Vienna, an offensive by critics who charged that the West was trying to impose its own conceptions on non-Western cultures and traditions. There is no doubt that the function of these charges—made particularly by representatives of China and Indonesia—was, in almost every case, not so much the defense of these cultures against a new kind of Western imperialism as the protection from outside scrutiny and condemnation of a variety of repressive practices or of state coercion that imposes on individuals a state-defined conception of what is good for them.

There is no need for the "universalists" to be on the defensive.[9] They could, and should, point out that the philosophy that inspires them is liberalism and that liberalism's concern for the ethical life of individuals is not a merely Western ideal, as its appeal in many non-Western societies shows. Nor is it universally embraced in the West, where a number of illiberal philosophies continue to do battle with it. They could also argue, in Rawlsian fashion, that political liberalism does not attempt to cover the whole range of an individual's life: it concerns itself only with the political sphere; indeed, one of liberalism's main concerns is to protect a sphere of private individual and group life in which a variety of philosophies and ethical projects can be pursued. But what the defense of human rights is above all aimed at preserving is this capacity of individuals to pursue their quests. What it particularly tries to rule out is measures and practices destructive of the individual's integrity and self-respect, and what it tries to ensure is a set of political conditions and institutions that promote the freedoms and the well-being of individuals—especially their right to define their own choices, private and public. Insofar as community standards or group practices meet such requirements, there is no conflict between local cultures and the philosophy of universal human rights. Insofar as these requirements are violated, no amount of arguing that these standards or practices are traditional, or result from widely shared religious or ideological codes, is capable of making them less destructive of individual integrity or autonomy and therefore less evil and more tolerable.

This reassertion of "universalism" does not mean that we can expect or should demand the immediate protection of all the rights listed in international agreements. But the problem of enforcement and tactics is precisely that of the latitude in carrying out the "wide duties" entailed by these documents; it does not lessen the duties themselves. Depending on the severity of violations in a given state, external pressure ought to ensure first a minimum of essential rights (which must include also a minimum of political rights, without which basic civil and economic ones risk being quickly jeopardized) and move on toward a fuller panoply only after these essential and basic rights have been established.

A second question concerns the effect of the international protection of human rights on state sovereignty. The principle of state sovereignty has been the cornerstone of world order for centuries and remains enshrined in the Charter of the UN. In a liberal conception, the justification for state sovereignty has to be derived not from what Michael Walzer has called the legalist paradigm—the rights possessed by states in the international order—but from the right of individuals to be protected from foreign oppression or intrusion, from their right to a safe political framework in which they can enforce their autonomy, pursue their interests, and assert their common designs. It follows that a state that is oppressive or violates the autonomy and integrity of its subjects forfeits its moral claim to full sovereignty. Both the steps taken in the past forty years for the international protection of human rights and recent practices by the UN or regional organizations such as the Council of Europe or the OAS, which make of the respect for human rights and the holding of free elections conditions for international recognition or assistance or legitimacy, all move in that direction.

As one author has observed, we are inching toward a two-tiered or two-class conception of the international order.[10] One class consists of those states that respect human rights and have political institutions based on the citizens' consent; these are the democratic states—still a minority, even after the recent "third wave." The second class consists of all the other states; they are the ones that are being, and need to be, pressured into enlarging their subjects' sphere of freedom and participation. "The external sovereignty of liberal states . . . has not been significantly altered by the human rights movement precisely because their internal sovereign structures are generally consistent with human rights norms. . . . Illiberal states, on the other hand, have experienced significant changes in their external sovereignty. They are, in many ways, the beneficiaries of far fewer legal entitlements than liberal states"[11]. Whether this is only a temporary condition, pending the transformation of nonliberal states into democracies (or at least into states that correspond to the somewhat mysterious ideal-type of "hierarchical" societies invented by Rawls)[12] remains to be seen. On the one hand, the reluctance of democratic governments to put a concern for human rights abroad at the top of their list of diplomatic objectives means that the transformation of illiberal states will continue to depend primarily on domestic developments. On the other hand, as we can now see in the former Soviet Union, the domestic transition from totalitarian and authoritarian regimes to liberal ones remains hazardous and tortuous. And yet, a liberal ethics of world order must subordinate the principle of state sovereignty to the recognition and respect of human rights; when one illiberal state is attacked by another, the defense of its integrity and independence against aggression must be accompanied by an international effort to improve its human-rights record. The principle of the individual's right to democratic self-government should be recognized as the highest principle of world order, with state sovereignty as a circumscribed and conditional norm.

The Right to Self-Determination

The next issue is that of self-determination—another principle that often clashes both with state sovereignty, insofar as it can lead to the disintegration of states, and with individual human rights, insofar as it is conceived as a collective right that may override the preferences and interests of individuals.

The principle of self-determination became an important element in liberal democratic theory when it became clear that the purposes of a liberal polity were not only to establish a framework of order and fairness in which individuals could lead their lives freely and in which they were consulted on decisions affecting their separate chances and their different lives. These purposes extend beyond the sphere of consent and participation into the sphere of common enterprises embraced and requested by the individuals as citizens. It is because of their desire to be not merely the subjects of a state (a set of rules and institutions) but the citizens of a political community (kept together by bonds not of obligations but of loyalty[13] and by a sense of common culture and common fate) that they have "invented" modern nationalism, that is, they have struggled either to blend all the elements of the preexisting state into an "imagined community" of distinctive symbols and features or to make the boundaries of the nation and those of the state coincide.

Not all modern nationalisms have been democratic and liberal. Jacobin and authoritarian nationalisms have often crushed individual rights. However, it is difficult for a democrat who believes in self-government, that is to say, in the individual's right to political as well as moral autonomy, not to acknowledge the force of the ideal of self-determination—of the desire to be governed by "our own" rather than by people felt to be alien. John Stuart Mill's argument about the connection between liberal democracy and national self-determination remains hard to refute. Where individuals acting together perform that "daily plebiscite" which, according to Renan, establishes a nation, the rejection of their right to national self-determination is a trampling of their will.

This does not mean that there can be no qualifications. First, precisely because the purpose is the unfolding of liberal autonomy, those who exercise their right to self-determination should be held to international standards of human rights. This means, in practice, that new nation-states born of secession should be recognized only on condition that they allow the monitoring of their practices with respect to human rights and also that the right to secession should be denied if the purpose of the new political community is the protection or perpetuation of illiberal injustice (such as slavery in the American South in the 1860s).

Second, it is necessary to take into account the effects of the moral imperatives we state. One effect of a rash of secessions breaking up heterogeneous states could be not simply "instability" (the forcible maintenance of the status quo could produce just as much, or more, chaos) but a calamitous decline in the life chances and opportunities of individuals both in the new state and in what is left of the old one. We see it tragically in former Yugoslavia. This is why the formation of new nation-states should be only a last resort: other alternatives to an untenable status quo ought to be sought, such as formulas of federalism or confederation or what the Dutch have called consociation (special provisions for nonterritorial groups).[17] Another problem arises when the state a seceding group wishes to create would be unable to perform the most elementary public functions ("maintain its roads and utilities, educate its children, preserve minimal domestic order, and provide basic public goods").[18] A thorough and fair examination of probable effects can hardly be provided by embattled or embittered parties. Therefore a reasonable exercise of the liberal principle of self-determination supposes a permanent preventive institutional machinery at the disposal of international and regional organizations, with full diplomatic support by leading powers and a capacity by the international or regional agencies to dispatch not only observers but, at the request or with the consent of the contenders, peace-preserving forces in explosive cases.

Even the triumph of liberal self-determination, respectful of individual rights, would still leave the world full of minorities—ethnic, cultural, religious, and so on—eager to protect their heritage and distinctiveness. Simple majoritarianism is not the alpha and omega of democracy: not only the individual but also distinctive groups of individuals need to be protected from majority coercion. It may happen that ethnic and cultural minorities eagerly seek assimilation into a melting pot, as in the United States, or accept integration into a unitary nation with a single official language, as in France in the nineteenth and most of the twentieth centuries (just as it may happen that a multiethnic and multicultural state functions harmoniously, as in Switzerland). But those minorities that resist the destruction of their specificity need to be protected. Here again, I am pleading not for "group rights" but for the right of individuals to form and maintain groups that give meaning to their lives, "become potential models and define potential roles, that we can adopt as our own."[16]

Precisely because political life does not—even for liberals—simply pit the individual against the state but, rather, entails complex relations among individuals, families, groups, and the state, there is no philosophical reason for equating the defense of individual integrity and autonomy against the state's Leviathan with the grant of rights to individuals only. This, however, was the original UN approach after 1945, because of the sense that prevailed then that the minority treaties of the interwar period had only encouraged mischievous manipulations by the countries that shared kinship with the minorities (such as Germany with respect to the Germans of Upper Silesia or Pomerania) and led to the disintegration of democratic states like Czechoslovakia. But on the other hand, the specific flaws of the interwar treaty system could be remedied, and it can be shown that at least during the Weimar Republic the existence of this regime played a moderating role on German revisionism.[15] On the other hand, general human rights may not suffice to protect the distinctive features and to assure the survival of ethnic or cultural minorities; these could be threatened by the blunt operation of majority rule in elections and in parliaments. "If Liberal equality requires equal citizenship rights, and equal access to a common 'field of opportunity,' then some minority cultures are endangered."[16]

Minorities need both access, through citizenship rights, to the state's process of decision making and guarantees against discrimination, especially in the form of limits to the ability of the majority to wipe out their culture or their resources. The right of the minority to speak its language, to have its schools, and to practice its religion, is legitimate in a liberal perspective, as long as the laws or treaties that recognize and organize a sphere of autonomy for a minority preserve, in turn, the right of individuals who belong to it not to have their lives and prospects defined exclusively in terms of their membership in this minority: if they want to send their children to the schools or churches of the majority, they must have the right to do so.

What is needed, then, in this important domain, is not just a broad international recognition of the rights of minorities but also specific legal commitments—constitutional or treaty obligations—made by the governments that represent the majority, reviewed by regional organizations or by the UN, and provided with mechanisms of appeal and redress set up under the auspices of these institutions. The recognition of new states in which minorities represent a sizable part of the population should be made dependent on the willingness of the new governments to accept such limitations. A degree of international supervision and intervention is necessary both to induce governments to deal fairly with minorities and to discourage the latter from excessive demands, intransigence, and blackmail. The respect of minorities, on the one hand, and their willingness to function within heterogeneous states, on the other, are the precondition for the preservation of interethnic or interreligious coexistence and cooperation within such states. The alternative, alas, is, all too often, ethnic or religious cleansing and tyranny.

The Rights of Foreigners

We have examined so far the principles that should guide an ethical international politics with respect to the treatment of individuals within a state and to their right to establish a new state. One of the most important contemporary issues concerns the treatment of foreigners who come to a country either as immigrants or as refugees. It is an issue of great empirical and legal complexity. The number of refugees worldwide has increased to more than twenty million, through domestic turbulence (Haiti), civil war (Cambodia, Bosnia, Somalia, Rwanda), international conflicts (the Gulf war, Afghanistan), decolonization, and flights from totalitarian countries. Immigrant workers have been attracted to advanced countries through a combination of population pressure at home and demand for manpower in the host countries; their skills, acquired there, and their remittances are important for the development of their countries of origin. The treatment both of refugees and of immigrants has varied from country to country, depending on the economic situation, the local culture, and the changing political climate.

Legally, the "regime" of immigrants is skimpy, limited mainly to provisions protecting the rights of workers; the right to grant or refuse entry remains an attribute of state sovereignty. There is an international regime for refugees, but it gives no guarantee of refuge: the granting of asylum remains a state decision, and the increase in the number of people claiming asylum has put enormous strains on the regime, with governments increasingly shifting to a narrow definition of what kind of persecution is a legitimate cause for seeking asylum and to long and restrictive procedures of verification. This is also an issue that—like self-determination—could become a major source of international conflict, especially when countries try to force states that "produce" refugees, or from which immigrants have come, to take them back or when states manipulate or arm refugees for their own purposes.

Over this issue, the clash of philosophies is particularly sharp—between "statists," who insist on the state's right to control entry and exit and to interpret the definition of refugees, and "cosmopolitans," who plead for open borders (with freedom of both exit and entry) and for granting refugees and immigrants a right to citizenship under certain conditions. Michael Walzer has tried to formulate a somewhat uneasy compromise.[19] Liberalism itself is, so to speak, not at ease with this issue; it involves a clear conflict between the rights of the citizens and those of the foreigners (there can be stiff competition for welfare benefits, jobs, and housing); and liberals, who have concentrated their thoughts on how to make of the state an ally and protector of individual rights and the expression of the citizens' will, have thought much less about the fate of the stateless and of those who are, in effect, between states.

My own principles are these: first, I believe that individuals should be recognized, by the states and by international agreements, to have a basic right of free exit (I know that many communitarians would not agree). Second, concerning refugees, I reject both Walzer's assumption that a state's right to determine the composition of its membership has priority over the rights of refugees and the assertion by states of a right to repatriate refugees forcibly for economic or political reasons, when these refugees have valid grounds for seeking asylum. My maxim, here, is that there is a duty to grant asylum whenever the refugees have a good reason to fear for their most basic rights through persecution in their country of origin; restrictions are justified only when the numbers become such that they constitute a threat to the domestic "system of equal liberty" the state tries to maintain, but this has rarely been the case.

Third, I recognize that the issue of immigration raises a number of major questions: is a state under any moral obligation to allow the entry of immigrants? What are the morally tolerable restrictions it can put on their entry? What are the rights of the immigrants once they are in the host country? How free and arbitrary can this country be in getting rid of them? My own normative position is that states ought to have a policy of immigration based on the principles of benevolence and mutual aid, insofar as entry is concerned (this is an argument against selective or preferential quotas); that immigrants whose presence is of a certain duration should be granted full civil, economic, and social rights and a minimum of political rights (the European Union has taken a first step in this direction, which dissociates citizenship from nationality); and that the states ought to have policies of national integration, or naturalization, based on the *jus soli*, not on the *jus sanguinis*. I recognize that, in practice, what President François Mitterrand once called the nation's "threshold of tolerance" is often much lower; and that for the kind of ethical policy I recommend to be practicable, it would require as complements effective international procedures for the settlement of interstate and even domestic conflicts capable of producing masses of refugees, as well as programs of international assistance to poor countries whose people would otherwise be driven out by misery. These complements are woefully inadequate at present.

Environmental "Rights"

Another set of issues has to do with the relations between human beings and nature in all its forms—air, water, land, and other species. Environmental ethics is concerned, in particular, with the effects of the population explosion and of industrial and technological development in a world in which the fear that needs will exceed resources leads to such dangers as the rapid depletion of existing resources, pollution, and climate changes. Here again, the problems may result in interstate conflicts—when food is used as a weapon or when states quarrel over water or over responsibility for pollution.

Some of the problems in this realm are problems of distributive justice that cannot be solved at the national level, because harm is spread across borders. What is raised, thus, is the issue of duties toward the inhabitants of other countries, especially in cases such as the "exporting" of pollution or the exploitation and exhaustion of resources that change the balance of economic endowments and possibilities. In the case of environmental damage caused by attempts of developing countries to industrialize and develop faster, their emphasis on their sovereignty is less convincing than their argument about the responsibility of multinational enterprises, or even international organizations, for fostering such policies.

The principles of a reasonable policy are clear and in conformity with the duties of distributive justice. The states from which the damage originates have the duty to take measures against, and to provide reparations for, damage created by their acts or their failure to act. This is a case of justice as fairness and reciprocity. In those environmental issues that pit countries of the so-called South (such as Brazil) against the North, the duties of the former are the same, but the advanced countries that require that such measures be taken have a duty to provide assistance—through aid or trade—in order to compensate the offending nations for their losses.

Some of the problems of environmental ethics are problems of intergenerational justice. If human beings indulge in unregulated growth (of population and resources) now, what will be left for our descendants? The debate about the rights of future generations is fierce. Some believe that since these generations have the same right to a livable environment as we do, we have a clear obligation to transmit one to them: this position is an echo of Edmund Burke's idea of an implicit contract among generations, an application of the duty not to harm others. Others have argued, unconvincingly, that the future generations' right does not yet exist or that we don't know what these generations will be like (Derek Parfit's "ontological precariousness"). I am unhesitatingly in the first camp.

Other problems go beyond the issues of rights and obligations among humans and pose interesting questions for deontologists and utilitarians alike. What, if anything, do we owe to species other than our own? or to the elements? Traditional ethics has concerned itself almost exclusively with human beings. In my opinion, the eloquent champions of "animal rights" and the zealots of a "land ethic" notwithstanding, there are no rights there. But we may have duties even when they are not the counterpart of rights—obligations toward sentient creatures that may not be capable of thought but are certainly capable of experiencing pain; and obligations, both moral and aesthetic, to leave to our successors a livable environment; hence, the duty to respect nature and to treat it not only as a resource but as an indispensable framework for our lives, choices, and plans. A "moral right to beauty" is an essential part of culture.

Conclusion

I have not dealt here with two of the thorniest and most important substantive issues of international politics: those involving violence (war and intervention) and those involving distributive justice within and among states. As indicated in brief discussion of human rights, above, how the principles outlined in this chapter are applied to concrete cases such as these—with what nuances, delays, and exceptions and through what coalitions, pressures, and inducements—is where most of the political difficulties lie. But it is important to lay out a framework of principles first: without them, "pragmatism" is left bereft of any sense of direction and rectitude. A recipe for a pudding is not a pudding; but there is no pudding without a recipe.

For all the issues raised, the central question is that of enforcement—of the principles listed and of the specific measures taken in order to apply them to a usually hostile and difficult reality. Precisely because states are so often the enemies of the individual rights that need to be protected or promoted, or else reluctant or unable to carry out the duties individuals should discharge across borders, the only way of preventing these principles from being thwarted or trampled is to build up, gradually, case by case, the capacity of international and regional institutions to supplement or substitute for the states, when enforcement directly by the states is impossible or risks being dangerously selfish. Obtaining the states' necessary consent to such a strengthening of international agencies; providing them with the financial, administrative, and technical skills necessary for the performance of public functions comparable to those that states normally carry out; and reforming their process of decision making so as to make it more representative and fair, without however, in the process, strengthening the forces of illiberalism within them—these are issues of enormous difficulty and importance.

Notes

Preface

1. Stanley Hoffmann, *The State of War* (New York: Praeger, 1965), and *Janus and Minerva* (Boulder, Colo.: Westview, 1986).

2. Stanley Hoffmann, *Duties beyond Borders* (Syracuse, N.Y.: Syracuse University Press, 1981), and *Janus and Minerva.*

3. Stanley Hoffmann, *The European Sisyphus* (Boulder, Colo.: Westview Press, 1995).

4. For the Yugoslav tragedy, see Stanley Hoffmann, "The Europeans and Yugoslavia," in Richard Ullman (ed.), *The World & Yugoslavia's Wars* (N.Y.: Council on Foreign Relations, 1996), and Stanley Hoffmann, *The Ethics & Politics of Intervention* (South Bend, Ind.: Univ. of Notre Dame Press, 1997).

Chapter 2: Hedley Bull and His Contribution to International Relations

1. Introduction to *Systems of States,* by Martin Wight (Leicester, Eng.: Leicester University Press, 1977).

2. Hedley Bull, *The Anarchical Society: A Study of Order in World Politics* (London, Eng.: Macmillan, 1977).

3. Hedley Bull, *The Control of the Arms Race: Disarmament and Arms Control in the Nuclear Age,* 2d ed. (New York: Praeger, 1965).

4. In "Strategic Studies and Its Critics," *World Politics* (July 1968), Bull states that being an adviser to a government is, for a scholar or a scientist, unbecoming or not depending on "what we take the moral nature of that government and its objectives to be" (599).

5. Hans Morgenthau, *Politics among Nations: The Struggle for Power and Peace,* 5th ed. (New York: Knopf, 1973).

6. Hedley Bull, "International Theory: The Case for a Classical Approach," in *Contending Approaches to International Politics,* ed. Klaus Knorr and James N. Rosenau (Princeton, N.J.: Princeton University Press, 1969), 27.

7. E. H. Carr, *Twenty Years' Crisis, 1919–1939: An Introduction to the Study of International Relations,* 2d ed. (London, Eng.: Macmillan, 1946).

8. Hedley Bull, "The Twenty Years Crisis, Thirty Years On," *International Journal* 24, no. 4 (Autumn 1969): 638.

9. Bull, "International Theory," 21.

10. Hedley Bull, "New Directions in the Theory of International Relations," *International Studies* 14, no. 2: 279.

11. On the basis of his remarks about game theory in "Strategic Studies and Its Critics," 601–2, one can presume that he would have been equally sarcastic about current attempts by champions of rational-choice theory to use game theory not just "to illustrate points that are independently arrived at" but "in order to determine solutions" to problems of international relations.

12. Bull, "International Theory," 20.

13. Hedley Bull, *Justice in International Relations,* Hagey Lectures, Oct. 12–13, 1983 (Waterloo, Ont.: University of Waterloo, 1984).

14. Hedley Bull, "The West and South Africa," *Daedalus* 111, no. 2 (Spring 1982): 255–70, 266.

15. Bull, "New Directions in the Theory of International Relations," 284.

16. Bull, *Justice in International Relations,* 13.

17. Hedley Bull, "Natural Law and International Relations," *British Journal of International Studies* 5 (1979): 171–81.

18. Hedley Bull, "Recapturing the Just War for Political Theory," *World Politics* 31, no. 4 (July 1979): 588–99.

19. Bull, "Natural Law and International Relations," 180.

20. Ibid., 181.

21. Ibid., 171.

22. Bull, *Justice in International Relations,* 13.

23. Bull, "The West and South Africa," 269–70.

24. Hedley Bull, "Society and Anarchy in International Relations," in *Diplomatic Investigations,* ed. Herbert Butterfield and Martin Wight (London, Eng.: Allen and Unwin, 1966), 35–50.

25. Hedley Bull, "What Is the Commonwealth?" *World Politics* 11, no. 4 (July 1959).

26. Bull, "Society and Anarchy," 48 ff.; *The Anarchical Society,* 262.

27. Bull, *Justice in International Relations,* 14.

28. Hedley Bull, "Civilian Power Europe: A Contradiction in Terms?" *Journal of Common Market Studies* 21, nos. 1–2 (Sept.–Dec. 1982), 150–51.

29. Hedley Bull, "The Grotian Conception of International Society," in Butterfield and Wight, *Diplomatic Investigations,* 51–73.

30. This analysis is derived from his essays in *The Expantion of International Society,* ed. Hedley Bull and Adam Watson (Oxford, Eng.: Clarendon Press, 1984), and *Intervention in World Politics,* ed. Hedley Bull (Oxford, Eng.: Clarendon Press, 1984).

31. Bull, *Justice in International Relations,* 10–11.

32. Bull, *The Anarchical Society,* 276 ff.

33. Bull, *Justice in International Relations,* 12.

34. Cf. Hedley Bull, "Arms Control: A Stocktaking and Prospects," *Adelphi Papers,* no. 55 (Mar. 1969): 11–20.

35. Bull, *The Control of the Arms Race,* 48.

36. Hedley Bull, "The Scope for Soviet-American Agreement," *Adelphi Papers,* no. 65 (Feb. 1970): 1–15.

37. Hedley Bull, "Future Conditions of Strategic Deterrence," *Adelphi Papers,* no. 160 (Autumn 1980): 13–23.

38. Ibid., 16.

39. Bull, *The Anarchical Society,* ch. 5 (esp. 104).

40. Cf. Hedley Bull, "A View from Abroad: Consistency under Pressure," *Foreign Affairs,* supplement, *America and the World 1978,* 445–46.

41. Hedley Bull, "The Great Irresponsibles: The United States, the Soviet Union, and World Order," *International Journal 35,* no. 3 (Summer 1980): 437–47.

42. Bull, *The Control of the Arms Race,* 212.

43. Bull, "Strategic Studies and Its Critics," 602.

Chapter 3: Ideal Worlds

1. See chapter 5, below.

2. See Joseph Nye, *Nuclear Ethics* (New York: Free Press, 1986).

3. John Rawls, *A Theory of Justice* (New York: Columbia University Press, 1993), 246.

4. John Rawls, "The Law of Peoples," in *On Human Rights,* ed. Stephen Shute and Susan Hurley (New York: Basic Books, 1993), 52–53.

5. Rawls, *Theory of Justice,* 246.

6. Ibid., 245.

7. Rawls, "Law of Peoples," 42.

8. John Rawls, *Political Liberalism* (New York: Columbia University Press, 1993), 15.

9. Rawls, *Theory of Justice,* 11.

10. Ibid., 2.

11. Rawls, *Political Liberalism,* 34.

12. Ibid., 34.

13. Ibid., 5–6.

14. Ibid., 49.

15. Ibid., 56ff.

16. Ibid., 202.

17. Rawls, *Theory of Justice,* 377–79. See especially Charles Beitz, *Political Theory and International Relations* (Princeton, N.J.: Princeton University Press,

1979), and Thomas Pogge, *Realizing Rawls* (Ithaca, N.Y.: Cornell University Press).

18. Rawls, "Law of Peoples," 54.

19. Michael Walzer, *Just and Unjust Wars* (New York: Basic Books, 1977), 5. In Walzer's conception, states derive their rights from the consent of their citizens, and he assumes a "fit" between the former and the latter. But if there was no such fit, foreign states could intervene only to help a national group secede, not to help a people overthrow its tyrannical government (thus, they could help East Timor, or Chechnya, or Tibet but not, say, the Shiites in Iraq—or the fundamentalists in Algeria).

20. Rawls, "Law of Peoples," 51.

21. Rawls, *Political Liberalism,* 40ff.

22. Rawls, "Law of Peoples," 50.

23. Ibid., 56.

24. Onora O'Neill, "Justice, Gender, and International Boundaries," in *The Quality of Life,* ed. Martha C. Nussbaum and Amartya Sen (Oxford, Eng.: Clarendon Press, 1993), 303–23, 312. See also O'Neill's essay, "Ethical Reasoning and Ideological Pluralism," *Ethics* (July 1988): 705–22.

25. Rawls, "Law of Peoples," 56.

26. Ibid., 56.

27. Rawls, *Political Liberalism,* 6–7.

28. Rawls, "Law of Peoples," 76.

29. Ibid., 66.

30. See, for instance, Charles Beitz, "Patriotism or Cosmopolitanism?" *Boston Review* (Oct.-Nov. 1994), and Yael Tamir, *Liberal Nationalism* (Princeton, N.J.: Princeton University Press, 1993).

31. Steven Lukes, "Five Fables about Human Rights," in Shute and Hurley, *On Human Rights,* 19–40, 21, 30.

32. Michael Walzer, *Thick and Thin: Moral Arguments at Home and Abroad* (South Bend, Ind.: University of Notre Dame Press, 1994), 8.

33. Ibid., 18.

34. Michael Walzer, "The Politics of Rescue," *Dissent* (Winter 1995): 18.

35. Ibid., 81.

36. Ibid., 83.

37. Ibid., 103.

38. Rawls, "Law of Peoples," 46.

39. Ibid., 50.

40. Ibid., 68.

41. Rawls, *Political Liberalism,* 15.

42. Rawls, "Law of Peoples," 68.

43. Ibid.

44. Rawls, *Political Liberalism,* 145.

45. Ibid., 146–147, 171.

46. Ibid., 11.

47. See Stephen Holmes, "The Gatekeeper," *New Republic* (Oct. 11, 1993): 39–47.

48. Rawls, "Law of Peoples," 53–54.

49. Ibid., 51.

50. Ibid., 69.

51. Rawls, *Political Liberalism,* 109.

52. Rawls, "Law of Peoples," 61.

53. Thomas Pogge, "An Egalitarian Law of Peoples," *Philosophy and Public Affairs* (Summer 1994): 195–224.

54. Rawls, "Law of Peoples," 79.

55. On Pogge, see "An Egalitarian Law of Peoples." Bertrand Guillarme's critique is in chapter 10 of his still unpublished doctoral thesis ("Rawls: La justification contractualiste de la démocratie libérale," Institut d' Etudes Politique, Paris, 1994), a careful and systematic exegesis of Rawls's thought.

56. Rawls, "Law of Peoples," 80.

57. For an Asian's refutation of the so-called Asian point of view, see Yash Ghai, "Human Rights and Governance: The Asian Debate," *Australian Yearbook of International Law* 15 (1994): 1–34.

58. Rawls, "Law of Peoples," 78.

59. A similar thought is expressed by Fernando R. Tesøn, in his critique of Rawls's essay from a Kantian perspective, "The Rawlsian Theory of International Law," *Ethics and International Affairs* 9 (1995): 79–100. "For the Kantian, the relationship between liberal and illiberal states can only be a peaceful modus vivendi and not a community of shared moral beliefs and political commonalities" (98).

60. Rawls, "Law of Peoples," 76.

61. Ibid., 71.

62. Ibid., 73.

63. Ibid., 77.

64. Ibid., 76.

65. See Sissela Bok, "The Search for a Shared Ethics," *Common Knowledge* 1, no. 3: 12–25. See also Frances V. Harbour, "Basic Moral Values: A Shared Core," *Ethics and International Affairs* (1995): 155–70.

66. For such an attempt, see Onora O'Neill, *Faces of Hunger* (London, Eng.: Allen and Unwin, 1986).

67. Rawls, *Political Liberalism,* 101.

68. See Judith Shklar, "The Liberalism of Fear," in *Liberalism and the Moral Life,* ed. Nancy Rosenblum (Cambridge, Mass.: Harvard University Press, 1989), 21–38.

69. Rawls, *Political Liberalism,* 22.

70. Rawls, "Law of Peoples," 69.

71. Guillarme remarks that Rawls's formulation leaves dangling the issue of

the rights of exiles and stateless people, who are not "clearly the members of any given society" ("Rawls: La justification contractualiste," 416). Judith Shklar had planned to write a book on exile.

72. We are not far from Onora O'Neill's suggestion (see fn. 16) to begin "with the thought of a plurality of interacting and divers agents" and with the principles that can be adopted by them, a procedure that rejects both "idealization" and relativism.

73. Shklar, "The Liberalism of Fear," 34–45.

74. I am grateful for the comments and criticisms of Bertrand Guillarme, Percy Lehning, and Daniel Philpott, whose essay, "Sovereignty" (*Journal of International Affairs* [Winter 1995]: 353–68) raises important issues for international theory.

Chapter 5: The Crisis of Liberal Internationalism

1. Tony Smith, *America's Mission* (Princeton, N.J.: Princeton Univ. Press, 1994).

2. Woodrow Wilson, quoted in Tony Smith, *op. cit.,* 88.

3. Michael Walzer, "The Politics of Rescue," *Dissent* (Winter 1995).

Chapter 7: A New World and Its Troubles

1. See John L. Gaddis, *The Long Peace* (New York: Oxford University Press, 1987).

2. William H. McNeill, "Winds of Change," in Nicholas Rizopoulos (ed.), *Sea Changes* (New York: Council on Foreign Relations, 1989), 163–203; Robert W. Tucker, "1989 and All That," ibid., 204–237.

3. On this distinction, see my *Primacy of World Order* (New York: McGraw-Hill, 1978). I realize that the distinction is, in reality, far from perfect. In the realm of economic interdependence, states try to combine the logic of competition (the quest for relative gains) with that of a world economy that has rules and a dynamism of its own. Chaos or crises caused in that realm, either by aggressive state competitiveness or by economic recessions and dislocations, call spill over into the traditional arena.

4. On this shift, see Carl Kaysen, "Is War Obsolete? A Review Essay," *International Security* 14, no. 4 (1990): 42–64.

5. I am referring to Francis Fukuyama's notorious essay, "The End of History?" *National Interest,* no. 16 (Summer 1989): 3–18.

6. See Joseph Nye, *Bound to Lead* (New York: Basic Books, 1990), chap. 6.

7. For such a prophecy, see John J. Mearsheimer, "Back to the Future: Instability in Europe after the Cold War," *International Security* 15, no. 1 (Summer 1990): 5–56.

8. Miles Kahler, "The International Political Economy," in Nicholas Rizopoulos, *Sea Changes* (New York: Council on Foreign Relations, 1989), 94–109.

9. James Fallows, Chalmers Johnson, Clyde Prestowitz, and Karel van Wolferen, "Beyond Japan Bashing," *U.S. News and World Report,* May 7, 1990, 54–55.

10. Edson W. Spencer, "Japan as Competitor," *Foreign Policy,* no. 78 (Spring 1990): 165.

11. Charles W. Maynes, "America without the Cold War," *Foreign Policy,* no. 78 (Spring 1990): 13.

12. John Zysman, "Redoubling the Bet," BRIE Working Paper 38, University of California, Berkeley, Jan. 1990, 20.

13. Richard N. Gardner, "The Comeback of Liberal Internationalism," *Washington Quarterly* 13, no. 3 (Summer 1990): 23–39.

Chapter 8: Delusions of World Order

1. See chap. 7, this volume.

2. See Michael Doyle, "Kant, Liberal Legacies, and Foreign Affairs," *Philosophy and Public Affairs* 12, no. 3 (Summer 1983): 205–35, and 12, no. 4 (Fall 1983): 323–53.

3. See Michael Walzer, *Just and Unjust Wars* (New York: Basic Books, 1977), chap. 6.

4. I. L. Claude, *Power and International Relations* (New York: Random House, 1962).

5. See the powerful argument along these lines in "Conscienza cristiana e guerra moderna," *La Civiltà Cattolica* (a Jesuit magazine published in the Vatican), July 6, 1991.

6. See Stanley Hoffmann, "Avoiding New World Disorder," *New York Times,* Feb. 25, 1991, and Lincoln P. Bloomfield, *International Security: The New Agenda* (Minneapolis: Hubert H. Humphrey Institute of Public Affairs, University of Minnesota, 1991).

7. As John Steinbruner has pointed out, modern technology encourages offensive strategies (even for defensive purposes), and the kinds of arrangements that might be reassuring to potential enemies (both sides agreeing to an equal density of force deployments and equal firepower) would require a fundamental shift in the way in which states are used to ensure their security: they would have, in cases of violations by rivals, to rely on external guarantees, rather than on their own accumulated might, or on their alliances. Steinbruner, "The Consequences of the Gulf War," *Brookings Review,* 9, no. 2 (Spring 1991): 6–13.

8. William Hyland, "Downgrade Foreign Policy," *New York Times,* May 20, 1991.

9. Brian Urquhart, "Learning from the Gulf." *New York Review of Books,* Mar. 7, 1991, 34–37. See also his further argument for a rapid deployment force, under Article 43, to intervene in conflicts such as those in Yugoslavia and Somalia, "Who Can Stop Civil Wars," *New York Times,* Dec. 29, 1991.

Chapter 9: The Price of War

1. "The Gulf Crisis," *New York Review of Books,* Dec. 6, 1990, 8–17.

2. Many supporters of a war see it as an opportunity for eliminating Iraq's nuclear capacity. But (1) the cost in innocent lives may be prohibitive, given the dispersion of those facilities; (2) establishing the precedent of the "right" of a group of states to destroy preventively the nuclear potential of a country, without an explicit UN mandate, would be extremely dangerous; (3) as Brzezinski and others have stated, deterrence, which has worked against far greater powers, remains an effective substitute for preventive war. Israel could deter Iraq, and the United States as well as other nuclear states could provide a nuclear guarantee to countries threatened by Iraq's nuclear capacity; (4) the combination of deterrence, a strict embargo on components of a nuclear force, and a negotiated system of arms control could suffice. Such a combination was effective against a much more serious threat for forty-five years.

3. Zbigniew Brzezinski, testimony excerpted in *New York Review of Books,* Jan. 17, 1991, 9.

Chapter 10: In Defense of Mother Teresa

1. Michael Mandelbaum, "Foreign Policy as Social Work," *Foreign Affairs* 75, no. 1 (Jan.–Feb. 1996): 16–32.

2. For further elaboration, see chap. 11, this volume.

Chapter 11: The Politics and Ethics of Military Intervention

1. See Stanley Hoffmann, *Duties beyond Borders* (Ithaca, N.Y.: Syracuse University Press, 1981).

2. Hedley Bull, *The Anarchical Society* (London, Eng.: Macmillan, 1977), chap. 9.

3. See Arthur Schlesinger Jr., "Back to the Womb," *Foreign Affairs* 74, no. 4 (July–Aug. 1995): 2–8.

4. Francis Fukuyama, "The End of History?" *National Interest* (Summer 1989): 3–35; and Samuel Huntington, "The Clash of Civilizations?" *Foreign Affairs* 72, no. 3 (Summer 1993): 22–49.

5. See Benjamin R. Barber, *Jihad versus McWorld* (New York: Random House, Time Books, 1995); John Lewis Gaddis, "Toward the Post–Cold War World," *Foreign Affairs* 70, no. 2 (Spring 1991).

6. Michael Ignatieff, "The Seductiveness of Moral Disgust," *Social Research* 62, no. 1 (Spring 1995): 91.

7. That domestic and international affairs are increasingly related has become blindingly obvious in two respects: economic interdependence in a world where trade negotiations now aim at nothing less than transforming the domestic economies—hence the social values and practices of the parties—and the effects of domestic political changes, especially revolutions, on foreign-policy behavior.

8. J. Bryan Hehir, "Expanding Military Intervention: Promise or Peril?" *Social Research* 62, no. 1 (Spring 1995): 49.

9. See chap. 5, this volume.

10. Michael Walzer, "The Politics of Rescue," *Social Research* 62, no. 1 (Spring 1995): 55.

11. Ibid., 59.

12. J. Bryan Hehir, "The Ethics of Intervention: Debating the Norms and Deciding the Cases," unpublished paper, Oct. 1994. Parts of this paper appear in "Intervention: From Theories to Cases," *Ethics and International Affairs* 9 (1995): 1–13.

13. Arnold Wolfers, *Discord and Collaboration* (Baltimore, Md.: Johns Hopkins University Press, 1962), chap. 5.

14. Walzer, *Politics of Rescue,* 60.

15. Otto Kallscheuer, "And Who Is My Neighbor?" *Social Research* 62, no. 1 (Spring 1995): 112.

16. See also Stanley Hoffmann, *The Ethics and Politics of Humanitarian Intervention* (South Bend, Ind.: Notre Dame Univ. Press, 1997).

17. Olara A. Otonnu, *Keeping the Peace in the Post–Cold War Era,* Report to the Trilateral Commission, no. 43 (New York: Trilateral Commission, 1993), 75.

18. Commission on Global Governance, *Our Global Neighbourhood* (Oxford, Eng.: Oxford University Press, 1995), 90.

19. I have not argued for a third criterion (or a much broader definition of the second): intervention in order to promote democracy. The promotion of democracy is an admirable "milieu goal" (especially if one is persuaded that democracies do not fight one another). But on ethical grounds, I am not convinced that it is a goal that always trumps the value of sovereignty and that intervention of a coercive kind is always a morally appropriate method. Also, as indicated above, "should implies can"; I do not believe either that there is yet enough of a consensus behind such a criterion nor enough of a possibility of installing and preserving democracy, from the outside, in countries that have never experienced it. Too much emphasis on the (worthy) goal of democracy may detract attention and efforts from the defense of human rights, even in areas that are not ready yet for democracy. Moreover, when the overthrow of democracy is accompanied (as it was in Chile in 1973 and Haiti in 1991) with massive violations of rights, the second criterion applies. It applies especially when the democratic government that has been overthrown had been established under international auspices or protection, as in Haiti.

20. Commission on Global Governance, *Our Global Neighbourhood,* 90 ff.

21. See Rosalyn Higgins, "The UN Fifty Years On," which argues for clear categories in the *European Journal of International Law* 6 (1995) 445–460, and chap. 12, this volume.

22. After war broke out in Croatia, and as Bosnia was moving toward independence, the European Community did not go beyond sending observers to

Bosnia, and the UN, unlike in the former Yugoslav Republic of Macedonia, did nothing preventatively. On Yugoslavia and Somalia, see *Enforcing Restraint,* ed. Lori Fisler Damrosch (New York: Council on Foreign Relations, 1993). On Yugoslavia, see also Susan L. Woodward, *Balkan Tragedy* (Washington, D.C.: Brookings Institution, 1995). On Somalia, see Terrence Lyons and Ahmed I. Samatar, *Somalia* (Washington, D.C.: Brookings Institution, occasional papers, 1995); and the special report of the U.S. Institute of Peace, "Restoring Hope: The Real Lessons of Somalia for the Future of Intervention." On Rwanda, see *Death, Despair and Defiance* (London, Eng.: African Rights, 1994).

23. See Thomas G. Weiss, "Intervention: Whither the UN?" *Washington Quarterly* 17, no. 1 (Winter 1994): 109–28.

24. See the text in *United Nations, Divided World,* ed. Adam Roberts and Benedict Kingsbury (Oxford, Eng.: Clarendon Press, 1993), 476–80.

25. Ottonu, *Keeping the Peace,* 76.

26. Hoffmann, "The Ethics and Politics of Humanitarian Intervention," ch. 1.

27. Tom J. Farer, "A Paradigm of Legitimate Intervention," in Damrosch, *Enforcing Restraint,* 327.

28. Hehir, "The Ethics of Intervention."

29. Higgins, "The UN Fifty Years On."

30. See Alex de Waal's remarks quoted in Kallscheuer, "And Who Is My Neighbor?" 123; and Geoffrey Best, *War and Law since 1945* (New York: Oxford University Press, 1994), 239 ff.

31. See Brian Urquhart, "For a UN Volunteer Military Force," *New York Review of Books,* June 10, 1993, 3–4.

32. For a more elaborate analysis, see Stanley Hoffmann, "The Europeans in Yugoslavia," in *The World and Yugoslavia's Wars,* ed. Richard Ullman (New York: Council on Foreign Relations, 1996), and Stanley Hoffmann, *The Ethics and Politics of Humanitarian Intervention* (South Bend, Ind.: University of Notre Dame Press, 1997), ch. 2.

33. See Weiss, "Intervention," 115–16.

34. Damrosch, *Enforcing Restraint,* 379; Lyons and Samatar, *Somalia,* 39 ff.

35. These comments were made in a lecture delivered at the seminar on Ethics and International Relations of the Center for International Affairs at Harvard University, Cambridge, Mass., 1994.

Chapter 12: Thoughts on the UN at Fifty

1. See chap. 5, this volume.

2. See Brian Urquhart, *Ralph Bunche* (New York: Norton, 1993).

3. Stanley Hoffmann, *The Ethics and Politics of Humanitarian Intervention* (South Bend, Ind.: University of Notre Dame Press, 1997).

Chapter 13: The Passion of Modernity

1. Liah Greenfeld, *Nationalism: Five Roads to Modernity* (Cambridge, Mass.: Harvard University Press, 1993).

Chapter 14: Nationalism and World Order

1. Ernst B. Haas, *Nationalism, Liberalism, and Progress* (Ithaca, N.Y.: Cornell University Press, 1997), 1:35.

2. Ibid., 46–53.

3. See Bull's classic, *The Anarchical Society* (London, Eng.: Macmillan, 1997).

4. See Bull's lectures on justice at the University of Waterloo.

5. See Michael Joseph Smith, *Realism from Weber to Kissinger* (Baton Rouge: Louisiana State University Press, 1986).

6. Association des Amis de Michel Debré, *Une passion pour la France: Hommage à Michel Debré* (Paris, 1997), 177.

7. See my analysis of Morgenthau in *Contemporary Theory in International Relations,* ed. Stanley Hoffmann (Englewood Cliffs, N.Y.: Prentice Hall, 1960).

8. Eric Hobsbawm, *Nations and Nationalism since 1780* (London, Eng.: Cambridge University Press, 1990).

9. Linda Colley, *Britons* (New Haven, Conn.: Yale University Press, 1992).

10. Liah Greenfeld, *Nationalism* (Cambridge, Mass.: Harvard University Press, 1992).

11. See chapter 11, above; also see Stanley Hoffman, *The Ethics and Politics of Humanitarian Intervention* (South Bend, Ind.: University of Notre Dame Press, 1997).

12. Such roots—fragile and withered—did exist in Germany after 1994 and, to a lesser extent, in Japan.

13. See Daniel Philpott, "In Defense of Self-Determination," *Ethics* 105, no. 2 (Jan. 1995): 352–85.

14. Dominique Schnapper, "The European Debate on Citizenship," *Daedalus* 126, no. 3 (Summer 1997): 207–11.

Chapter 16: Nation and Nationalism in America Today

1. I have dealt with this in *Gulliver's Troubles* (New York: McGraw-Hill, 1968) and *Primacy or World Order* (New York: McGraw-Hill, 1978).

Chapter 17: Principles of a Liberal Ethics

1. See the critiques by Will Kymlicka in *Liberalism, Community, and Culture* (Oxford: Clarendon Press, 1991), chap. 3, and William A. Galston, *Liberal Purposes* (Cambridge University Press, 1991).

2. Galston, *Liberal Purposes*, 296.

3. See Rex Martin, *A System of Rights* (Oxford: Clarendon Press, 1993). When I talk about "legally defined and protected rights," I refer both to states' constitutions and codes of laws and to international agreements.

4. Stanley Hoffmann, *Duties beyond Borders* (Ithaca, N.Y.: Syracuse University Press, 1981), chap. 3.

5. Amartya Sen, "Freedom and Needs," *New Republic*, Jan. 10–17, 1994, 31–38.

6. See Roger J. Sullivan, *Immanuel Kant's Moral Theory* (Cambridge: Cambridge University Press, 1989), chap. 6.

7. See John Rawls, *Political Liberalism* (New York: Columbia University Press, 1993), chap. 3, 99 ff., for a listing of these differences. For Rawls, Kant's doctrine is one conception of the good, "in which the ideal of autonomy has a regulative role for all of life" (99). What Rawls seeks is an "overlapping consensus" on justice as fairness, attractive to believers in other conceptions of the good as well.

8. Ibid., 19.

9. See B. Kansikan, "Asia's Different Standard," and A. Neier, "Asia's Inacceptable Standard," in *Foreign Policy*, no. 92 (Fall 1993): 24–51. I agree with Neier's rebuttal of Kansikan but not with his belief that the fight for human rights can somehow be kept nonpolitical and dissociated from the promotion of democracy.

10. Gregory H. Fox, "New Approaches to International Human Rights: The Sovereign State Revisited," in *State Sovereignty*, ed. Sohail H. Hashmi (Philadelphia: University of Pennsylvania Press, 1997), 128.

11. Ibid.

12. These are nonliberal polities that are peaceful, based on an impartial conception of justice, provided with political regimes that entail "a reasonable consultative machinery," and respectful of basic human rights—clearly an ideal-type. See John Rawls, "The Law of Peoples," in *On Human Rights*, ed. Stephen Shute and Susan Hurley (New York: Basic Books, 1993), 41–82.

13. See Judith Shklar, "Political Obligation and Loyalty," *Political Theory* 21, no. 2 (May 1993).

14. For a range of suggestions, see Gidon Gottlieb, *States Plus Nations* (New York: Council on Foreign Relations, 1993).

15. Daniel Philpott, "In Defense of Self-Determination," *Ethics* 105, no. 2 (Jan. 1995): 14.

16. Kymlicka, *Liberalism, Community, and Culture*, 17.

17. See Peter Babej, "Weimar's Revisionism and the League's Minorities System," Ph.D. diss., Harvard University, 1994.

18. Kymlicka, *Liberalism, Community, and Culture*, 152.

19. Michael Walzer, *Spheres of Justice* (New York: Basic Books, 1983), 31–63.

Credits

Chapter 2 is the revised text of the 1985 Cyril Foster lecture, delivered at Oxford University on October 17, 1985, and published under the same title in *International Affairs* (London) (1986): 179–95.

Chapter 3 is the revised text of an article published as "Dreams of a Just World," *New York Review of Books* 42, no. 17 (Nov. 2, 1995): 52–56.

Chapter 4 is the revised text of a lecture in honor of Bernard Brodie, given at University of California at Los Angeles, June 1995.

Chapter 5 is the revised text of an article published under the same title in *Foreign Policy* (Spring 1995): 159–77. Copyright © 1995 by the Carnegie Endowment for International Peace.

Chapter 6 is the revised text of an article published under the same title in *Atlantic Monthly*, October 1989, 84–96.

Chapter 7 is the revised text of an article published under the same title in *Sea Changes*, ed. Nicholas Rizopoulos (New York: Council on Foreign Relations, 1990), 274–92.

Chapter 8 is the revised text of an article published under the same title in *New York Review of Books* 39, no. 7 (April 9, 1992): 37–43.

Chapter 9 is the revised text of an article published under the same title in *New York Review of Books*, 37, nos. 1–2 (January 17, 1991): 6–9.

Chapter 10 is the revised text of an article published under the same title in *Foreign Affairs* 75, no. 2 (March-April 1996): 172–75.

Chapter 11 is the revised text of an article published under the same title in *Survival* 37, no. 4 (Winter 1995–1996): 29–51.

Chapter 12 is the revised text of an article published in *European Journal of International Law* 6, no. 3 (1995): 317–24.

Chapter 13 is the revised text of an article published under the same title in *Atlantic Monthly*, August 1993, 101–8, as a review of *Nationalism: Five Roads to Modernity*, by Liah Greenfeld (Cambridge, Mass.: Harvard University Press, 1993).

Chapter 14 is the revised text of a paper presented at the Nobel Symposium, Stockholm, September 1997.

Chapter 16 is the revised text of an article published as "More Perfect Union: Nation and Nationalism in America," in *Harvard International Review* 20, no. 1 (Winter 1997–1998): 72–75.

Chapter 17 is a draft for a forthcoming volume on ethics and international relations by Stanley Hoffmann and Michael J. Smith.

Index

About the Author

The preeminent scholar of world politics in both the United States and Europe, Stanley Hoffman is the Paul and Catherine Buttenwieser University Professor at Harvard University, where he has taught since 1955. He was the chairman of the Center for European Studies at Harvard from its inception in 1969 until 1995. He is also an essayist for the *New York Review of Books* and the Western Europe review editor for *Foreign Affairs*.

Born in Vienna in 1928, Hoffman lived and studied in France from 1929 to 1955. He has taught at the Institut d'Études Politiques of Paris, from which he graduated, and at the École des Hautes Études en Sciences Sociales.

He is the author of numerous books on French and international affairs, including *Contemporary Theory in International Relations* (1960), *The State of War* (1965), *Gulliver's Troubles* (1968), *Decline or Renewal: France Since the 1930s* (1974), *Primacy or World Order* (1978), *Duties Beyond Borders* (1981), *Dead Ends* (1983), *Janus and Minerva* (1986), and *The European Sisyphus* (1995), and *The Ethics and Politics of Humanitarian Intervention* (1997). He is the coauthor of *In Search of France* (1962), *The Fifth Republic at Twenty* (1981), *Living with Nuclear Weapons* (1983), and *The Mitterrand Experiment* (1987); and the coeditor of *The New European Community* (1990) and *After the Cold War* (1993).